Executive's Portfolio of Model Speeches for All Occasions

Dianna Booher

PRENTICE HALL
Paramus, New Jersey 07652

Prentice-Hall International (UK) Limited, *London*
Prentice-Hall of Australia Pty. Limited, *Sydney*
Prentice-Hall Canada, Inc., *Toronto*
Prentice-Hall Hispanoamericana, S.A., *Mexico*
Prentice-Hall of India Private Limited, *New Delhi*
Prentice-Hall of Japan, Inc., *Tokyo*
Simon & Schuster Asia Pte. Ltd., *Singapore*
Editora Prentice-Hall do Brasil, Ltda., *Rio de Janeiro*

©1991 *by*

Dianna Booher

10   9

Library of Congress Cataloging-in-Publication Data

Booher, Dianna Baniels.
    Executive's portfolio of model speeches for all occasions / by
Dianna Booher.
        p.   cm.
    Includes index.
    ISBN 0-13-296989-0
    1. Communication in management—Handbooks, manuals, etc.
2. Occasional speeches—Handbooks, manuals, etc. 3. Public
speaking—Handbooks, manuals, etc.   I. Title.
HD30.3.B66   1991   90-47272
658.4'52—dc20   CIP

ISBN 0-13-296989-0

PRENTICE HALL
Career & Personal Development
Englewood Cliffs, NJ 07632
A Simon & Schuster Company

On the World Wide Web at http://www.phdirect.com

Printed in the United States of America

Acknowledgments

I want to express my appreciation to all the great speakers who've motivated me to emulate them and who serve as role models for all of us.

Particularly, I want to thank those individuals who've given permission for their speeches to be included in the Appendix. Although the choices were difficult, my criteria for inclusion were a variety in style, the occasion of delivery (be it routine or auspicious), the ideas presented, a flair for appropriate word choice, and an appeal to the emotions.

In the "Openings" and "Closings" categories, some of the ideas are original; some are tidbits that have been floating around for years—their origins known only to God. Those have not been credited to any particular source. Nevertheless, I'm grateful to have heard or read each story repeated somewhere by someone.

Victor Books, publisher of my earlier book *The Confident Communicator*, has graciously agreed to let me repeat ideas from that work on handling question-and-answer periods and practicing delivery techniques.

Last of all, I want to thank my capable staff for listening to my material as I tried out each speech: Some lines worked and some didn't. But then, what else is a great staff for?

A special thanks to my assistants Chris O'Shea and Janet Houston-Spore for their help in manuscript preparation. All errors that have crept in are probably my own.

Dianna Booher

How This Book
Will Help You

The picture becomes clear in your mind's eye. Just slightly silver at the temples. A twinkle in your eye and a modest grin from ear to ear. You scan a glowing crowd of smiling faces, eyes full of admiration. The applause swells in your ears as you back away from the podium and amble back toward your seat at the luncheon table. Afterward, members of your audience file by your table to shake your hand and tell you how much they enjoyed your perceptive comments—comments they'd like to make themselves if they were as articulate as you.

Fade into the end of the well-wishers line. Your most distinguished guest—your mentor, your CEO—lets a grin spread to the corners of his mouth as he slaps you on the back. "Couldn't have expressed it better myself! Superb. They were with you all the way."

The picture fades, and reality looms larger. The results you're sure of—you know what you want. The problem becomes how to get there. How do you get started on your topic? Where do the ideas come from? How do you find that apt phrase or perfect illustration that says it all? Where does the emotion come from?

"I'd love to be a speaker—if it weren't for preparing the speech." This sentiment is common to many extroverts. Even those who love to find themselves in front of audiences must go through the time-consuming process of putting together a script. And for those who don't relish the idea of gripping a podium before a group of colleagues, speaking is a two-part nightmare: the preparation *and* the delivery.

No matter how you categorize yourself—an extrovert who loves the limelight, or a behind-the-scenes person who considers speaking before an audience an imposition—this book can help.

It provides complete "off-the-rack" models for all business occasions. With minor revisions on names, places, and dates, or the insertion of specific details, these speeches are ready for use today or tomorrow.

You'll notice that other speeches necessarily include names and details specific to an occasion—such as those in the "Eulogies," "Farewells," "Retirements," and "Introductions" sections.

If you need only a slight nudge in the appropriate direction, use these models to generate an outline of your own ideas. Skimming the key points of a speech similar to the one you'd like to give will start your own creative juices flowing. Take the speech skeleton and simply add meat to the bones with your own experiences, illustrations, readings, or observations.

Or start with your own outline of key points and skim these speeches for illustrative stories, quotes, or apt phrasing.

Finally, turn to Part II for general tips on fine-tuning your ideas for your specific audience and the how-tos of a perfect delivery.

Those speakers who seem to think on their feet so easily rarely do. That is, those natural-sounding speakers have a repertoire of key points, apt phrases, quotes, and stories for almost every occasion. When preparing to speak, they pull out their mental portfolio and deliver their well-categorized and polished sentiments with ease.

You can do likewise. With over 180 speeches, you can build your own repertoire of ideas for all occasions, both business and personal. Some of the scripts are based on ideas from actual speeches delivered by executives serving major corporations across the nation. Their experience can become yours with little effort.

The Apostle James observes: "The tongue can be sharper than a two-edged sword." Your ability to express yourself can be your plan of attack to stay on the cutting edge of your profession. Your tongue may be the sword to slay the dragons of fear or waste or mediocrity. Or your speech may be the sword that leads your colleagues to the front lines of productivity, quality service, and growth.

Nothing makes you more visible in the corporate world than the ability to express yourself before a group. With the help of this book, you'll no longer be a face in the audience, lamenting, "I wish I'd said that." You *can* say that! This book will take the pain out of preparation and put you behind the podium in half the time.

Contents

PART II: General Tips for Speechmaking   235

APPENDIX: Real Speeches   275

PART I: MODEL SPEECHES

Achievements

GENERAL GUIDELINES

- Lead the audience to appreciate the achievement with a history and details of the distinction and with names of other individuals or corporations who have excelled in this way.
- Mention the effort, time, or expertise this distinction required.
- Express pride in the individual or the company's contributions.

(For employee's distinction)

- Create a desire in the audience to emulate the honored employee's achievement.

(For company's distinction)

- Share the credit with employees who have contributed to the company's achievement or distinction of honor.

TO ANNOUNCE DISTINCTION
OF AN EMPLOYEE

1

Audience: employees and family members of honoree
Message: We are proud of you and value you as an employee.
Tone: formal
Timing: 4 minutes

"The only thing that is universal is incompetence; strength is always specific!" observed author Charles Garfield about his study of peak performers. To be sure, we can be specific about (honoree)'s strengths. This morning, I'm pleased to announce to you that (bestowing organization) has named him this year's winner of the prestigious (title) award for his outstanding contribution to the field of science.

For those of you who may be unfamiliar with this award, it recognizes excellence specifically in the field of (type) research. This award was established by the (name) Foundation over 20 years ago in recognition of scholars who have furthered our knowledge of [explanation of research] and developed practical applications of that knowledge in business.

In short, the award symbolizes man's commitment to seeking truth about our world. The foundation's ultimate goal—and indeed ours as well—is to make that truth practical in ways that will lift or lighten the suffering of others. To bring us all an improved quality of life.

Although, as Andrew Jackson concluded, "One man with courage makes a majority," many through the years have taken up the cause to eradicate problems from our world. Others whose names you will recognize share this particular honor with (honoree), having been previous recipients of this award:

[Insert names of prominent past winners.]

While all of us, I'm sure, would like to be able to contribute to our fellowman in such a way, Theodore Roosevelt drew lines around those who deserve recognition:

The credit belongs to the man who is actually in the arena, whose face is marred by dust and sweat and blood; who strives valiantly; who errs and comes short again and again, who knows the great enthusiasms, the great devotions, and spends himself in a worthy cause; who at the best, knows the triumph of high achievement; and who, at the worst, if he fails, at least fails while daring greatly, so that his place shall never be with those cold and timid souls who know neither victory nor defeat.

(Honoree) has been in the arena. And I'm sure he would be the first to tell you that not all of his attempts throughout his career have resulted in immediate successes. Someone has said that to achieve, we must be obsessed by it. (Honoree) has been obsessed because his obsession is to benefit others. He had false starts and hit dead ends in several trails he followed. But trial and error is the essence of scientific research. Nevertheless, his victories are specific. His research has resulted in the development of a device to [insert explanation of achievement].

As other peak performers do, (honoree) excels because of his specific strengths—his thoroughness, his tenacity, his curiosity about "what ifs," and his insight about his research results.

We as a company salute him for those traits and this distinction. As lecturer Elbert Hubbard put it: "One machine can do the work of 50 ordinary men. No machine can do the work of one extraordinary man."

The Biblical proverb of Solomon says, "Like apples of gold in settings of silver is a word spoken in right circumstances." In closing, we hope as his employer we have spoken the right words of encouragement at the right time. We want to recognize (honoree)'s achievement, as well as encourage him and each of you to pursue excellence in whatever field you have chosen. We look to people such as you for a brighter future.

2

Audience: employees, family members of honoree
Message: We are proud of you and value you as an employee.
Tone: informal, light
Timing: 3 minutes

Good morning, everyone. (Honoree), if you have to get up this early in the morning, it should be for a good cause, correct? Well, besides the hearty breakfast, we want to offer you our congratulations.

To let the rest of you in on our secret, (honoree) has been chosen by (awarding organization) as (title of award). We are thrilled by this distinction. Not only will it give (honoree) the big head, it will bring recognition to our company as being a group of managers bright enough to hire her.

To set the record straight, (honoree) was not the only candidate for the award. In fact, the panel of her colleagues made the selection from over (number) professionals nominated nationwide for this distinction. Another thing we should set straight: the selection criteria involved more than someone who had attended meetings. Much more, to be exact.

As I talked to the panel of judges, I discovered quite a rigorous checklist. Individuals chosen for this honor must have proven themselves by capable leadership and mentoring of colleagues, by community service on behalf of the organization, by contributions to the body of knowledge we call "sales and marketing," and finally by her own sales record.

With these criteria before them, they ended up with (honoree)'s name on the top of the list. For (number) years running, she has served as the chairman for the Professional Development workshops that provide know-how to her colleagues in the field. She has spearheaded the community drive for relief funds to go to victims of the (type) disaster. And for (number) years, she has filled positions on city-wide United Fund committees. Both (name of two magazines/journals) have published articles she's contributed this year. Articles that have certainly brought recognition to our own company and industry, as well as adding to the sales and marketing expertise of her colleagues across the nation.

In her spare time, she's also sold a few (products). Seriously, (honoree) has been our own top sales rep in her division for (number) consecutive years, adding $X to our gross revenues. Aiming for achievement, she has hit the target of success.

I'd say that's quite a To-Do list you started with, (honoree).

You've made us very proud as a company. We wish you well in your personal goals and in your future professional goals. (Awarding organization) knows a winner when they see one. So do we. Keep up the good work and thank you for keeping us in the limelight.

TO ANNOUNCE DISTINCTION OF YOUR OWN COMPANY

3

Audience: employees of the company
Message: We appreciate your contribution to our company's distinction in this area.
Tone: formal
Timing: 2 minutes

"Give, and it shall be given unto you: good measure, pressed down, and shaken together, and running over . . ." wrote Luke, the Apostle. We have given and now we are receiving. I'm pleased to announce to you that our company has just received the (title) award. Not only are we thrilled by this recognition of our contribution to the field of art, we are thrilled by the fact that we could donate the money, time, and talent of so many of you to this worthwhile project.

Giuseppe Mazzini, the Italian patriot, has aptly put it:

> The moral law of the universe is progress. Every generation that passes idly over the earth without adding to that progress remains uninscribed upon the register of humanity, and the succeeding generation tramples its ashes as dust.

You can be proud as employees to have added to that progress in our community's support of the arts, to have contributed to that record of civilization that will outlive us. Artists look at things through *their* eyes. They make those things and ideas visible to us that we might not otherwise learn about ourselves and our world. Our sensitivities and our revelations grow with each generation. We as a company have contributed to that knowledge; you as individuals have contributed to that knowledge.

By giving, we have received recognition as a company with foresight and a commitment to the local community.

And that brings me to my closing thought: A company is nothing more than its employees. Our honor is yours individually. Thank you for your talent, and we encourage your continued support of the arts as you attend performances at (theater) and tour the (name) Art Museum.

4

Audience: employees of the company
Message: We are achieving, thanks to you.
Tone: informal
Timing: 2-3 minutes

Today, we have just shipped the one-millionth (product) out our front door. It's great to be CEO of an organization that cares about quality and productivity. We've set in place policies that produce quality, and you've contributed the craftsmanship and the commitment to productivity.

You've heard it said that the optimist sees a glass that is half full. The pessimist sees one that is half empty. Comedian George Carlin says that he sees a glass that's twice the size it needs to be. Your own attitudes are a reflection of how you see life in general and how you see your job specifically. I think we have a lot of George Carlin clones around here. You look at designs or procedures that are inappropriate for the tasks and then make the necessary corrections. That's what you've become known for—an eye for detail, improvement, and innovation.

Steel magnate Charles Schwab concluded, "All successful employers are stalking men who will do the unusual, men who think, men who attract attention by performing more than is expected of them." Lee Iacocca has agreed: "The kind of people I look for to fill top management spots," he says, "are the eager beavers, the mavericks. These are the guys who try to do more than they're expected to do—they always reach."

We here at (corporation) have both kinds of employees—the support people who follow well and who daily do more than is expected of them and the "eager beaver" executives who lead the way in new directions.

You here at this (city) plant have become team players in the best sense. That is, your commitment to pull together has helped you avoid the vast wasteland of mediocrity. Instead, your team spirit has molded you into "cream of the crop" employees, in a group that can act as a role model to others in our industry we've left far behind.

Through training, communication, cooperation, and commitment, you've turned an assembly line into a customer's line—a line of workers who think like customers think and who work like customers would work if they were building their own products. You demonstrate an understanding of quality, waste-reduction, and increased efficiency. In short, you understand profit and you are the real door to our future.

I'm proud to stand before you on this historic day for our company. Keep up the good work. Together we are going to dominate the next decade.

Anniversaries

(Of tenure of employee or organization)

- Mention the anniversary and what you are doing or plan to do to commemorate the occasion—ceremony, dinner, certificate, gift.
- Give a historical perspective to lead the audience to appreciate the long tenure.
- Include several specific accomplishments or contributions of the individual or organization.
- Express your confidence in the individual or organization's future plans and successes.

(Of past tragedy)

- Mention the anniversary and how you plan to commemorate the occasion—donation or memorial.
- Express regret for the tragedy and gratitude for any individuals' values or sacrifices surrounding the incident.
- Offer appreciation for any positive community response at that time and mention good that has come from the tragedy.
- Challenge the audience to remember and uphold the values and principles evidenced in the course of the tragedy.

ANNIVERSARY OF LONG-TERM EMPLOYEE

5

Audience: family, peers, and supervisors of long-term employee
Message: We appreciate your loyalty and attitude.
Tone: informal, light
Timing: 2 minutes

Before we wrap this program up, we have one other agenda item. (Name), would you please come to the front here with me. You're a distinguished employee, having just completed your (number) year with us at (corporation).

I guess you know us just about as well as you know your own family. At least, you spend about as much time with us. From our best estimates, we figure you've walked (number) miles into and out of the building. You've eaten approximately (number) lunches here. You've made at least (number) elevators trips from floor to floor. And you've cashed (number) paychecks—that's counting back when we paid people every week.

Well, here's one more to cash—a little bonus for a lot of hard work. Please take it as a token of our appreciation for your faithful consistency on the job. Your attendance record is splendid. Day in and day out, you've been here to get the job done—and done well, according to your supervisors. They say performance depends on attitude. So from your record, we conclude that you have a great attitude about life in general. A positive mental attitude is the right attitude in any given environment or decade. Let's hope you're contagious.

Our company is people. And as our representative during these past (number) years, we figure you've spread a little good cheer to thousands of people who've walked through our doors.

Thank you. From all of us, congratulations.

6

Audience: family, peers, and supervisors of long-term employee
Message: We appreciate your consistency and talents.
Tone: informal
Timing: 3 minutes

Someone has said that when you hire people who are smarter than you are, you prove you are smarter than they are. Well, I don't know that we're in any intellectual race, but we did find a talented individual (number) years ago when (name) walked into our offices trying to convince us of the same.

(Name), at the time you reported for work here, the hit song was "(title)." "(Movie title)" was playing to large audiences in our movie theaters. A loaf of bread cost (number) cents. A new Chevy cost (number) dollars. The average home cost (number) dollars. And the average employee made (number) dollars a year.

Times were hard. But you didn't let that deter you from excelling in your university studies and preparing to take on the corporate world here at (corporation). And take it head on, you did. You wrestled with operations for about (number) of those years, cutting costs in your department by X percent over the (number) years. Then you struggled with engineering until you had developed a few patents, (number) to be exact. Then you finally took up managing, where you've supervised directly or indirectly some (number) people.

We'd have to sum it up this way—talent and loyalty. We admire that. It's like the little old lady who, in time of war, kept her poker ready in case the enemy approached her house. When asked what she thought she could do with such a mild weapon, she said, "Well, I could certainly show them whose side I'm on."

(Name) has shown us whose side he's on time and time again. He's always been on the side of innovation, quality, and ethics—no matter who else in management or otherwise lined up.

So here you are, (name), (number) years later. What has come of your life here? A loaf of bread is $1.05. A new Chevy costs $16,000. The average new home costs $92,333. And the average employee makes $24,556 a year.

I ask you: Are you better off today than when you started here with us? If not economically, I hope you're a better person for having worked here, learned here, associated with friends here.

I know we're certainly much better off for having had you around. Thank you for your contributions and your commitment to growth and excellence.

7

Audience: family, peers, and supervisors of long-term employee
Message: Thank you for your contributions.
Tone: informal, light
Timing: 2 minutes

Someone has said that "growing old is a habit that a busy man has no time to form." During the (number) years (name) has been with us, that's certainly been the case. (Name) has a reputation for boundless energy, great enthusiasm, long hours, and hard work.

Experience gained over time is something we value here at (corporation). Often in our culture we focus on the young—their idealism, their energy. But I don't think we give enough attention to the wisdom of years and experience. Good judgment comes from experience—and experience comes from poor judgment. I don't know that you, (name), can recall any uses of poor judgment over the years, but I'd suspect you might. To temper that, however, let me be quick to add that we remember the good judgment, the leadership, the talent, the successes.

They say that *education* is what you get from reading the small print in a contract. *Experience* is what you get from not reading it. Well, (name), you've learned much around here, but your learning is far from over. You may agree with former president Harry Truman. This is how he put it: "The only things worth learning are the things you learn after you know it all." From your experience, I'm sure you, in turn, have taught and will continue to teach others. We thank you.

Please accept this (gift) as a small token of our appreciation. Congratulations and best wishes for years and years of more experience, health, and happiness.

ANNIVERSARY OF AN ORGANIZATION

8

Audience: staff, alumni, and friends of a university
Message: We are here to recommit ourselves to education as we rededicate this school.
Tone: formal
Timing: 3-4 minutes

Anniversaries are as American as Mom, apple pie, and baseball. They are a celebration of the past and a pep rally for the future. The founders of this university certainly must have enjoyed exercising their rights and their God-given talents to foresee a need for their university in this particular part of our country. (Name of founder) saw something worth doing when he saw the need to emphasize science in this university and the need to locate it here in (city)—in a state that has contributed so much to history through the years.

It's our state that has sent such leaders as (name), (name), and (name) to Congress. It's our state that has turned out over (number) national merit scholars in the last ten years alone. It's our state that has shown the world how to manufacture and produce the best (product) in the world. From Mozambique to Rio De Janiero, people use our (product).

The founders also had the foresight to see the impact this university would have on bringing industry into the state. Most of these companies have made their headquarters right here in our city. Their growth is our growth. Our growth is theirs.

And most important, the object of the university is to prepare our youth to educate themselves throughout their lives. Its students are taught to lead creative, sensitive lives of contribution. Our university has never been an expense to the community or to its students—only an investment.

The mission of the university has become more relevant and more urgent with each passing year. With scientific advancements such as (type) and (type), we can see the importance of continuing our research. We intend to find a cure to diseases and other problems that threaten us. We want to advance our knowledge in all areas by exploring our universe.

And our facilities themselves—the decor—have kept pace with the nature of our noble scientific missions. Through donations by (name) back in (year), the (name) and (name) buildings were renovated. Then in (year), (name) contributed $X to the face-lift of (building). Following these major changes, our alumni organization has seen to it that (building) and (building) have kept up with the spirit of the university. Both these buildings have undergone major renovations during the past (number) years.

This university has been a pioneering organization in a field of study that has directly changed the way we live.

That's why this anniversary takes on such significance to the community and to those of us who work here. The vision back in (year) was a challenging one. Through the decades, our alumni have contributed to the local, national, and world economy. The faculty and staff can be proud of the part they've played in preparing students to enter rewarding careers and in advancing our civilization.

We resolve to keep that achievement and that ideal before us as community and university leaders. Thank you for celebrating with us today.

9

Audience: employees of one's own organization
Message: I'm excited about our future. Thank you for contributing.
Tone: formal
Timing: 4-5 minutes, depending on insertion of details about accomplishments

The innovative people and the technical excellence we are celebrating today emerged from a tragic accident (number) years ago. In (year), when the company was only (number) years old with a balance sheet still bleeding red ink, a random act of terror [or mention other tragedy such as fire, hurricane, disease] destroyed much of our facility here and injured many people in leadership positions. A tragic beginning to a very bright future.

But the board of directors of (name of organization) didn't look back. Even through difficult economic times and months of uncertainty, those leaders found a way to plan and build a new and better facility. This one that now houses your work includes state-of-the-art equipment. It provides a pleasant working environment for growth and expansion.

Your commitment to the goals of excellence is based on more than (number) years of progress generated by thousands of dedicated people who were determined to move forward. You, the people who now work here, know better than anyone else how important process and product innovations are to profit and to our community at large.

I'm excited about the work we do here. I'm excited about forming closer and closer partnerships with each other as corporate citizens, with customers, and with suppliers. We are committed to providing the highest quality products at the lowest cost.

As evidence of that commitment, here's what we've been about for the past (number) years.

[Insert details of advances in the past—new products and services and statistics on their acceptance in the marketplace.]

The spirit is still glowing—the spirit in the hearts of the founders of this organization over (number) years ago. That spirit still lives in those employees here who make better things happen for a brighter tomorrow. We recognize that spirit. We respect it. We appreciate it.

I'm an optimist when it comes to the future of our organization. You've heard it said that the pessimist is the guy who, when opportunity knocks, complains about the noise. Thank goodness that's not the style of those who work here. Competition to our employees simply means opportunity—opportunity to cooperate and improve quality and responsiveness.

I look at our product designs for the coming years and see a wide-open window of opportunity for us. I say the last (number) years have positioned us better than ever to come out winners. I say the rest of the decade will be a time of great innovation and excitement in the area of (industry) services and products. I say let's put on a face of enthusiasm and walk with a spring in our step.

I say, let's move out and ahead!

10

Audience: members of professional or civic club

Message: We have contributed to the community; let's pause and reflect and then move ahead.

Tone: formal

Timing: 5-7 minutes, depending on insertion of details about past accomplishments

Today, I confess that I've been daydreaming—both reminiscing about the past and predicting the future. These may be inappropriate activities during a Sunday morning sermon or a management meeting, but quite right for this time in the life of our club. We're celebrating a birthday, an anniversary. This club was founded exactly (number) years ago.

Now most of you weren't around to remember the setting on that date, so let me brief you.

Economically: Times were difficult. The average worker received $X annually for his labor. A Sunday newspaper cost (number) cents. The national debt was only $X.

Historically: President (name) had just taken office and promised an end to [insert] and the beginning of a new era. An era in which every American could expect [insert].

In the scientific arena: (Name) had just found a cure for (disease) and other scientists had just discovered the link between [insert] and [insert].

Technology: (Corporation) had just put (product) on the market. It promised to revolutionize the way we [insert].

In the arts: (Movie title) was the leading movie of the year. And I'll spare you the lyrics of (song title), but it was the hit song that blared from our radios. One of the most popular books read by business persons of the time, (book title), explained how the world was headed for [insert].

Reminiscing isn't an entirely wasted activity, you understand. It provides perspective. It photographs the past in an effort to predict the prosperity of the future.

Clearly, we as club members have been responsible for our past deeds on this historical, economic, scientific, technological, and artistic stage. When some clubs and businesses are planted, it takes time for them to bear fruit. Sometimes five years, sometimes ten. But (name of club) has been fruitful for the community and for its members almost since its inception.

Here's what your members have accomplished during the past (number) years for our city and our state:

[Insert details of club's accomplishments, such as civic and cultural contributions, educational opportunities for its members and the community, charitable contributions.]

As you can see, through the years, the leadership of this organization hasn't just asked you to put your names on the roll and bring your bodies to meetings. We've asked you to put your heart into our purpose and bring your ideas and enthusiasm for hard work in serving the community.

Anniversaries are a time to take stock. To look at our strengths and our weaknesses. Yes, we have a few weaknesses. I would hope that in the next few years, we can improve the way we [insert]. That is no less a goal for the individual member than it is for us as a group.

At the end of my reminiscing, I've come to these conclusions: There is much we can contribute to the future of our city and its citizens. You have a right to be proud as club members. Let's congratulate ourselves and then move ahead to the next big project.

ANNIVERSARY OF PAST TRAGEDY

11

Audience: all employees of an organization
Message: We remember these people who met a tragic death.
Tone: formal
Timing: 2 minutes

Today marks the anniversary of one of the greatest tragedies to occur here at (corporation). It was one year ago that an unfortunate, mentally deranged individual entered our building and gunned down 12 of our finest employees. To the individual who committed such a horror, the act was random and without meaning.

But to us—those people who knew, worked with, and loved the individuals who met their death—the act has taken on meaning.

We have grieved. We have prayed. We have asked ourselves over and over how we could have prevented it. We have tried to take precautions to prevent forever a recurrence. We have suffered from the emptiness their deaths leave.

We pause now, today, from our everyday tasks—our phone conversations, our meetings, all our planning and interacting—to remember them as they were: Energetic. Fun-loving. Talented. Compassionate. Committed to families. Committed to their fellow workers. There is pain, but there is also joy that we had the privilege of knowing and working with them through the years.

Because each of you as an individual is important to us at (corporation) and because human life is sacred to us as a nation, we resolve to remember and honor these who have died. We look forward to the day when such tragedies are no longer part of life, to a brighter day for us all.

Awards

GENERAL GUIDELINES

(To accept)

- Express appreciation for the recognition.

- Mention why the achievement was important to you, if appropriate. What does the award symbolize to you? What is your driving force? Your goal? Benefits to others from work in this field?

- Share the credit with other individuals or groups who have contributed to your achievement; however, avoid a laundry list of unrecognizable names.

- Be modest; don't boast of all your efforts and accomplishments on the road to success.

- Display emotion appropriate for the occasion. An audience will value genuineness, but will suspect insincerity if you display gushy overexuberance about routine presentations.

- Thank your audience for caring enough about you or the award to attend.

(To present to an employee or an organization)

- Elaborate on the overall commendation or achievement. What is the history of the award? What are the criteria for selection of recipients?

- Explain specifically why the recipient deserves the award. Comments from others, statistics, superior results—all these specifics show the recipient that you understand the hard work, time, ability, or attitude necessary to his or her success.

- Offer your congratulations.
- Be enthusiastic, avoiding the sound of a routine presentation.

TO ACCEPT AS AN INDIVIDUAL

12

Audience: employees, industry and media representatives
Message: Thank you for this recognition.
Tone: formal
Timing: 2 minutes

Thank you so much. I'm pleased and yet humbled to accept this award. Be assured that I accept it, recognizing the contributions of those who have gone before me in the field. Jacob Riis, the Danish-born journalist and reformer, has observed:

> When nothing seems to help, I go and look at a stonecutter hammering away at his rock perhaps a hundred times without as much as a crack showing in it. Yet at the hundred and first blow it will split in two, and I know it was not that blow that did it—but all that had gone before.

I have not struck all those 101 blows myself. As Thomas Edison added, "I start where the last man left off."

Many others such as (name, name, and name) have developed great ideas, put them into action, and served as role models to the rest of us. My work has been an add-on to theirs.

I accept this award on behalf of all these who have given of their time and imagination to prepare the path. I hope that together we—those predecessors as well as some of you in the audience—have made this organization a better place to work and this community a better place to live.

My goal is to see [insert details of the mission] happen before the end of our decade. It's not an easy goal. It's not one set lightly. The facts say that [insert statement of ultimate goal] can become a real possibility. With determination, motivation, leadership, and cooperation we can stretch ourselves. We can become the driving force others only hope to generate behind their own efforts. I offer my encouragement to any and all who want to join in working toward this end.

The ultimate goal line—the accomplishment that our world can hail as worthwhile—stands within our grasp if we keep learning, moving, growing, working. I pledge all my energy toward that end.

Thank you for caring about our progress as a group. Thank you for recognizing me in this meaningful way as I "strike a blow or two" against the problems that threaten to keep us from success. I look forward to meeting the next stonecutter to step forward.

13

Audience: business associates
Message: Thank you for this recognition.
Tone: informal, light
Timing: 2 minutes

Thank you. If, as Shakespeare said, "Praises are our wages," I feel as if I just got a raise. A very hefty one at that. After all, this is a big event for me—my Boy Scout award for knot-tying constitutes my resume at this point in my career. And though I'd like to take sole credit for this achievement, in all honesty, I can't.

You've heard it said that the big potatoes are on top of the heap because there are a lot of little potatoes holding them up. Certainly, I don't think I've become "big potatoes" on the pile, but I have had several people holding me up. They've made my work look awfully good.

Without the help and encouragement of these people, I'd still be determined—but not quite where I wanted to be. Publicly, I want to recognize (name) for career advice along the way. To recognize (name) for the time she spent with me as a sounding board about [insert details]. To recognize (names) for their leadership and confidence in me as I struggled.

Thank you. Thank each of you who had a part in selecting me for this award. To me, this award symbolizes the value we as individuals and as a group place on the quality of our workmanship. My mom always said to me—as I'm sure yours did to you—"If it's worth doing, it's worth doing well." She usually referred to piano practice and recitations for the school play. But today that adage has taken on new meaning. Your coming tonight confirms to me that you, too, embrace that value. That you, too—when you do things—do them well.

Mark Twain once gave some advice that I've taken to heart: "Keep away from people who belittle your ambitions." You know, some people do rain on everyone's parade of ideas and goals. But the really great people—the superachievers—always make others feel great. They pump people up rather than let the air out of their parade balloon. There are no "small potato" people in this group. You're great, and you've made me feel great about this accomplishment.

To be recognized by one's peers is the highest honor in any category. Despite my flippant opening, I don't take this recognition from you lightly. Thank you very sincerely.

14

Audience: employees, civic associates
Message: Thank you for the recognition.
Tone: formal
Timing: 1-2 minutes

Thank you so much for this plaque and the award it signifies. There's a distinguished group of people who've been honored in this way in the past, and I'm somewhat baffled at my good fortune to be joining them. My emotions are mixed: Surprise. . . . Pride. . . . Humility. . . . Gratitude.

As you can see by the graying temples, I've been around for a long time and I've seen this organization grow—from temporary headquarters and a membership roster of (number) to this very ample office complex and a membership of more than (number). And those statistics do not even begin to reflect the community projects completed during these past (number) years.

This award is simply a good reminder that the spirit of capitalism, justice, and democracy rests on our energies to make the community better and safer. We can all be grateful that community service has become synonymous with America.

Yes, this organization has grown—in size and in commitment.

And I like to think that I, too, have grown as an individual because of my involvement with you in these professional and civic affairs. I have simply done my small part as a corporate and private citizen—as each of you has. Ultimately, the strength of our nation rests on the character and commitment of each of us individually. And a basic part of our character is formed as we contribute to our fellowman.

Thank you very much for this recognition.

15

Audience: employees, civic associates, and the press
Message: I don't feel so smart, but I'm honored to receive this award.
Tone: informal
Timing: 2-3 minutes

I'm very honored to receive this award naming me Manager of the Year. The arduous screening process that your committee went through—just described by (name)—adds an extra dimension to the honor. That is, that the selection was made by many of you, my peers, flatters me and makes it especially meaningful.

Receiving an award, however, always makes you a little more thoughtful and deliberate about your future actions. For example, if my peers seem to think I'm a good manager and role model, then what have I been doing right?

So I began to think about all the recent decisions we've made at (company): The acquisition of (company name). . . . The introduction of our new product line, the (name). . . . Our involvement in the community's (cause) fund drive.

Of course, none of these management decisions was made without excellent advisors—both personal friends and admired employees who have worked almost around the clock for months on some of these projects at (company). (Name), (name), and many others who've been involved know how very much I've appreciated their contributions to my career and the growth of (company).

Nevertheless, you notified me that *I'd* been selected for this honor. And I was and am flattered.

In fact, I became so enamored of my wisdom in these business decisions that I started to pontificate with my two teenagers at home. I figured they should get a head start in the business world, so I began to outline some of my theories of management to them. And in their naive but straightforward way, they were quite capable of spotting some flaws in my arguments. If you've ever tried to explain the welfare mess, our national debt, or some of our trade agreements to your own kids, then you understand. All in all, explaining my management decisions to my kids was not a process without some pain.

And what all this says, of course, is that I'm glad you didn't scrutinize my record as thoroughly as do my children. I'm more than pleased to trust your judgment.

This is a prestigious award from a prestigious organization. I thank you sincerely.

16

Audience: civic associates
Message: Thank you for your own work for this cause.
Tone: formal
Timing: 3-4 minutes

Thank you for inviting me to join you today to accept this award. It symbolizes many things to me: primarily that we are not alone in the world, that human beings do care about each other.

I'm not going to say I don't deserve this award—because I identify with Golda Meir's advice. She said: "Don't be so humble—you're not that great." So I'll just accept the award as a symbol of your graciousness in recognizing those who've helped your cause in some small way.

But I want to focus on you and your group and to commend your efforts. You've come a long way in providing our citizenry with the encouragement and information they've needed through the past decade. You've taken many small steps at the local and regional level. And all these steps have lead to an impressive national effort and result. As a group you have [insert details of their accomplishments].

Your future growth is extremely important. Your growth must continue for those people you serve. Your growth is good business. And what's more, your growth is morally right.

From the well-known politicians and business people of our past, which do we remember most? The people who made their millions? Rarely. Most frequently, we proudly recall those we've labeled humanitarians or statesmen. Those who have risen above self-interest to meet their social responsibilities. Ben Franklin, for his work on gaining and preserving our liberty. Andrew Carnegie, for our free public library system. H. Ross Perot, for his patriotism that inspires others.

Organizations such as yours make us all aware of what our role as human beings is—what we owe to each other and to future generations. You are doing one small task at a time, and these tasks pay off immeasurably over the long haul.

I'm especially proud of my small role in helping cast the spotlight on your organization. But more so, I'm especially proud of you who make up an organization that gives our citizens an opportunity to be their best selves. As Hemingway once said, "The world is a fine place and worth fighting for." I think we all need to sacrifice a little of ourselves for what we believe in. You are building a better (city) and a better America. Thank you for that and thank you for this award.

17

Audience: business and civic associates
Message: Our profession deserves attention.
Tone: informal
Timing: 2-3 minutes

Thank you. I'm deeply honored to receive this (name of award). You've heard the old phrase "dyed in the wool," such as "She's a dyed-in-the-wool Republican," or "She's a dyed-in-the-wool entrepreneur." Well, in accepting this award, I'll have to say that I'm especially pleased that you, my peers, have selected me because I'm a "dyed-in-the-wool (profession such as engineer)."

For years, we as a professional group have just assumed that the rest of the world understood how complex our jobs were and understood how much we contributed to the improvement of society. But I'm no longer sure that's true. In the press, we see a lot of (profession) bashing. They—whoever the "they" happens to be—say we're insensitive to the end result of our thinking and our progress.

Yet, those making these very statements continue to enjoy [insert a few key accomplishments of the profession]. All of these are a direct result of our work as a group.

I want to take this opportunity tonight to lead us all to reflect on our accomplishments as a group of professionals. Let's start with ways we've increased productivity over the last 20 years.

[Insert details.]

And as for quality, let's recount the marked improvement in that arena. Specifically, we've discovered a new way to

[Insert details].

In today's world, from time to time, almost any profession finds itself under fire. But people under fire—just like steel—have been known to achieve great things. There's little consensus on where our country and our world are headed. So we're probably going to have to continue to make our own assumptions and determine our own path as we go along. But such a situation doesn't frighten me. I think that we as a professional group will continue to lead the way to a better America.

To all of you as my peers, my sincerest thanks for attending tonight and for the honor you've given me with the presentation of this award.

TO ACCEPT ON BEHALF OF AN ORGANIZATION

18

Audience: employees, industry and media representatives
Message: We are glad to do our part for this cause.
Tone: formal
Timing: 4-5 minutes

On behalf of the men and women of (company), which I represent here tonight, we are honored to receive this year's (name of award). We as an organization appreciate the opportunity to help those who so very much need our support and encouragement.

For too long, many people in our nation have allowed themselves to become self-centered and satisfied. They have become detached from the society that has nurtured them. We at (company) have to continually remind ourselves that we all have a stake in the moral and social well-being of our society.

Like you as an organization, we at (company) are in the service business in another arena. We see ourselves as a company with a mission beyond that of earning a profit. By no means am I implying that profits are bad; only through profits can companies continue to offer such community support.

But I mean that our mission is service— even in our profit-making business activities. We feel that our products and services at (company) make people's lives better, healthier, more pleasant. As a corporation, we have a primary responsibility to carry out the basic function of business—to make a profit. And we have a host of "citizens" to please—stockholders, employees, customers, and the public at large. But our experience has taught us that corporate involvement in social causes does more than help people who receive a check for medicine or receive a bed to sleep in for the night. Our involvement actually strengthens our ability to make a profit.

In other words, profit and community service go hand in hand. Good works continue to be one of the best ways to build goodwill.

In addition to the involvement with your organization, you may or may not be aware of our work with the (name of organization) to provide [insert details on service to community].

A second way some of our managers have chosen to serve their community is through an organization called (name), which has the goal of [insert details].

Then individually, some of our employees have devoted considerable energy on company time to become involved in (names of causes or organizations).

In monetary terms, our contributions to (type) research this year have totaled more than (number) dollars—a figure we're proud of and a figure we feel we owe the community for allowing us a safe, pleasant lifestyle as residents.

But we do not intend to stop there. Rather, we have established a strategic plan to pursue social goals in several new arenas in the coming years—involvement that your own family may benefit from at some time in their lives.

To sum up our strategy at (company), we encourage people to help people. We want to solve people problems as well as profit problems.

Certainly, we are aware that other corporations have conscientiously undertaken similar projects to help the community. They, too, are anxious to participate in finding solutions to the problems and social ills around us. But I also want to encourage those companies who may not be so involved to dig deep into their own reserves of employees and dollars to seek out the answers to the challenges we face in our community. We all must become more active and more committed than ever to community service—which is, when you come down to it—individual service.

To those individuals and companies who have not yet become involved in the community, I offer this observation: Employees who participate in such programs become better people—they shape their character with sound moral values,... increase their energy and zest for the job and life in general,... and broaden their knowledge about human nature and community affairs. All become more valuable employees.

A free society will work—if we work at it. Thank you for recognizing the contributions of our employees with this award. We pledge to you to continue our efforts in the community.

19

Audience: professional and civic associates
Message: We are honored that you recognize our success.
Tone: formal
Timing: 4-5 minutes

Thank you. I accept this (name of award) on behalf of a great team of professionals at (company). Standing here behind the podium with this award in hand, I think I know how it feels to be an Olympic athlete or an Academy Award winner. As you've already heard tonight, many great organizations have been recognized before ours and no doubt many successful ones will come after. Nevertheless, this is our moment, and we are thrilled to stand in the spotlight.

To us, the award symbolizes the quality we value in the way we serve our customers. When we discover a major quality problem, we appoint a task force to search out the causes for the problem and to propose some solutions. But for the little quality problems—those that occur once in every thousand times—we know we can depend on our people individually. They must notice them in their specific work assignment and bring them to the attention of management or correct the deficiency themselves. In other words, our people have gone nuts about quality.

We also are happy about our growth record over the past five years. But we don't necessarily measure our own growth in terms of dollars. We have added (number) employees during this period and have expanded our research in [insert details] to alleviate the ongoing problem of [insert details]. Finally, we've laid out some firm plans for community involvement—plans that are quite ambitious, but do-able.

That's what this award means to (company) employees. A culmination of much energy, talent, and commitment to be the best in all arenas.

But I want to focus on a larger stage now—our industry. I think we should congratulate ourselves as an industry on making it through the last few years. For starters, beginning in (year), we saw problems such as [insert details on one or more problems]. We accepted them as challenges to make us more efficient and creative.

The stakes were high. The mission was worthwhile. The obstacles were monumental. But we found the critical resources—industry professionals such as you who have devoted the time and leadership necessary to turn the situation around for the world. Top-management, middle-management, and first-line supervisors have worked side by side in our companies. Volunteer leaders of our trade associations have done their part in collecting and shaping our individual energies. And this united effort has been successful.

Our progress is worth celebrating. We at (company) are celebrating this honor you've given us. And we want to encourage you to celebrate your part in the survival and indeed the improvements that have taken place because of the past challenges. We have communicated with our employees. We have communicated with our customers. We have communicated with our representatives in Congress and the public at large.

Thank you for presenting us at (company) with this award to recognize our hard work. We're proud to be honored as an organization with a philosophy of excellence and a tradition of anticipating crises and managing changes.

And we as an industry—you in the audience specifically—have a right to be proud of how far we've all come. And as we're reminding ourselves at (company), we have to continue to be alert to the opportunities—and the pitfalls—ahead. In the end, the customer will win.

TO PRESENT TO AN EMPLOYEE

20

(On academic distinction/continuing education or training)

Audience: professional associates and family members

Message: You as a group are to be commended for your time, effort, and ability in furthering your education and developing your skills.

Tone: formal

Timing: 2-3 minutes

They say you can always tell luck from ability by its duration. Luck may have been the reason behind an exam or two here or there, but ability alone is the foundation of success through (number) months of this (name of program) intensive training program.

The program, begun by our CEO himself almost (number) years ago now, involves intensive pre-study and development of case studies to be reviewed before an individual is even accepted for participation. Then after acceptance, the participants are required to complete (number) class hours of study, to develop more than (number) case studies, to participate in (number) weeks as an intern, and then to complete an intensive final test of knowledge and behavioral accomplishments.

From the program's inception, it was not designed for the faint-hearted, for the drifter, for the individual contented to be "just one of a group." Therefore, it was no surprise to friends and coworkers who know you well, when each of you volunteered to enter the program to focus on developing these new skills and thinking processes.

Many of you have already distinguished yourselves at the various universities across the nation. But we are here to present all of you with the (name of award) in recognition of your continuing efforts to excel in your chosen field.

Who cares? The gathering here tonight of your colleagues and family and friends. We care about your dedication and struggle. We care about achievement. We care about excellence.

Charles Garfield, in his book *Peak Performers*, identifies those celebrities like gold medalists and astronauts as well as the "average Joes" who stand head and shoulders above their colleagues at work. Upon completion of his studies, Garfield wryly observed these commonalities about his interviewees: "Some people make things happen, some watch things happen, and some wonder what happened."

By your effort during this training program, you clearly have identified yourself as part of the group that will make things happen. To paraphrase another, "There is no future in any job; the future lies in *you* who hold the job." You, as graduates of this program, are the business leaders that will make your companies profitable, that will make your communities progressive, that will make your world civilized and prosperous.

Congratulations on your achievement. We hope this program and this recognition certificate will be part of an ongoing, richly rewarding career and life.

21

(On publication)

Audience: employees and other business associates
Message: Thank you for putting our company in the spotlight by publishing.
Tone: formal
Timing: 3 minutes

Why her? Why (name)? Why have editors considered her work worthy of publication? What do editors and editorial boards look for in selecting work to be published in their pages? First of all, they want to be on the cutting edge of new ideas and new technology. Then they want to recognize the first and the best—the fresh thinkers, the brightest minds. Third, they want to be clear with their readers. They demand a writing style that communicates rather than confuses, . . . that elucidates rather than obscures, . . . that motivates rather than denigrates.

For all these reasons, editors nationwide have chosen to bring (name)'s work to the forefront of the industry, to the attention of those who can benefit from it and build a bridge from it. Within the last (number) years, (name)'s work has appeared in these prestigious journals:

[Insert journal titles here, along with titles of the articles.]

And publication always brings prestige for those who publish and the organizations they represent.

New York pop artist Andy Warhol has quipped: "I am a deeply superficial person." Well, there's nothing superficial about (name). Although publication in the national media always brings with it a certain degree of personal gratification and recognition, (name)'s work has been motivated by more than a need to see her name in bright lights or by-lines. More than anything else, she deeply cares about our progress in the field of [insert details of contribution to her field].

Her caring has not been without profit. Our company could not have paid for the kind of advertising and media attention that (name)'s publications have produced. We have benefited from inquiries on new products and our new technology. We have become known as an innovator, with calls from investors wanting to underwrite our future growth. We have strengthened our current clients' confidence in what we offer. Even from our competition, we have received congratulations.

Therefore, it is with pleasure and gratitude that I recognize (name) for her contributions to our organization and to the industry as a whole. (Name), congratulations on such achievement.

22

(For suggestions implemented within the organization)

Audience: business colleagues within one's own department
Message: We appreciate this suggestion; it will increase our productivity and save us money.
Tone: informal, light
Timing: 4-5 minutes, depending on insertion of details

Paperwork. What most people consider the drudge part of their jobs. Paperwork threatens to devour our budgets and time, demoralize our staff, confuse our customers, sap our creativity, and reduce our overall productivity. (Name) has done something about it in his department. You're all waiting breathlessly to find out exactly what his paperwork secret is—to find out how to clear your own desk of clutter. Well, let me keep you in suspense a moment longer about the details.

As you know, we began two years ago to solicit your suggestions on how to improve your job and the bottom line. "If there's a way to do it better, find it" became our motto. Our suggestion committee plastered the walls with reminders of our campaign for suggestions. With their good PR and your willingness to think creatively, the program has elicited over (number) suggestions that have resulted in a savings to the company of over $X. Not to mention increased satisfaction from our customers and our employees themselves.

Just to remind you of some of the suggestions that have been implemented during the past two years, let me mention:

[Insert several programs or changes that have been put into effect, along with the persons who initiated the ideas.]

So you can see that the people who have made this program work have done an excellent job in making this a better place to earn a paycheck.

Those committee members who review suggestions perform a valuable service for all of us. They must thoroughly check out the suggestion and the numbers to verify that the idea really will work well in our environment and fit our overall purposes. And they have done that with (name)'s suggestion.

Here's (name)'s suggestion in a nutshell: To reduce the paperwork we all shuffle weekly, we should eliminate the (title) report altogether and streamline the (title) weekly reports from your department by presenting all the information on a simple one-page graph. Roughly, the committee estimates these two changes will save us $X annually. Your department manager will receive more details shortly about the hows and whens.

Someone has said that there's nothing quite as embarrassing as watching an employee do something you assured him couldn't be done. Well, we're embarrassed. More specifically, we are embarrassed that we didn't think of it sooner and we're proud that (name) brought the idea to our attention.

(Name), please join me up here. [Pause until recipient joins you in front of the group.] I'm pleased to present to you this check representing a portion of the savings we will realize because of your idea. We did have second thoughts about this, however. After all, to a fellow who doesn't like paperwork, we're handing him more paper—a check. We could have wired the money, I suppose, but we thought you'd forgive us just this once for adding to your paper clutter.

Thank you sincerely, (name). Employees such as you keep all of the rest of us on our toes. Creative thinking and commitment to do an excellent job deserve our congratulations.

23

(For business or civic achievement)

Audience: business associates, industry and media representatives
Message: We admire your achievement.
Tone: formal
Timing: 5-6 minutes

Good afternoon. My personal welcome to all of our guests on behalf of the Chamber members. My happy task is to announce the winner of this year's CEO of the City Award presented by our local Chamber of Commerce.

Just to give you a little history on the award, we initiated this annual recognition as a response to a lull that had fallen across our city in the 19—s as our economy suffered and gasped for air. When things are darkest, we all tend to chime in with the doomsayers and focus on what's wrong with our corporations and economy. This award was established as a way of redirecting our thinking to what was right and continues to be right about the successful corporations based here.

In selecting this year's winner, our panel of judges, composed of our Chamber leadership and their committee chairs, reviewed files of candidates nominated at large from our membership. As a member of that panel myself, I can assure you that the selection process and investigation were thorough. Of more than (number) candidates nominated, we have chosen (name), CEO of (corporation), as the individual who represents the very best of corporate leadership in (city). And maybe even in the state or nation, though we didn't research that far.

What are the measures of great leadership? Someone has defined it this way: "A leader is anyone who has two characteristics: First, he is going somewhere. Second, he is able to persuade other people to go with him." That's an oversimplification, but I think you will agree that (name) has persuaded others to go with him.

In his tenure with (corporation), he has taken the company from $X in revenue and (number) employees to $X in revenue with more than (number) employees. Their balance sheet shows consistent growth. They have logged (number) consecutive years of record earnings. Their revenues have tripled in the period he has been at the helm. The stock price has doubled in the past (number) years, and the company has a X percent return on equity. All this in a period of recession for our city and their industry in general.

You can't argue with success. We are today recognizing consistency of success and the degree of difficulty of the task itself. In the words of management guru Warren Bennis, "Leadership is the capacity to translate vision into reality."

Another mark of a leader, in addition to financial success, is strong ethical values planted in the corporate culture. At (corporation), they believe in the dignity of the individual and a higher purpose for business than simply profit. The level of trust built into their value system is the glue that holds procedures and policies together and sets the daily environment for progress.

A third mark of leadership is clear communication from the top down and from the bottom up. In the wisdom of Peter Drucker: "Management is not being brilliant. . . . Management is craftsmanship. Most of the time it is hard work to get a very few simple things across so that ordinary people can do them." At (corporation), they get things across very well—in both upward and lateral directions. Their employee-suggestion campaign serves as a model for anyone. And their monthly reporting system is a model in efficiency and clear communication about goals and accomplishments.

Clearly, (name) has led his company to financial success. But that financial success is only one mark of a leader. (Name)'s leadership has also been evident in promoting an ethical culture and clear communication. In a phrase, he has translated vision into reality at (corporation).

Education and experience alone can't make us all leaders. But they can teach us which leader to follow. (Name) is a front runner; he has given us, as well as his own employees, someone to follow.

On behalf of our panel of judges, I'm pleased to name him as CEO of the City for 19—. (Name), you have our admiration and our congratulations. May the future be even brighter.

TO PRESENT TO AN ORGANIZATION

24

Audience: employees, industry and media representatives
Message: We admire and appreciate your success.
Tone: formal
Timing: 6-7 minutes

Good evening, ladies and gentlemen. Thank you for allowing me the privilege of being with you tonight at your (number) Annual (name) Awards program. We've all come to honor (corporation) for its literacy work across the nation this past year. As recipient of this year's award, your company—in the judgment of our nominators and selection committees—has done the most to advance our understanding of the literacy problem and its effects and to give us momentum in resolving it. Not only has (corporation) donated $X to the Literacy Foundation, but your company has also granted sabbaticals to (number) key employees to support their personal involvement in the programs here in our local community.

Illiteracy threatens to

[Insert statistics and details about illiteracy in the business community and how it affects the workforce.]

But why would this corporation and these few individuals personally take on the burden of doing something about the problem?

Why would they spend hours reading research notes and other literature to educate themselves about the growing crisis?

Why would they postpone or miss other business opportunities to meet together to plan and strategize about what has worked in other cities and what our local community needs and would respond to?

Why would they as individuals miss family events and get-togethers with friends and business associates to travel to other cities to observe other literacy programs firsthand?

Why would they as individual employees spend their lunch hours interviewing those unfortunate people who cannot read or write, who cannot communicate on a very basic level?

In other words, why would such a program generate the feelings of "more than just a job"?

The answers to these questions lie in the kind of corporate culture (corporation) has established. In the kind of values the management there holds. In the caliber of individuals they employ and the attitudes they hold.

In our day and age, many people consider boredom—or at least un-emotional involvement—as a mark of sophistication. Many think it's ple-beian to show enthusiasm for almost any idea, event, or cause.

I suggest another tag for that attitude other than sophistication. I suggest that we as managers and employees become bored in direct pro-portion to our loss of interest in other people and pursuits higher than ourselves and the bottom line. The biggest booster of boredom and com-placency is selfishness. . . . Selfishness.

This corporation and these individual representatives whom we've come to honor tonight have not become lulled into self-centeredness by complacency or abundance. They have not looked out their office windows at the need and muttered, "Somebody ought to do something."

They have done something.

They have written big checks. They as individuals have crisscrossed our nation. They have studied models of excellence and then have come home to plan, organize, and implement them in our own city. They have been responsible for the success of (name) programs that have taught (number) of our citizens to read and become fully functioning members of our workforce and of society.

And we should never forget that these programs represent individual lives changed. Today because of their donations and painstaking work: A grandmother can read her newspaper. . . . An indigent mother can use the want-ads to find work. . . . A high-school dropout can take the GED exam and earn his diploma. . . . A father can read the map to take his children to Disneyland. . . . A sweetheart can select a greeting card for her loved one. . . . A husband can upgrade his skills and make a better life for his family.

(Corporation) and these individuals have my admiration for what they have accomplished and for the commitment that leads to such ac-complishment. We are celebrating some of the very qualities that make us human—our abilities to reason, to discover, to learn, to pass on knowl-edge.

I commend these individuals and salute their corporation. (Names of recipients), the award you are receiving tonight on behalf of your cor-poration is an encouragement to continue your efforts to fight illiteracy. We hope you will also regard this award as a symbol of our gratitude for illuminating the darkness of those individuals your programs have touched. Your company not only revolves around money and machinery; it has shown concern about purpose and people. We hope those thoughts bring you great satisfaction.

Benedictions

GENERAL GUIDELINES

- Express thanksgiving for past and present opportunities.
- Recall the qualities of the retired, deceased, or otherwise honored individual.
- Look forward to the future with confidence.

RETIREMENT

25

Audience: business or civic associates
Message: Bless this individual as she continues to contribute.
Tone: formal
Timing: 1 minute

At the closing of these shared thoughts about our friend and colleague, we are reminded once again about how time slips by. How days slip into months and years of career and achievement. We thank You, Lord, for the privilege of working with (name) through the years. For her example of enthusiasm, integrity, dedication, and compassion. As we continue to work at our individual tasks, thank You for the way she has contributed to our professional and personal growth.

We also ask Your special blessings on (name). In her retirement years, grant her rest, peace, and pride in her career accomplishments. We ask that You also continue to give her good health and many years to continue her personal contributions to the lives of friends and family. Bless her as she serves in whatever way You lead.

RECOGNITION OF ACHIEVEMENT

26

Audience: business and civic associates
Message: Bless us in this achievement.
Tone: formal
Timing: 2 minutes

As we are gathered here today to present these scholarship funds to (name) University, we seek Your blessings on our efforts and intentions.

We are mindful this money collected throughout the nation from friends and alumni of the organization is but a token of the love we hold for learning. As paper, the money is nothing. But at work in the lives of young people, we know it means a future for the individuals involved and a contribution to society and to all of us.

To those scholarship recipients, the money will bring hard work, respect for authority, appreciation of knowledge, development of skills, and a manner of livelihood. For society, these scholarships represent a quest for more knowledge, a desire for the cures to the diseases that afflict us, a prevention of economic and industrial evils that plague us, a hope for a better life for generations to come.

Thank You for the blessings on us individually and collectively— blessings that have allowed us to work and see the financial rewards of that work.

Thank You that our resources are enough to meet our own needs and to share.

Thank You for giving contributors a charitable spirit and foresight about this need.

Thank You for giving leadership in this academic community to oversee the uses of this money.

And finally, thank You for the dedication and determination of those young people who will achieve because of these scholarships.

Bless us together.

CIVIC MEETING

27

Audience: civic group
Message: Bless us as we solve problem issues.
Tone: formal
Timing: 1 minute

Dear Lord, we ask Your presence and blessings on our time together tonight. We have come to express our concerns about the welfare of our community. . . . To learn from each other. . . . To grow in spirit and in character. . . . To find Your will for our lives and neighborhoods.

We thank You for the opportunity in this country to assemble ourselves at any time and at any place to discuss our concerns as citizens. We are mindful that many in our world do not enjoy such freedom.

Grant us the wisdom to carry out decisions within Your will. Bless us as we continue to conduct our business with dignity and sensitivity.

28

Audience: business or civic group
Message: Bless us as individuals as we grow in our professional and personal lives.
Tone: formal
Timing: 1 minute

Our Heavenly Father, bless this food that we have enjoyed tonight and its nourishment for our continued strength and health. We also ask that You bless all those who have so capably handled the details of this event to make the evening profitable and meaningful for all of us.

Thank You for the ideas and insights that have been shared. Help us to use them to grow as business professionals and as family members. Enrich our lives because of our attendance and contributions among this group of friends and associates.

We thank You for Your provisions and Your ongoing protection. Keep us mindful that we are in Your service while on this earth.

MEMORIAL FOR DECEASED

29

Audience: business or civic group
Message: Bless the ongoing contributions of the deceased's memory.
Tone: formal
Timing: 1 minute

Please bow your heads as we each in our own way remember (name). This memory, of course, Lord, will not be our last. We acknowledge Your right and power both to give life and to take it. We accept Your sovereignty in our lives, even when it may bring us heartache and even when we may not understand the reasons.

We ask that You as an all-compassionate God help us to carry on (name)'s work that we have gathered here to commemorate. As we have talked about and remembered his contributions to the community, family, and friends, we ask that you inspire us to do our part in seeing his efforts come to a successful reality.

Particularly, we ask Your blessings on (name of favorite project) that he loved and worked with. Help those individuals who benefited from his efforts there continue in their progress to regain hope and stability for their lives. Help those in leadership to bring others into the causes for which (name) worked so diligently.

We trust confidently that today (name)'s spirit is at rest with You, his Maker. And we thank You that his example and memory is still among us, his friends.

30

Audience: business or civic group
Message: Bless the family of this individual and the ongoing contributions of the deceased's memory.
Tone: formal
Timing: 1-2 minutes

Dear Lord, (name) has been Your faithful servant on earth for many years. She has served long and well. As we as friends and business associates have gathered to remember her contributions to our lives, we ask that You particularly be near her family.

Rather than lessen the pain of the loss of a loved one, the years seem only to heighten our appreciation of that great loss. Specifically, we ask Your guidance for her son and daughter as they settle matters of (name)'s concern. Those of us who know her children well know that their adult lives have already produced gain in the world. Much of that, we know, is a direct influence from their mother's life.

And then as business associates, we realize that many of our successes on the job are a result of (name)'s direction, advice, and knowledge.

Together we are thankful for her contribution and example before us. Those of us who didn't get an opportunity to express our appreciation to her directly ask particularly that Your spirit grant her that knowledge in the afterlife.

Even now, her compassion in word and deed continues to glow within us. As she has honored us with her life, we ask that You help us honor her and her family today.

Thank You for Your eternal provisions for us all.

Dedications

GENERAL GUIDELINES

(Of a business facility)

- State the specifics of the occasion—where, when, why, how—this facility has been established.
- Point out benefits of the facility to the workers and the community.
- Call attention to the contributions of those who worked to make the facility ready.
- Recognize the responsibility of those who will work there and express confidence in them and their future use of the facility.

(Of a memorial for a deceased employee or civic leader)

- Recall virtues or contributions of the one to be memorialized and lead the audience to an appreciation of that person's values.
- Call attention to any obstacles this person overcame and how remarkable the achievement or contribution was.
- Mention the effects or significance of this person's life.
- Encourage the audience to emulate those virtues or qualities or to uphold those values and support those causes that the deceased considered important.

(Upon presentation of a memorial gift)

- Express appreciation for the contributions or values of the memorialized individual.

- Mention the significance of this individual's life to you or to the organization.
- Present the gift as symbolic of your sentiment.

OF A NEW FACILITY

31

Audience: employees, members of the community and the press
Message: We are proud of this new facility. It will benefit our workers and our community.
Tone: formal
Timing: 6-7 minutes, depending on insertion of details about facility design

We are dedicating a new (type) facility here, our (name of plant). Planning such a move is just like planning a new product or a new service—it's expensive and it's risky. But it's also exciting and challenging.

Why the excitement over a building? It represents our industry leadership and our focus on technical excellence. We intend to continue to build the quality in—not add it on.

The quality has been built into the design. We have the latest technology in our computer systems and in our

[Insert details about state-of-the-art technology in the facility.]

And you've heard much lately about quality customer service. We've also built that into the design. The building layout invites customer interaction. You noticed when you arrived today that the parking lot is not one big expanse of parking slots, but a group of slots near each of our (number) entrances. You also noticed the reserved signs—not for our management, but for our customers.

Inside, our idea was the same. As you tour the building, you'll see the various seating areas that encourage our representatives to visit with our customers in comfort and still retain the convenience of a desk and office equipment within reach of their fingertips.

Not only will our customers like the design—so will our employees. Their safety and comfort has also been uppermost in the minds of our planners.

[Insert details about safety and other features that add to a pleasant working environment for employees.]

In short, the environment is designed to encourage customers to tell us what they want, and to encourage employees to think innovatively in producing those products and providing those services. We want to help our employees work smarter and gain a sense of satisfaction in knowing that we care about the atmosphere and quality of their work life.

For the community, this facility means another corporate neighbor is on the doorstep. We've worked diligently with city planners to lay out the grounds and entrances and exits to improve, rather than hinder, the traffic flow.

We hope the community will also appreciate the increased tax base—significant dollars for its schools, parks, and other projects. New jobs also are a part of the picture as we expand.

All this—the better environment for our employees,... the inducement for our customers to speak their minds to us,... and the involvement and contribution to the community—is both exciting and challenging.

We have numerous people to thank. (Name) and (name) have been responsible for [insert specific details].

Our thanks also go to (name) and (group) for their involvement and forward thinking with regard to [insert specific details].

It takes special people to launch any new undertaking such as this. These are special people, as are many of you in the audience who will show up at these doors next (day) morning to give your best.

This is our day of celebration—our exciting challenge to maintain our innovation and leadership. Thank you for coming to be a part of it.

32

Audience: employees, community and press representatives
Message: We are celebrating our expansion.
Tone: formal
Timing: 6-7 minutes, depending on insertion of details about the facility design

Today is the (number) chapter in the ongoing saga of (corporation). I say (number) chapter because this is our (number) such facility in the United States. The first was opened in (city) over (number) years ago with no less fanfare than this.

But I must say that the celebrations certainly get larger as we grow. We have a proud heritage of excellence and a future that knows no bounds.

I want to define "state of the art" as it applies here today:

[Insert details of the facility's construction and layout.]

Anyone who tours these grounds and sees firsthand the design details and investigates the thought processes behind those details can't help but be impressed. More important than the striking appearance of this building is what goes on inside.

We are here to dedicate a symbol of the present and a promise for the future. Our present reads like this: With over (number) employees, we have become the leader in the (type) industry. Our products span the shelves of your local stores. To mention a few:

[Insert product names, particularly those that may not be well known to the general public.]

As you can now see, we help you put food on your table, maintain your physical fitness, travel from place to place, and entertain yourselves.

This building and these products result in a higher quality of life. We can now produce them in a shorter lead time with lower production dollars.

This facility replicates our past image of a growing, innovative, customer-oriented company. That's the past.

Now about that promising future I mentioned earlier: Within (number) months, we plan to have hired (number) people to fill jobs here. There will be both hourly and salaried groups of people who will help us maintain our traditions of quality.

And it goes without saying that we are committed to being a good corporate citizen. We want to join your organizations, shop in your city, attend your churches and synagogues. We plan to put down roots and become family.

How big a job has it been to move us—this (corporation) family—into town? A tremendous one. From day one, (name) has been at the helm of this ship. He has seen our ship come in. In fact, he launched it. This effort and final facility involved the culmination of (number) months of planning and coordination.

Under his leadership have been several first mates who've racked up a few planning hours themselves. (Name). . . . (Name). . . . (Name).

But of what value would all this planning be without the workers here?

People power—of that we have plenty. It will be the creativity, commitment, and integrity of these people who will make a contribution to the community and to the industry.

By their hard work, energy, and enthusiasm, they have been, and will continue to be, a winning team. They—our people—will as always write the last chapter to our story. This is an important day for these people as they set the pace for the complex world we compete in.

Yes, we are proud of our past and make a promise to the future in this city. This spirit—on display in this new facility—will lead us into the next century. Thank you for celebrating with us.

OF A MEMORIAL
FOR A DECEASED EMPLOYEE

33

Audience: family, employees and civic associates
Message: We remember her contributions to our corporation and to our personal lives.
Tone: formal
Timing: 3-4 minutes

Winston Churchill said it best: "We make a living by what we get, we make a life by what we give." As those of you gathered here today will agree, (name) made a life. Her sudden and tragic death grieves us, but it also focuses our thinking on what is good and right about our spirit here at (corporation). I can't think of a better example of that spirit than (name).

She didn't just make a living here; she made a life. First, she offered her friendship. To those who worked around her most closely, she was known affectionately as "(nickname)." You could not attend a day-long meeting or seminar with (name) without her asking about your family, your vacation, or your health. Not routine were your answers, either, because as you talked to (name), you got the sense that she really listened to what you said,... that she really cared about your happiness and well-being.

And she valued each employee and client who passed through her door as an individual of worth, and she dealt with them all that way.

(Name) didn't just make a living here; she made a life. She offered her integrity. Integrity is what you have when no one else is looking.

No detail was too small for her to handle. No risk was too minimal for her to give the pros and cons full consideration. No financial decision was too large that honesty did not count.

(Name) didn't just make a living here; she made a life. She offered her compassion. Many of you will remember her efforts in helping the community to rebuild after the (tragedy). She was also involved in our own annual charity efforts such as (names of campaigns). Pain and suffering pricked her heart, and she did more than bleed. She acted on behalf of those who needed her financial support and her personal energy in [insert details of the cause].

We honor her today by placing her photograph and a small plaque about her work here in our hallway. It's our hope that those who pass by every day will be reminded of her contributions here at (corporation).

We also encourage you to emulate her commitment to make a life—not a living. To give rather than to receive.

Employment here is more than a paycheck. It is friendship, integrity, and compassion toward our fellowman. We honor (name) today and want her family to know that we share in their loss and respect their wife and mother's contributions to our lives.

OF A COMMUNITY MEMORIAL FOR CIVIC LEADER

34

Audience: family, members of the community and the press
Message: We remember his leadership.
Tone: formal
Timing: 4-5 minutes, depending on the insertion of details about the upcoming artistic performances

A traveler met three stonecutters along a road and asked each what he was doing. The first man responded that he was cutting stone. The second said that he was shaping a cornerstone. But the third proudly smiled and said: "I'm building a cathedral."

(Name) lived his life to build cathedrals. Whether it was the (name of project) or the (name of project), he always saw the big picture. It's been said that a manager thinks about **today** and *tomorrow*. A leader thinks about *the day after tomorrow*. And to his credit, (name) was a man who thought about the future—in both his business and his civic roles—and could communicate that vision to others.

We have gathered here to rename this building in his honor. Although it's not a cathedral, what goes on inside will change the lives of those who enter. Their horizons and their appreciation of the arts will bring them to a better understanding of life itself—our roots and man's longings from earliest time.

This museum and performing arts theater will also bring new life to our present-day city. Attention and commitment to the arts, such as this building represents, increase our city's competitive edge as a destination for new industry, new businesses, and new families.

Such commitment to art isn't a luxury; it's a necessity. The image of a city is tied to its citizens' and its neighbors' perceptions of its leadership. (Name), whom we honor today, was the instigator of that image. Through his untiring efforts over the past few years, he led (number) local businesses to contribute $X to see that this center was established.

But his efforts did not stop with construction. He also shared his vision of attracting some of the top artists in the country to perform here. By stimulating a partnership between the arts and the corporate community, he has fostered the image that our city is emerging as a cosmopolitan, international center.

Over the next year, we have scheduled these upcoming events in this center:

[Insert details of upcoming programs and events.]

We encourage you as corporations to purchase season tickets and make them available to your employees and clients as your further contribution to the city and to the arts.

What has been good for the city as a whole has also been good for the individual citizen. As a result of (name)'s leadership, we have a place for our children and our grandchildren to visit and to enrich their understanding of the world. To be specific, their understanding of themselves.

As a cathedral builder, (name) created that vision and communicated that vision. "Monuments are the grappling-irons that bind one generation to another," said the French moralist Joseph Joubert. We are pleased to dedicate this building to (name)'s memory—to bind his efforts to this symbol of our appreciation of the arts.

UPON PRESENTATION OF A MEMORIAL GIFT

35

Audience: family, business and civic associates
Message: This gift will support the causes for which they worked.
Tone: formal
Timing: 4-5 minutes

I consider it a pleasure to be here today representing (corporation) to help you move closer to that (city) memorial honoring the (group of people).

In a sense, we are too late. This recognition of their efforts in (cause) is long overdue. As they gave their lives in their attempts to rescue their fellowman, their decision was swift. Where there was suffering, they jumped in to alleviate it. We should be no less swift with our recognition of their sacrifice.

They have made a contribution to our community in more ways than their heroic efforts to save those victims of the tragic (act). Their contribution, you might say, was also in their attitude. Their decision to get involved, though a quick one, wasn't necessarily a thoughtless one.

On the contrary, with thought and deliberation, these individuals made their decision to fight for another's right to live. There was no regard for poverty or race. There was no regard for station in life. There was no regard of personal gain.

Instead, their minds riveted on the desperation before them and the chance for survival of another human being.

Why did they do it? A Dutch woman, Miep Gies, risked her life daily for more than two years to shelter the Frank family during Hitler's reign of terror. Why? What is it that drives some men and women to risk their lives for another? Social scientists can't tell us—other than to say that these people long to see satisfying results. In other words, they care. And they want to reverse the bad situation.

With this memorial, we are acknowledging their caring and sacrifice and commending their courage.

You may wonder why (corporation) would be so vocal in support of this particular memorial. The answer is simple: We strongly believe that this is both the history and the future of America.

Let me explain. It has not always been so in America that such value was placed on the dignity of all human life. While our cultures and backgrounds have always been diverse, we as citizens have not always embraced each other in brotherly love. There have been lines of religion, race, and riches. But sacrificial acts like this prove that we are indeed moving toward what Martin Luther King called "one America."

That's no small endeavor. These (number) individuals whom we are memorializing today have taken another step over that line into our future. They have sacrificed their lives so that others—young and old, rich and poor, Protestant and Jew—could carry the baton further.

We as a corporation are stepping forward to set the record straight. We value the lives of these victims. We honor the deaths of those who gave. We want that new America. We are thrilled to see this memorial planned.

Let me challenge other corporate citizens of our state and our nation to participate in celebrating such a value system wherever they see it displayed.

It is with pleasure and admiration that I present to you our check for $X to construct the memorial that marks the spot where (number) individuals valued another's life above their own.

36

Audience: family, business and civic associates
Message: We acknowledge the sacrifice of this individual for the public's welfare.
Tone: formal
Timing: 4-5 minutes

We are here today to honor officer (name), who gave his life for what he believed in—the law. (Name) was killed in the line of duty while investigating a drug operation in our city. Neither danger nor fear prevented him from carrying out his mission. His sacrifice reminds us all of the commitment made by all our law enforcement officers every day on their jobs.

Please reflect with me a few moments on the meaning of his sacrifice. His commitment.

First of all, his commitment involved being a role model for lawful conduct for all our citizenry. His personal life was above reproach where the law was concerned. How can one enforce a law that he or she does not respect in personal, daily life?

Second, (name)'s commitment involved moral courage. He knew well as a member of the police force that you can't please everybody all the time. But he did not let public opinion—as it is expressed on various issues in the daily papers—deter him from upholding the law as it is written. In split seconds, he had to make judgments about an individual's rights as they balance against the safety of the public at large. Not easy decisions. One who makes them is not without thought or courage.

Third, (name)'s commitment meant service to the public. Your children go to school each day without fear for their lives. Your teenagers attend movie theaters and shopping malls without thought that they may be mugged on their way to and from. Your homes and your businesses do not need 24-hour guards around them when you leave for fear that your belongings will be gone when you return. Our nation's highways are safe for your travel from state to state. Our museums are open for your pleasure as you browse to entertain or educate yourselves.

Oh, I'm not saying that our city is without drug peddlers who would devour our children, muggers who would attack our teens, or burglars who would steal our belongings.

I am saying that fear of such horrors is not ever-present in your minds. And it is the presence of our public servants and their commitment to your safety and well-being that gives you peace of mind about your loved ones and your possessions. And as we fill our streets and our hallways with more officers like (name), that peace of mind will be even more pervasive in our world.

Officer (name) committed himself as a role model for personal observance of the law, to moral courage in the face of opposition, and to the welfare of the public. He made his commitment knowing the risks involved in his job.

We applaud that commitment, the courage it exemplifies, and the safety it affords. Likewise, with respect we present this check for $X to his family—his wife and children. This money, we hope, will make their lives easier in the face of their loss.

Mrs. (name) and children, his memory and his sacrifice will not be forgotten.

Eulogies

GENERAL GUIDELINES

- Express grief over the loss, but avoid going into specific details of the tragedy or illness.
- Offer specific praise of the deceased. If you didn't know the individual well, pass on remarks or observations from others.
- Close with gratitude for the deceased's contributions in life.

37

Audience: business or civic group, family members
Message: Let's focus on living.
Tone: personal, yet formal
Timing: 3-4 minutes

Rather than our own death, it is the death of a friend that hurts us. But it's not of death that I want to talk today. While good men die, their contributions do not. I have chosen to talk about living and giving.

"A successful man," observed Albert Einstein, "is he who receives a great deal from his fellowmen, usually incomparably more than corresponds to his service to them. The value of a man, however, should be seen in what he gives and not in what he is able to receive."

In one word, (name of deceased) was a man who gave.

He gave us encouragement. I've never known a decision so heavy, a deadline so pressing, a crisis so confusing that (deceased) could not put a spring in my step when I walked out of his office. He had a way of putting things in perspective that made the situation bearable, if not actually beneficial.

Someone has said that a good way to judge a man is to see which he would take if given a choice—a light load or a strong back. Through no choice of his own, (deceased)'s situation required a strong back. And along the way, through his own experience and heartaches, he developed a soft shoulder and an encouraging handshake.

He gave us time. He attended meetings just to offer emotional support when we needed it with clients and bosses. He handled paperwork that piled up when we had to be out of the office on other business. He phoned us at home to ask about our sick parents or children. He strolled into our offices and took a few minutes or a few hours to become a sounding board for plans and decisions.

He gave us laughter. I recall the time I told him he was like a father to all of us at the office. With his quick wit, he responded, "Does that mean I have to take out the garbage?" Even in this time of sadness and great loss, that line—and many more just like it—brings a smile to my face and, I'm sure, to yours.

Yes, (deceased) gave us encouragement, time, laughter. Only the time is gone. The encouragement and the laughter will remain.

As he often did in his business travels, (deceased) departed from life as from a hotel, not as from his home. As a dedicated Christian, his eternal home is with his Maker. Adlai Stevenson once commented about a man and his contribution: "It is not the years in a life that counts; it's the life in the years." (Deceased) lived. We will miss him.

38

Audience: business or civic group, family members
Message: This person will be missed.
Tone: formal, yet personal
Timing: 3-4 minutes

Too soon, (name of deceased) has left us. Our lives will be empty in places that his energy once filled. Poet John Donne analyzed the void this way: "Each man's death diminishes me, because I am a part of mankind." But I, as many of you do, feel the loss on a much more personal, individual level.

We are gathered here this morning in the presence of his family and his friends and his God to say that here was a life that demands notice. . . . A life that exemplified kindness. . . . A life that illustrated the Golden Rule. . . . A life that inspired emulation. . . . A life that burned so that others' paths were lighted. He was living proof of just how fine a person can be.

Our sorrow is lessened only slightly with the comforting thought that we had the privilege to know and work with (deceased) over the years. As a respected professional and a community volunteer, (deceased) contributed in innumerable ways to our careers and our personal lives. For those fortunate enough to work with him on a daily basis, we saw these traits and behaviors in his life:

He exuded enthusiasm for almost any task at hand. (Deceased) zipped into the office every morning ready for whatever the day held, ready for whichever one of us had a difficult decision at bay. With equal energy, he volunteered many hours to his community through the Boys Club of America and the Shriners organizations.

Aside from his enthusiasm, he trusted others and he himself could be trusted. Until the day of his death, he never broke a promise to me within his control. And he gave me his complete trust on a handshake. I have even purchased and sold property on his behalf solely on his spoken commitment.

He led. A short statement, but long on meaning. Although there are many definitions of leadership, (deceased) led our staff in such a way that he exemplified rather than defined leadership. He never gave us a project that he didn't pursue with equal fervor. He never asked us to devote time and energy to something to which he did not make an equal, if not superior, commitment. He identified personal and corporate values and then upheld them in every situation—without compromise when they might cost him.

And as other leaders do by definition, he inspired. We wanted to work as (deceased) worked. . . . To be enthusiastic like (deceased). . . .

To trust as (deceased) trusted. . . . To be admired as (deceased) was admired. . . . In brief, we all at one time or another, in some way or another, have aspired to be like (deceased).

Was he selfish of his reputation among us? Not in the least. He never missed an opportunity to mentor us in the ways of his success. Always graciously, he shared what he knew of the business, of the world, of family life, of personal living. And he knew volumes.

Yes, he has left a void that we cannot fill. We resolve to cherish his memory. We want his family to know that we will miss him, too. Our hearts and prayers are with you at this most difficult time.

39

Audience: business or civic group
Message: The deceased achieved far more than the average.
Tone: formal
Timing: 4-5 minutes

Members of the family, friends, acquaintances. . . . There always comes a time at the end of all of our lives when we must leave those of us on earth and give an account of our labor. The Apostle Paul in his letter to the Romans declared, "Every man must give an account of himself to God."

That account is long for (deceased). Few among us achieve so much. Many of great genius sow seeds of progress that blossom only after long years. (Deceased)'s seeds have already bloomed in our lifetime.

The (deceased) Foundation has pumped new life into our nation's research efforts to cure diseases that cripple and kill. It was (deceased)'s dream that we find a cure for cancer in her century. The dream still burns in the hearts of many scientists today. The foundation has also provided scholarships to promising medical students and talented artists.

The (name of theater) has also become a visible monument to (deceased)'s enrichment of the arts to our lives. The brick-and-steel structure, as well as the talent that performs there, reflects to the community the contribution of the arts in making us a civilized nation.

As a member of numerous boards and agencies, she helped shape policies that have radically improved our political and financial situation in the world. Few of us are untouched by those morals and principles that have shaped our corporate lives and our political policies.

During her (number) years, she traveled to (number) countries and spoke to millions about freedom, about the importance of art, about corporate charity as the answer to the threat of disease.

The many magazine and journal articles that have featured her achievements and analyzed her persona bear witness to her contributions. The written words testify to her knowledge and dedication to the causes she espoused.

Hear her now, as in 19--, she admonished the graduating class of (university) about their responsibilities to their fellowman: And I quote. [Insert quote here.]

Through these published records, she continues to inspire those of her generation and those who will come after.

If I have painted her as larger than life, it is because she was. As we can say of few people, the entire world is a better place because she has lived.

And even with this long account of achievement, I dare say (deceased) can look her Maker in the eye and say truthfully that she achieved with the utmost integrity. She challenged her enemies without malice or vengeance. She treated her friends with compassion and love. No one can ever say that her work has hindered the work of God in the world.

In summary, (deceased) has provided an example of what one determined, talented, caring individual can do for mankind.

40

Audience: business or civic group, family members
Message: The deceased's personal qualities contributed to our lives.
Tone: formal, personal
Timing: 4-5 minutes

(Names of family members present), friends, business associates. . . .

When we here at the office heard of (name)'s death, we were shocked and saddened. We stopped. We stopped our problem-solving, . . . our concerns for the work getting done, . . . our push toward all deadlines. Infinitely more important than such routine matters is dealing with the loss of one who had become almost like a family member to us at work.

Mrs. (name) and children, let me try to tell you what we knew of your husband and father in his dealings with us, his work friends. First of all, (name) was a brilliant businessman. People from all over the country—the competition, state agencies, trade associations, our branch offices—have both written and called our offices to express condolences.

Your husband and father was not only a brilliant businessman; he was also a good listener. Many of us remember hours sitting in (name's) office, asking his advice on work and personal matters. Things big and small. Like where to invest money as well as where to attend church. He listened to our concerns and offered advice freely.

Your husband and father was honest. He never stole a trade secret, equipment, or productive time from the organization. No debtor ever called our offices to seek repayment. His word was his bond. We didn't have to ask for a confirming memo or letter on decisions (name) made. When he told us something, we could believe him.

Your husband and father was compassionate. He came to our homes in time of death in our families. He visited and sent flowers and notes to our hospital beds and those of our families. He contributed his money to worthy causes.

In fact, I'm often reminded of the time (name) had just returned from a three-week tour of our Japanese plants. When he arrived at the office suffering jet lag and learned of my own mother's death, he climbed back on a plane and flew across the country to express to me his availability to cover my work assignments, his assurances that I would still have a job two months later after I settled lengthy estate matters, and his personal support and advice on family concerns. Then he traveled all night to a New York meeting the following day, ever mindful that his work associates were continuing to count on him there. I never knew (name) to refuse compassion to anyone in a time of need.

Your husband and father was loyal. He never told us, his employees, one thing and our colleagues and bosses something else. When we were right, he stood up for us. When we were wrong, he helped us see the other side—often to our benefit.

Your husband and father had a great sense of humor. He shared the latest Aggie jokes with us. He saw the light side of every situation. And he kept reminding us in our times of desperation with deadlines that it was, after all, just a job.

I'm sure you, more than we at work, know this side of (name)—his brilliance, his listening attitude, his honesty, his compassion, his loyalty, his humor. A reputation for only a few of these virtues is in itself a good fortune for his family.

But I wanted this group gathered together in his memory to know that we, his friends at the office, also knew him as more than a dedicated professional. We loved a genuinely warm individual—one we will miss greatly.

Simply remember that for all these virtues, (name) has not gone unrewarded by his sudden death. Death is, after all, only the side of life that we can't see from earth's shores. Who knows what God has in store for His child. We ask God's comfort on you, his family, in your time of sorrow.

41

Audience: business and civic group
Message: This person was a capable administrator.
Tone: formal, impersonal
Timing: 1 minute

Ladies and gentlemen. . . .

This is a difficult moment for us as we pause to reflect on (deceased)'s death. At such times we are often at a loss for words to express the value of someone's life, particularly someone who has served with such a capable hand and committed heart.

I knew (deceased) as an outstanding administrator. Her achievements are recorded on the walls of our building—her legacy of technical expertise, integrity, frankness about and courage for a cause she believed in, and a value system that cannot be denigrated. She was a woman we will not forget. Our collective memories will continue to hold her in high regard.

Pause with me now and, in your own way, reflect on what traits we need to emulate and what tasks remain for us to accomplish here as a group.

Farewells

GENERAL GUIDELINES

(To the person leaving)

- Comment on the value of the relationship to you personally or to the group.
- Expand on personality traits, talents, or achievements that you appreciate or admire. Be specific with your praise.
- Avoid remarks that may upset an employee who is leaving under unpleasant conditions.
- Express best wishes for the person's future plans.

(From the person leaving)

- Recall specific benefits or satisfaction from your association with the group.
- State your confidence in the person replacing you and in the satisfactory completion of any ongoing projects.
- Mention your future plans in an upbeat manner, if they are not too personal.

TO BOSS LEAVING
ON A FAVORABLE NOTE

42

Audience: all employees of the company
Message: This high achiever deserves recognition.
Tone: formal
Timing: 2-3 minutes

An assertive blond twenty-two-year-old fresh from (university) knocked on our doors in 19—. We put him to work as a junior accountant to give him a basic dose of what the world outside the classroom really involved. And he proved to be a quick study, moving up through the department in (number) other positions, until he told us he finally had the numbers game down and wanted more responsibility. Well, we agreed to give it to him during the next (number) years as he moved from accounting to operations to marketing and finally to executive vice president of marketing, his current position.

(Name), let me assure you that your association with (company) has been more than a long one—it has been a valuable one. Under your tenure here in various capacities, our company has grown from annual revenues of $X to $X. We've gone from (number) employees to (number) employees. No longer headquartered in a single building in Atlanta, we now have offices in (number) cities in (number) countries. Much of that growth is directly attributable to your talents.

Along with these achievements, we as a group have come to appreciate your personal style. They say the best executives are the ones who have the good sense to select good employees to do their job, and the self-restraint to give them room to do it. We have seen both characteristics—the ability to hire and train excellent staff and the management style to let them do their jobs well and with personal pride.

Having talked to several employees and colleagues who've worked closely with you through the years, I've heard these labels and phrases frequently: Energetic. . . . Fast-thinking. . . . Honest. . . . Tactful. . . . Caring. . . . Committed. . . . Inspiring. . . . Ready to share the credit. . . . Capable. . . . In short, I'd say you've had a dynamic career with (company), and the company will continue to profit from your personal contributions for years to come.

We want to take this opportunity to express formally our best wishes to you in your new position. As you take the reins as CEO of (new company), we will keep our eyes on their balance sheet. You can be assured that we'll look forward to seeing your name in the national media, industry articles and meeting proceedings, and in your own company annual reports.

A hearty thank you for your contributions here and best wishes from all of us at (company).

43

Audience: business associates
Message: You're a nice guy; you deserve the best.
Tone: informal; light
Timing: 3-4 minutes

In putting our heads together about what to say to (name) before he leaves, I intended to comment on his leadership abilities, his strategic planning tactics, his motivational drive, and maybe his technical expertise. But I didn't get very far as I talked to different people—those who work with him every day. Instead, I kept getting comments about his personality.

That's not to say, of course, that we don't value his leadership, planning, motivation, and technical expertise. Those are a given. But what comes to mind most often—and what will continue to surface as we get along without him around here—are those individual qualities unique to him as a supervisor.

First of all, his witticisms and humor have brought us all through some pretty difficult and daring times. Do you remember the time Fred mistakenly shredded the plans for the new Monroe plant? We were all about ready to commit hara-kiri as we tried to reconstruct them from memory. But after the crisis, in his low-key way, (name) dashed off a department memo containing an application for employment in Ollie North's office.

And then there was the Stanwick crisis. But I won't go into details about (name)'s hurried trip to New York, where he was the only person to show up for the canceled sales meeting. Let's just say both Judy and Marion kept their jobs.

Second, there's his concern for all of us as individuals—both personally and professionally. Many of us can attest to the fact that he almost literally "taught us all we know" about the business. (Name), you've fought for our raises and more responsibilities for the department. You've budgeted for the latest, state-of-the-art equipment for us to turn out our best work.

You've nominated us for the training courses we've needed to hone our skills. You've answered about every technical question that could surface—and a few that never surfaced. You've seen that we were treated fairly in restructuring maneuvers around here. And, much to your credit, you've opened some doors for us in other departments and personally groomed us to move up and on.

On a personal note, you've made us each feel that we've contributed to the overall success of our team. Through divorces, diseases, and deaths you've shown understanding and support.

In addition to your sense of humor and your concern for us as individuals, there's one final personality trait—or should I say "quirk"—I should mention. Your habit of wearing both navy and black socks—at the same time! Please, (name), before you report to the next job, will you remember to turn on the lights in the morning as you get dressed?

And speaking of your new job at Herrington: We do wish you the best. Although they may not know it yet, they are getting much more than your resume details. They're getting a super guy who knows his job and also treats his employees with class. Thanks, (name). We wish you the very best.

TO EMPLOYEE LEAVING
ON A FAVORABLE NOTE

44

Audience: colleagues in immediate department
Message: You're the life of the party. We'll miss you.
Tone: informal; light
Timing: 2-3 minutes

It's not the job—it's the people. I think most of you will agree with that sentiment. So, George, we're trying not to think about how much we'll miss you around here. But before you report to that new position in Dallas, I think maybe *you* should think about how much you're going to miss *us*.

Have you thought about how you'll know where to park without Eileen announcing which mornings Security plans to make rounds to ticket illegally parked cars?

Have you thought about where you'll eat breakfast on Fridays when you have no group of colleagues gathered around our box of shared donuts? McDonald's can't compare.

Have you thought about how you'll remember who's on what intercom number without Maria's reminders?

Have you thought about how you'll have to deal with all that devastating peace and quiet without the squeaky elevator outside your corner office?

Have you thought about whose umbrella you'll borrow when you forget, misplace, or break yours? And if you do find one, it probably won't be as handy as Jim's is to grab on the way out the door.

Have you thought about how confusing a newly organized desk can be—no familiar piles of paperwork just where you've left them for the past 48 days?

Have you thought about whom you're going to get to solve all your problems and make all your decisions without this able group of advisors?

Have you, George, given all this adequate thought? On the other hand, it may be too late to change your mind about leaving—I hear that once they process your paperwork around here, you're history.

Seriously, you're a super salesperson—exceptions, none. And you're a nice guy to have around. We're going to miss you in the day-to-day routine, as well as when we're trying to reel in the big fish with a new product line. When you report to your new manager at Sedton, reserve the right to fly back here from time to time and help us out.

But we'll plan to see you in the interim at various conventions and trade shows. Keep a little time free for us to catch up on details and dinners.

Best wishes with your new territory.

45

Audience: colleagues in immediate department
Message: You're talented. Best wishes in your new job.
Tone: informal, serious
Timing: 1-2 minutes

Let me have your attention for a couple of moments as we begin and then we want you all to stay awhile and chat with Susan before you go back to the job.

Susan, the gathering and good food are in your honor this afternoon. On behalf of the group, I want to express to you our appreciation for your work here. The training program you designed for our administrative staff has to be one of your finest contributions. I understand that you designed the program, hired the instructor, and publicized the benefits to bosses. As all of you know, we continually have a waiting list for the program—excellent evidence that you did a superb job from conception to delivery.

A second achievement that has gained our admiration is your building relationships with our local and national trade associations. Five years ago, we were virtually unknown in our industry. Today, by your volunteer committee work—most often involving after-hours time—the industry has taken notice of who we are and the services we can provide. We owe that recognition to you.

As far as individual contributions you've made to each of our personal and professional projects, I'll leave that to each individual to express.

But on behalf of the group, in closing, we are happy for your success in landing a position in a completely new career field at Alladin. With the talents and creativity you've shown us in the last five years, we know you'll be effective in any direction you choose to go.

Thank you for your contributions here. The department is a much better one because of your efforts. Our best.

TO EMPLOYEE LEAVING ON AN UNFAVORABLE NOTE

46

Audience: colleagues in immediate department
Message: We hope things work out well for you elsewhere.
Tone: informal
Timing: 2 minutes

For those of you who are new in the group, Marsha came to work for the company about three years ago—first in Purchasing and then here with us in Contracts. Her duties have included everything from dealing with suppliers, to handling shipping procedures and problems, to negotiating large contracts with our best customers. You'll agree that all those tasks spell frustration from time to time and demand much attention to detail. We appreciate the effort and time required to handle such work.

You've done an admirable job, Marsha. Knowing your meticulous work habits, I'm sure your replacement will have no difficulties in picking up where you left off. I dare say he or she will find every "t" crossed and every signature line authorized.

We do want to offer our emotional support as you move to Nebraska to care for your parents. Most of us will eventually have to make similar difficult decisions about career and family situations. Our hearts and prayers go with you and your family in the move. If we can make things easier for you in tying up particular details here, please call on one or all of us.

We will miss you. Keep in touch with someone here to let us know when you decide to resume your career. We admire your courage in this transition and expect great things from you in the future.

Good luck and God bless.

FROM EMPLOYEE LEAVING ON A FAVORABLE NOTE

47

Audience: colleagues in the immediate department or larger group
Message: I'm excited about my new position.
Tone: informal
Timing: 2-3 minutes

The rumor's true—I've lost another job. They've found someone to untangle my excesses here and I'm moving on to a new challenge. That challenge, as a (position) at (new company), will be to keep my head above water while I learn to swim to safety in the murky economic tides. The new job will certainly stretch my abilities, but I've always been one to jump overboard and *then* ask if there are life rafts anywhere. In a word, I'm excited about the big plunge.

I appreciate this get-together, however, to say good-bye formally to each of you. You may not have realized it at the time, but many of you have contributed to my developing "water wings" in the last (number) years. First, (company) taught me quality customer service. Most companies talk about it; (company) people practice it—every day.

Individually, the (number) managers who've mentored me during my work here—(names of managers)—have provided leadership, know-how, and emotional support to handle the various projects I've been assigned. Those qualities are never to be taken for granted in any work environment. In all honesty, I have the highest regard and admiration for their professionalism and talent.

Others of you, also, have taught me to swim upstream. (Name) has been invaluable in supplying "the way we've always done it" tips to help me get into new projects and find approaches that have worked well for the company in the past. (Name) has contributed to my appreciation of organization and keeping things on the time line—happening when they should. And many others of you in the office have been gracious to lend your support in a crisis.

I have appreciated all your contributions to whatever successes I've had here.

Having had a chance to visit with (name), who will be assuming my duties next week, I'm confident that she will excel in the areas I did and certainly outperform me in tasks I haven't even attempted. The (ongoing project) sounds well under way, and I'll be eager to hear your successes there.

You're a very talented group of people. I'm lucky to have been associated with such a team. Thank you for what you have contributed to my professional growth. And thank you for your friendship.

FROM EMPLOYEE LEAVING ON AN UNFAVORABLE NOTE

48

Audience: colleagues in the immediate department or larger group
Message: I'm leaving, but don't feel sorry for me. I don't regret the decision.
Tone: formal, distant
Timing: 2 minutes

After "I heard you're leaving," the following phrase is usually, "What are you planning to do?" So I thought I'd take a few moments to outline some of my plans. The entrepreneurial bug has bitten me as it has so many others recently. Within the month—after some rest and relaxation—I plan to open my own computer consulting service, catering especially to small businesses. We will offer a full line of services—analyzing their tasks, developing special programs for their specific applications, and providing installation and training.

The decision has been made after years of dreaming and months of deliberation. The timing feels right. The opportunities in the computer consulting area seem more than ample. And my associates and I are eager to begin pocketing the profit from our own efforts.

One of the most difficult things about beginning a new business, of course, is the camaraderie of past friendships. I'll miss those.

Thank you for your interest in my career and for the experience I've gained through my affiliation with each of you and the company.

Thank you for coming to say good-bye.

Fund Raisers

GENERAL GUIDELINES

(Kickoff to project)

- Get attention for the cause.
- Request participation. Be explicit about what you need or want them to contribute, but assure your audience that any contribution is welcome.
- Mention the benefits of involvement and success.
- Include testimonials from people who have contributed to the cause or from recipients of the money or services.
- Predict a successful campaign/project.
- Show excitement. Avoid sounding as though this is "business as usual" or that your own participation is just "part of the job."

(Celebration of success)

- Share the evidence of your successful fund raiser/project.
- Express appreciation to all those who have contributed in every way—especially those behind the scenes.
- Remind them of the benefits/uses/outcome of the contributions.

KICKOFF TO A PROJECT

49

Audience: business or civic groups
Message: This cause deserves your money.
Tone: informal
Timing: 6-7 minutes, depending on insertion of two testimonials

There's no such thing as a free lunch, they tell us. As you might have guessed from your invitation to this morning's event, there's no such thing as a free breakfast either. I hope you've enjoyed your ham and biscuits and whatever else. But in exchange, we want you to reach for that wallet.

But not with reluctance as did one society lady who was caught by a beggar coming out of a big charity ball. When the beggar asked the woman for money to eat, she snapped, "I spent $100 for a ticket tonight and $3,000 for this gown. How can you dare ask me for money after what I've already contributed?"

Well, we didn't ask you to get all dressed up this morning in a tuxedo or hire a limo to come downtown—or even buy your breakfast ticket. The company has graciously provided the food. But we *are* going to ask you to open your hearts for the work of (name of agency).

Since 19—, (agency) has been providing a shelter to the homeless of our community. They feed, clothe, and shelter over (number) individuals each year. And the help doesn't stop there. After the immediate crisis in these situations, they provide support in finding long-term solutions. Training. . . . Help with jobs. . . . Counseling with families into which these individuals must return.

All of this effort is dependent on people like you. This agency does not receive funds from any governmental or state agencies, which can only do so much.

Any time individuals such as you first learn of a charity or cause, the questions are often: "Do they do any good? Will my money be used in a worthwhile way?"

From personal experience, I can give you the answers to both questions: Yes. Let me share just two brief success stories of theirs, with names changed to protect privacy.

[Insert two testimonials of individuals helped by this agency.]

So, I repeat: Their efforts have met a growing need in our community and continue to do so with the help of caring people. Sir Francis Bacon long ago concluded: "In charity, there is no excess."

The voices of abused women and children, . . . of mentally unstable individuals, . . . of those suffering from unavoidable misfortunes and illnesses . . . cry to the rest of us for compassion.

Let's answer with personal involvement to those with whom we come into contact. Let's answer this morning with our pocketbooks. Let's answer with hope.

Whatever you can afford will make the difference in someone's life. $5,000. $1,000. $500. $100. $25. With your dollars, together we can buy someone—a specific individual in our city—a future.

Any such charity is twice blessed—it blesses the one who gives and the one who receives. In my way of thinking, unless an individual is a recipient of charity, he or she should be a contributor to it.

Thank you for your compassion. And I'm looking forward to what this one group of concerned individuals can do.

50

Audience: business or civic groups

Message: This cause is worthy of your support.

Tone: informal

Timing: 7-8 minutes, depending on insertion of success stories

Money. The lack of it has brought organizations to their knees. The abundance of it has created selfishness and greed. Money. Everybody wants some. Nobody has enough. However you feel about money—its lack or abundance, as a curse or a blessing for the individual—as a group, we need it.

You're going to hear from (name) in a few moments about the exact details of our project, but first I want you to get the big picture. The why of our get-together and campaign.

We need funds for [insert overview of project goal].

We know exactly how much we need—$X. And we know exactly how we're going to get the money—hard work. An impossible task, some may think, to raise that much money among a group such as ours in such a short time.

That's what the pessimists think. They hear the numbers, see the obstacles, feel the competition for our dollars, and then go home with a sigh. Ballgame over. Rained out. Lack of interest. If you're of that train of thought—and I doubt we have any of those with us in this group—please hide the pessimism behind a smile and don't voice that feeling. A naysayer can rain on a lot of people's parades—simultaneously if they're high enough in the organization for their words to pitter-patter downward.

But fortunately the vast majority of people around here are of another caliber—optimists.

I base my optimism on the increasing generosity of America—of individuals and corporations. Volunteerism and charity are concepts firmly rooted in our national heritage. We are a giving people—some of us by nature, some of us by experience. We have seen what a few dollars and a few well-placed efforts can accomplish.

No, you're not pessimists. I can see it now on your faces: Energy. . . . Enthusiasm. . . . Anticipation. . . . Confidence. . . . You're positive thinkers, who put your efforts behind your words. In fact, many of you have already spent hours strategizing, planning, devising, and scheduling. Today's event is just the first step in our success story.

We're not the only group that has tried such a fund-raising campaign. Let me tell you a story or two about what other organizations similar to ours have accomplished.

[Insert success stories at other locations.]

But back to us, here at (name of organization.) We want you to visualize with us what these funds can do for us as a group and what they can do for you as individual employees.

First, [insert details of project benefits].

It's a planned process.

As Emerson put it: "All our progress is an unfolding, like the vegetable bud. You have first an instinct, then an opinion, then a knowledge, as the plant has root, bud, and fruit." Likewise, we simply have to trust our instinct over reason at this the front end.

We've talked. Now's the time to act. There's a place for each of you on the team. For your dollars and for your personal involvement in reaching others to contribute. We ask that you dig into your own pockets . . . and then that you talk to your colleagues to spread your enthusiasm. Some people just need a bigger push than others to see the goal line.

To provide funds for [insert program goals]. That's the *why*. Now, here's (name) to give you the *how* details, the game plan.

CELEBRATION OF SUCCESS

51

Audience: business or civic groups
Message: Thank you for your contributions; the world will be a better place because you cared.
Tone: formal
Timing: 3 minutes

Someone has quipped that most Americans drive last year's car, wear this year's clothes, and live on next year's income. Well, I don't know about the veracity of that statement—I suppose it's true for many of us. But this I do know: Despite the state of your own bank account, you have not let selfishness seep in.

I'm so pleased to announce that we have collected $X for the (agency). We didn't meet our rather high goal, but we came within a whisper—95 percent. With sheer courage and determination, we set a goal higher than we could *easily* reach. (X) percent higher than we've raised in past campaigns. A goal that would push us in a bad economy. In my way of thinking, $X is a tremendous accomplishment.

Volunteerism is on the upswing. You have been generous with lending your skills and expertise to these efforts. We're proud to have talented volunteers such as you—but then we knew you would do well in this arena because you've already proven yourselves to be the finest paid employees. We can't alleviate all the problems our community is facing— but you have gone a long way with this project.

$X is no small sum for a group our size. This $X represents food, clothes, shelter, and, for some, skills training and a job.

Some people who were once cold are now warm. Some people who were once in rags are now neat and cleanly dressed. Some people who went to bed hungry have full stomachs this morning. Some people who were once filled with hate now understand love. Some people whose self-esteem had hit rock-bottom can now hold their heads higher when they enter the workforce. Some who once despaired now have hope.

Although those individuals will never learn your names and will miss the opportunity to say thank you, I want to speak for them.

First of all, I want to express my appreciation to (name) for bringing this need to our attention. He spent several hours in trips around the city to check out the work the agency does and to interview the directors and members of the staff. Thank you, (name). Would you agree that in helping others we also nourish our own spirits? As the old epitaph goes, "What I gave I have; what I spent, I had; what I kept, I lost."

In short, I stand before you to say that I'm proud to be a member of such a group. You are a group of unique individuals—people who care deeply about their community and who are willing to work hard to do something about that concern. Each one of you has made an important contribution. The money collected represents the depth of genuinely compassionate people. God bless you for your giving.

52

Audience: business or civic groups
Message: Thank you for your contributions; let's celebrate the
benefits.
Tone: informal
Timing: 3-4 minutes

A dollar goes a long way now. You can carry it around for days without finding a thing it will buy. Well, we're carrying around lots of dollars now, and we've found something to buy. Thanks to your efforts, we have collected a total of $X to build a [insert details of project].

Money flows to great ideas. And (name of campaign) has been a great idea. This tremendous response evidences that fact. With these funds, we as employees will now be able to

[Insert benefits or results of the effort.]

That's not to say the project has been easy or the task has been without lavish effort and loving sacrifice on the part of many. First of all, I want to commend (name) for her leadership throughout the entire campaign. No emergency was too big or detail too small for her personal attention and time.

The others involved have headed committees, which are the hands and feet of any organization. And able-bodied committees these individual teams have been! The committee chairs included

[Insert all those who chaired committees.]

Finally, let me thank each of you who served on a committee in any way. These committee chairs will agree with me, I'm sure, that it's rather difficult to lead if there's no one to follow. You individually and we collectively have made this effort a success. The employees and other professionals here for years to come will reap the benefits of your farsightedness and your energy.

Let's celebrate. Give yourself a hand. [Lead in applause.]

Graduation
Addresses

GENERAL GUIDELINES

- Congratulate the graduates on their academic achievements.
- Outline some obstacles and challenges they face in the future.
- Encourage them to make the world a better place.
- Aim for a fresh approach, avoiding an overly formal tone and graduation cliches such as "Commencement is a beginning" and "Today is the first day of the rest of your life."

53

Audience: graduates, family, and friends
Message: This is how I see the world and your part in it.
Tone: formal
Timing: 17-18 minutes

Thank you for inviting me to address you on this occasion.

You will have many birthdays, many dinner parties, many Fourth of Julys. But you will have only one university graduation—a rich event of a lifetime. Many of your friends and family members and I, as well as you, hold this one thing in common—an appreciation for knowledge and how it can enrich our lives. I congratulate you for your efforts, your families for their sacrifices, and your professors for their dedication to excellence.

That's the shiny side. The dim side—just in case any of you have already forgotten—is the No-Doz, the coffee, the retyping and reprinting of the reports always due the day before yesterday.

But whether you remember the dim side or the shiny side of your college years, only your own efforts will brighten or tarnish the memory from now on. University lectures behind you, you will be the authors and speakers of the future. I believe strongly that each generation's achievements can overshadow the last.

Many of you are anxious to say this academic party's over and to proceed to the next one—to be held in corporate America. But stop. . . . Reflect. . . . Before you break down the door to get to that first job, take this time to strategize, to plan exactly where you want to go and how you'll get there.

I invite you to stop and think about the changes that you should consider before you knock on the first office door and apply for that first job. Confucius admonished us, "Choose a job you love, and you will never have to work a day in your life." Great advice. But these are days of so many choices that the selection is difficult. Every graduating class "wakes up"—pun intended—to a new world every spring. These changes—or trends—will affect what you look for and what you accept in a job and career.

A primary phenomenon in corporate America is our grappling with a global economy. The price of cabbage in Kansas affects Singapore housewives. The price of microchips in Japan affects workers in Muleshoe, Texas. For years, we saw "Made in Japan" on too many labels. Those labels now bearing "Made in the USA" carry more respect than they once did. Because of the intense competition, we have had to become more concerned with our quality and our cost. In today's marketplace, innovative ideas, scientific discoveries and technology, management techniques, and investment money move quickly from one country to the next. Competition is keen. It demands to be reckoned with.

The second trend in corporate America is the information explosion. When we transfer data from a vendor's database to ours, the information is old before the last printout rolls off the printer. Just to stay up on the job—to stay informed—you will find yourself inundated with professional journals, general-interest news magazines, specialized newsletters, stacks of correspondence, and brochures on new products and services that will make you more efficient. You will spend hours of your day reading, interpreting, analyzing, responding to, digesting all that information. You will be tempted to hide from the mail carrier, but you'll learn that what he or she brings to your desk or doorstep is vital to your job. You have to keep up.

A third trend in corporate America is *change*. Universal, never-ending, complex change. We have some hi-tech crystal balls and resident astrologers. We call them computers and staff analysts. They both crunch mundane statistics, trends and predictions of what we need to be doing in the immediate and long-term future. With these hi-tech crystal balls, these resident astrologers can predict—with a great deal of certainty—that things will continue to change.

What that means to you is that you must continue to educate yourself. For the dedicated, high-achieving individual, school will never be out. You will always be chasing knowledge. In my own corporation, our managers attend formal training at least (number) days each year. Many attend more often. Why? Because learning is their entryway to achievement and their handle on change. Our jobs change weekly, monthly. With mergers and acquisitions, we learn one job only to be handed another.

That's not easy. But there is a method to dealing with it, according to one chief executive officer of a large company. He had just been voted out of his job by his board of directors. So before he cleared out his desk and packed his briefcase, he prepared three large envelopes for his successor: "Just in case you run into the same kind of problems I've had, open these one at a time."

The new, young CEO appreciatively took them. But he felt confident he'd have no need of them because he'd graduated from a university such as yours—fully prepared for any situation. However, he stuffed them in his file cabinet, just in case.

About a year later, things did indeed get tough. The board didn't like the changes this new CEO had made, didn't like the budget allocations, didn't like the way the balance sheet looked. So the young man pulled the first envelope from the files and opened it. In big bold letters, it said simply: "Blame Marketing."

So he did, and things got much better. The bottom line saw black again.... Sales increased.... Profits improved.... Things were good for about another two years. Then once again, trouble developed. His superiors started asking questions he couldn't answer and raising issues he didn't want to face. So once again, he pulled open the file and reached for the second envelope. In big bold letters, it said: "Blame economic conditions."

So he did. Business once again turned around. The price of his stock went up. He felt creative and capable once again. But another couple of years went by, and he found himself in agony about the annual report. So the day before his annual stockholders meeting, he decided to open the third envelope. He found these words: "Prepare three envelopes for your successor."

As I said, working in an environment at three or four different jobs in a company that tries to hit a moving target can be challenging. You may be leaving here with an accounting degree and ten years from now you'll be selling insurance or working on a space-shuttle design. Your academic education may end with tossing your caps into the air, but your career education is just beginning.

To give you a personal example: My father had a (type) degree, and he worked for (number) years at one company where he managed engineering project after project. And I might add, with success. But success to him and his bosses meant the assignment of another important engineering project. And another. And another.

In my case, I have (type) degrees, but I've held a job as a (position), as a (position), and as a (position). Now, I'm in charge of seeing that [present responsibilities] happens.

You can expect the same, only more so. Several careers in your lifetime. In other words, you will need to learn to think like a generalist and acquire all the skills that entails. You will need to perfect your skills in writing, speaking, interpersonal relationships, time management, planning, budgeting, project management.

Let me say it this way: Learning is an attitude and a process, not a final destination. The people we now hire are not those with certain degrees but those with a desire to succeed, to achieve. To be ordinary is easy; excellence requires commitment.

A fourth trend is that corporations are really—really—embracing the idea that *people* matter. We're tossing out the bureaucratic procedures and policies that once governed people when management wanted them for their backs—their physical labor. Businesses have rediscovered that people have much to contribute with their minds and their spirits. Decisions are no longer made from above with no input from below. Management wants a workforce that is determined to think creatively and to improve the quality of the products produced and the services provided.

In return for people's creativity on the job, corporate America is taking on more of the responsibility to see that they provide well for their employees. They want them to raise happy, well-adjusted children. They want them to take care of their health. They want them to appreciate the arts. They want them to reunite their families and put down roots in the community. They want them to be a part of establishing family, community, and work traditions. It's been a good change—all for the well-being of the employee.

A fifth change in corporate America is the insistence on an increase in productivity—your productivity individually. You put in long hours at this university. But don't think that will end when you get a "real" job. The 40-hour work week is gone. Studies tell us that the average worker now spends 50-60 hours on the job. Because of all the trends I mentioned earlier—a global economy and increased competition to produce higher quality at a lower cost—management ranks are thinner. We're doing more with less. We're turning out more work with fewer workers. Your career success will depend on your commitment, investment of time, and energy to achieve. Your attitude will need to be that you get up every morning and ask yourself, "Can I do my job quicker, cheaper, better?" You will be rewarded accordingly.

Yes, you are putting on a business suit and buying a briefcase in the midst of profound changes. These changes will affect the way we live, love, and work for years to come.

We have a global economy.

Information explodes around us.

Change in the world and in your chosen career is inevitable; you will need to continue your lifelong education.

Businesses are focusing on people—their creativity, their unique ideas, and their personal well-being.

Competition demands increased productivity from everyone.

So what does all this mean specifically?

Well, it means that when you come to interview with my company and join hands to work with us, we want an open mind. We want you to listen to our problems, to hear our experiences, and to propose new insights. We want you to be disciplined. Long hours are the rule, not the exception. We want you to be dedicated. Caring about quality and doing a good job is as old as the Bible. "Whatsoever your hand finds to do, do it with all your might."

No one knows what the future holds for you in the face of these changes. That's good—a blessing from the good Lord. But one thing you do know, one thing you will always have a choice about. And that one choice is attitude. Only you can decide to be flexible, happy, healthy, productive, and successful in life.

We welcome you to corporate America. We're ready to give you a chance to show what you can do. We'll give you opportunities to succeed and to fail. We hope you'll take both. For in failing, you and we learn. We want your ideas on new products and services. We want your idealism.

We want your questions and challenges about things that are not working well now. We want your energy, your enthusiasm, your drive. In short, welcome to the real world.

As you travel, I wish you good health, people to love, time to enjoy.

54

Audience: graduates, families, and friends
Message: Here are my secrets to personal and career success.
Tone: formal
Timing: 18-20 minutes

Good afternoon, graduates, family, friends. . . .

Thank you for asking me to be a part of your celebration—a celebration of an ending and a beginning. To the graduates, congratulations on your academic achievements and on the friendships you've built while here at the university. Both will continue to enrich your lives through the years.

To the parents, congratulations also. You, too, feel a sense of accomplishment and pride in your graduate's completion of formal schooling. To the faculty, you should pat yourselves on the back. Who knows what great minds you've helped shape these past few years.

In thinking of what to say to you today, I talked to a friend of mine who's often called upon to address graduating classes, and I asked him for his suggestions. He responded with, "My advice to young people who are going out in the world today? . . . Don't go!"

I decided, however, to be a little more upbeat. In fact, I've chosen a Biblical pattern—the Ten Commandments. No, I'm not trying to play God, but I have put together a list of dos and don'ts. First, I want to give you the basis of these rules—the theory, if you will. Then the rules themselves.

Here's the theory part: Life isn't fair. . . . There's no such thing as a free lunch. . . . Some good deals aren't. . . . Money won't buy happiness. . . . No pain, no gain. . . . Talk is cheap. . . . Victory goes to the swift. . . . Pride goes before a fall. . . . No man is an island.

What's the matter, you've heard those theories before? Well, never mind. They're still true. So upon those theories, I've built my list of dos and don'ts. You've probably been hearing several of those lately also—how to dress for an interview, what to say when they ask you what kind of salary you want, and so forth. But here are the things that you really need to know after you land the job—the things we look for in people we will hire and promote, in people who will achieve much over their lifetime.

Here's my list—of things I've learned and am still learning, the things that may help you in the years to come:

Commandment 1: Be willing to pay the price. Today's preparation determines tomorrow's achievement. No one has cornered the market on family and career success. Anybody who walks into the store and pays the price can walk away with it. Someone once approached the great violinist Fritz Kreisler and offered this praise after a concert: "I'd give my life to play as beautifully as you do." The musician responded, "I did."

You graduates have already invested four or more years as a down payment, while some former high school classmates decided to spend these last four years elsewhere—most of them out already earning the living they will be earning for the rest of their lives. Don't throw that down payment away.

If you want to be successful in your chosen field, find out what it takes to be the best of the best. Time . . . Practice . . . Commitment . . . Sacrifice . . . There is a price. Success is never on sale; it's just a matter of deciding how much you want to pay.

Commandment 2: Be self-disciplined. Emerson said that our primary need in life is somebody who will make us do what we can. We've all had that somebody at some time or other. A parent. . . . A friend. . . . A teacher. . . . But from now on, you yourself will have to be that somebody. You will have to have the wherewithal to make yourself do what you're capable of. Discipline to put in the necessary hours. . . . Discipline to stay up to date in your field. . . . Discipline to read. . . . Discipline to use your time well. . . . Discipline to eat right and stay healthy. . . . Discipline to stay with a task.

Whether it's gluing a model plane together or researching marketing trends in retail clothing, follow-through marks success. Self-discipline is simply control. If you don't control yourself, *someone else* will. Or *no one else* will. Either case will be less desirable than self-control.

Commandment 3: Set some goals. That's not the same as being disciplined. Discipline is setting your alarm at 5:00 a.m. and making yourself get up when it goes off. Goal-setting is knowing *why* you set the alarm at 5:00 a.m. in the first place. . . . What did you plan to achieve? How did you plan to achieve it? If you've ever done any sailing, you know that finding the wind isn't always easy. If you don't have any plans to go any place special, then any wind is the right wind. But if you have a certain water-side restaurant that you want to make by noon, then you need to pick a *specific* direction and find the *right* wind. Winners expect to win in advance. Life, for them, becomes a self-fulfilling prophecy. Choice, not chance, determines destiny. Make some choices; set some goals.

Commandment 4: Learn to get along well with others. HRD studies reconfirm over and over again that people do not lose their jobs because they don't have the technical know-how or skills. More frequently, the difficulty is that they can't get along with other people.

You may not please all the people all the time, but you can please most of the people most of the time—if in no other way but by being open to their criticism. Weigh it against others' considerations. People seldom improve when they only have their own yardstick to measure themselves by. I can assure you I've made more improvements in my own life and in my own business as a result of others' criticism than their praise.

Measure yourself with someone else's yardstick occasionally. If on your first job, your boss comments that you lose your temper too easily, and your parent or your spouse comments that you lose your temper too easily, and your friend comments you lose your temper too easily, it stands to reason that probably . . . you lose your temper too easily. When you hear such feedback, listen before you deny it. Evaluate it. Weigh it. Do you think changes are in order?

Regardless of criticism, to get along with other people, you have to care about them genuinely. Live the Golden Rule and you'll get the gold. The gold medal of love. . . . The gold medal of satisfaction. . . . The gold medal of peace of mind. . . . Friends are some of God's best gifts to us. We don't have friends in our lives until we make room. Until we learn to get outside ourselves and care about what's happening in another person's life and in the community at large.

Commandment 5: Be a dreamer. We've often heard George Bernard Shaw's distinction of men: "Some men see things as they are and say 'Why?' I dream things that never were, and say, 'Why not?'" We need men and women like you entering the workforce to say "Why not?" We need solutions to air pollution, disease, racial violence, poor product quality, impersonal customer service.

Dare to dream up some ways to resolve these problems and address these issues. Humanist James Allen says, "You will become as small as your controlling desire; as great as your dominant aspiration." In other words, to succeed beyond your wildest expectations, you have to have some wild expectations. I say, keep your head in the clouds. Dream.

Commandment 6: Take risks; don't be afraid to fail. Obstacles are those things you see when you take your eyes off your goals. And, believe me, if you ever get so cockeyed sure of something that you never see obstacles, you had better question whether the task is worth doing at all. So taking risks means evaluating the obstacles and determining that the chance for payoff is worth the risk.

The world is full of people who follow wherever the path leads; but we need people in the business world who will strike out where there is no path and then leave a trail.

Commandment 7: Stay informed. Justice Oliver Wendell Holmes said, "Man's mind, once stretched by a new idea, never regains its original dimensions." I hope that's true—that after your years here, your mind has been stretched so that you will never be satisfied to stop learning about what's going on around you.

Use every resource available to learn how business operates. One of the biggest realizations in going through school is that knowledge is "out there"—even if you haven't learned it all. You just have to have the "want to" to retrieve it and use it. You don't have to know everything about everything to hold a new job. You just have to have the drive and the enthusiasm to find out. Keep your eyes and your ears open for how people around you make decisions, act, refuse to act, make a profit, lose a profit. Analyze future trends as you put two and two together around you.

Someone has said of us knowledge-workers, "Wealth was once measured in gold. Now it's measured in what we know." Stay alert, informed.

Commandment 8: Be ethical. Know when to compromise and when to stick to your convictions. What you once knew to be right and wrong . . . is still right and wrong. The corporate world is having to learn all over again that being ethical is what's best for business and the bottom line in the long run. Compromise may come in many forms—insurance coverage, expense reports, toxic-waste decisions. Right has been and always will be right.

Commandment 9: Have some fun. You want to know how to have some fun every day of your life? Confucius said, "Choose a job you love, and you will never have to work a day in your life." For the most part, he was right. My job is fun—most days. And you'll find that every job has its days of drudgery. So on those days, you learn to play at something else. Keep other interests and other friends in your life. You need to laugh.

Commandment 10: Define success in your own terms. Someone has aptly observed, "Many people spend their lives climbing the ladder of success only to find, when they get to the top, the ladder is leaning against the wrong building."

I want to read you several definitions of success I've collected through the years. Listen to them. Pick one you like:

—"Happiness is a way station between too little and too much."

—"The good life is a process, not a state of being. It's a direction, not a destination."

—"Winning isn't everything—it's the only thing," according to Coach Vince Lombardi.

—"If a man has a talent and learns how to use it,... he has gloriously succeeded and won a satisfaction and a triumph few men ever know," claimed author Thomas Wolfe.

—Mack Douglas, a Baptist minister, defined success this way: "When a man has done his best, has given his all, and in the process supplied the needs of his family and his society, that man has succeeded."

—"Success is having something to be enthusiastic about."

—"Success has always been easy to measure. It is the distance between one's origins and one's final achievement," according to author Michael Korda.

—And with this one I'll focus on success in a reverse way—here's how John Charles Salak defines failure: "Failures are divided into two classes—those who thought and never did, . . . and those who did and never thought."

As I said at the beginning, you have to select the way you'll measure success for yourself. The axiom you want to live by. Write it down. Repeat it to yourself often. That'll help you translate success into specific job decisions.

Should you accept a job traveling most of the time? Well, that depends. Is your idea of success adventure and learning about the world around you? Or is it being home with your family every night? Should you join a certain professional organization and devote ten hours a week to it? Well, that depends. Is your idea of success to keep at it 10, 12, 14 hours a day to get that promotion? Or is your idea of success to network with friends more often? To join hands on community projects?

Your personal definition of success—if you have a firm grasp on it—will make many seemingly difficult decisions much easier through the years.

Here they are again—my Ten Commandments upon reaching graduation and entering the corporate world:

Be willing to pay the price.

Be self-disciplined.

Set some goals.

Learn to get along well with others.

Be a dreamer.

Take risks; don't be afraid to fail.

Stay informed.

Be ethical.

Have some fun.

Define success in your own terms.

Because I noticed some of you weren't taking notes on that list, I'll be briefer by deferring to writer Robert Fulghum to wrap this up for me: In one of his bestselling books, he wrote, "Most of what I really need to know about how to live and what to do and how to be, I learned in kindergarten."

Now, he tells us—after you've just finished college. Anyway, Fulghum continues:

> Wisdom was not at the top of the graduate school mountain, but there in the sandpile at Sunday School. These are the things I learned: Share everything. Play fair. Don't hit people. Put things back where you found them. Clean up your own messes. Don't take things that aren't yours. Say you're sorry when you hurt somebody. Wash your hands before you eat. Flush. Warm cookies and cold milk are good for you. Live a balanced life—Learn some and think some and draw and paint and sing and dance and play and work every day some. Take a nap every afternoon. And when you go out into the world, watch for traffic, hold hands, and stick together.

So when you get out there in the world—and you see the expectations and the problems, the challenges and the temptations, the discouragements and the opportunities—and you forget your professors' lectures, just try to remember kindergarten. The rest will take care of itself.

My personal congratulations to each of you. I wish you success as you improve the world.

Holiday
Celebrations

GENERAL GUIDELINES

- Mention the historic reason for the celebration.
- Express warm wishes for the season and the reason.

CHRISTMAS OR CHANUKAH

55

Audience: employees and family members
Message: Let the spirit of Christmas and Chanukah pervade the year.
Tone: sentimental
Timing: 3-4 minutes

Why do we see so many smiles at this time of year? Have you ever wondered why there is that twinkle in the eye of the man on the corner? The springy step of the lady at the deli? The elfish grin of little children as they peep at visitors who unexpectedly drop in?

Could it be that the man on the corner has just decided that he isn't in such a big hurry to attend his meeting after all because he'll have a holiday coming shortly? Could it be that the steps of the lady at the deli are springy because she just decided on the perfect gift for her son? Could the children be hoping each visitor has come with a new toy for them?

Why do we see so many smiles around (company) at this time of year? Could it be that the big project is nearing completion? Or the parking garage has more vacant slots? Or the stores are finally putting on sale the very thing on your spouse's wish list?

Well, whatever *your* smile means, I can tell you what generates mine. We've had a great year at (company) because of your hard work and creativity. You are a bright, innovative group who gives it your all every week of the year. It's just that we tend to reflect more on our good fortune of hiring you when we look at the year-end totals. Thank you for your efforts.

Some of us will be celebrating Christmas and some, Chanukah. Chanukah is called the Festival of Lights. A candle is lit each of seven nights to commemorate a miracle of light for the Jewish people. The Christian holiday celebrates the birth of Jesus more than 2,000 years ago. The origins of our feelings and celebrations at this time of the year are religious.

But these feelings do not have to stop at our door. . . . Or the synagogue door. . . . Or the church door.

Why am I smiling? Is it too far-fetched to believe that the miracle of love and light could spread from month to month until throughout the year we share the same smiles, warmth, and compassion for all people everywhere?

Is it possible that the poor could find food and shelter?
That the lonely could find companionship?
That the bereaved could find comfort?

That the frightened could find peace?
That the sick could find health?
That the hopeless could find hope?
Whether you celebrate Christmas or Chanukah, let me leave you with this thought: God has no hands but yours this season. A demonstration of charity and love is far better than a definition of them.

I'm smiling because, in short, I'm celebrating you as a group of employees. Your commitment. . . . Your cooperation. . . . Your charity.

As you do your part to make the sentiment of the season last, Merry Christmas, Happy Chanukah.

FOURTH OF JULY

56

Audience: general
Message: Let's celebrate freedom to make choices and changes.
Tone: sentimental
Timing: 3-4 minutes

Our momentous decision to choose freedom for ourselves led us to draft and approve the signing of the Declaration of Independence, July 4, 1776, thus severing our ties from Great Britain. It was a choice not to be forgotten. One year later, we celebrated in Philadelphia by adjourning Congress and participating in a ceremonial dinner, including fireworks and ringing bells. Those rituals have hung on—military parades, picnics, and patriotic pageants.

Why are we *still* celebrating? First of all, we celebrate our choice of freedom over tyranny and oppression. We celebrate that soldiers in past wars have agreed that democracy was worth dying for. We celebrate that as individuals we have rights that no one ruler can take away. And we celebrate the freedom to worship this week in whatever synagogue or church whose doctrines we believe. We celebrate the freedom to educate ourselves without restriction. We celebrate the freedom to hold a job and make whatever money our energy, health, and abilities will allow. We celebrate the freedom to pack our families into a car and drive across the country without asking anyone when or if. We celebrate the freedom to buy the best food and medicine science has provided.

But in addition to this celebration of choices, let's also remember that we celebrate the freedom to change. To become all that we can be. To improve the condition of ourselves and people the world over.

In our less-than-perfect world, we can change our skills and lot in life through education.

We can change our environment with legislation.

We can change our yoke of taxation with a vote.

We can change our health problems with research and cures. We can change our cities through compassion and involvement.

Yes, we may disagree about how to go about all the changes. Nevertheless, we are free to choose and change. To enjoy what we have now and to grow to what we can become as a nation under God. We celebrate freedom to choose and change. We are one body and one spirit against anyone or any government that threatens to take this freedom away.

We are one nation—black, white, brown. We are Protestants, Jews, and Catholics. We have Irish blood, Indian blood, German blood. We are intellectuals and of common thinking. We are lighthearted and somber. We are engineers and beauticians, artists and plumbers. We make our home in the East and in the West. We are liberal and conservative, rich and poor.

But one thing we have in common. We are Americans—one body and one spirit for freedom and against oppression. For choice and change, against restriction and stagnation.

Let's celebrate God's blessings on America. Let's celebrate the choice our forefathers made for independence. Let's celebrate the sacrifice of those who have died for that freedom. Let's celebrate our resolve to improve that which is not perfection in our country.

Let's celebrate the hope that all our brothers and sisters around the world can one day choose and change.

Let's enjoy ourselves today. We are Americans.

NEW YEAR'S DAY

57

Audience: general
Message: The new year is a time for focused growth.
Tone: lighthearted
Timing: 3-4 minutes

Remember those sayings your mother always used with you—someone has called them momilies. Your mother told you to be sure to wear clean underwear because you might be involved in an accident and end up at the hospital. Don't cross your eyes; they might stick that way. An apple a day keeps the doctor away. Pretty is as pretty does. Early to bed, early to rise makes a man healthy, wealthy, and wise. Never mind that that last one was borrowed from Ben Franklin. Your mother had your best interest at heart, and she was always tantalizing—or warning—you about what might lie ahead.

We may look back and laugh at mothers for such advice. On the other hand, we may wish we'd taken more of it.

But in either case, what do these momilies and New Year's have in common? Resolve and a determination to improve ourselves.

Every January for the last 12 years I've resolved to lose weight, eat healthier, exercise more, work smarter and harder, educate myself, renew old acquaintances, call or write Aunt Susie to tell her how much she has meant to me, cooperate with colleagues, pray regularly, and organize myself. So why do I stand before you overweight and flabby? Undereducated? Still out of touch with old friends and Aunt Susie? Stubborn with my colleagues? Unrepentant? Disorganized?

Focus. . . . I have lacked focus. It's not that you should ignore the urge to make New Year's resolutions. On the contrary. The New Year is a season for new beginnings. Black budgets. Flat stomachs. Blank calendars.

But what I'm suggesting is focus. In tackling the whole of what needs improving about ourselves, we diffuse our energy. On Monday, we eat a Snickers bar. On Tuesday, we call an old friend and the line is busy. On Wednesday, we clutter our desk. On Thursday we blow our stack at the gal at the next desk. On Friday, we skip the lesson in grammar and read only the pictures. So by the weekend, we've grown ashamed of our own weaknesses, . . . humiliated by our lack of self-discipline, . . . embarrassed by lack of results.

Have you been at that point? So have I. But the answer is not to give up, let up, check out. Instead, I think the answer is focus. Let the New Year's inspiration for change and self-improvement propel you toward only *one* or *two* changes for the better. Focus. I challenge you to never stop growing and to channel energy and determination for self-improvement into one stream.

If it's to get in good physical shape, set up a diet that you can realistically live with and schedule an exercise plan. If it's to get a better handle on your career, outline the new skills or knowledge you need and chart a plan to get you there. If there are relationships you need to renew, focus on daily time together and small acts of love and concern.

In trying to do everything, we often end up doing nothing.

Yes, the New Year is time for growth. But not both an apple a day **and** clean underwear—try one or the other this year.

Have a great New Year's Day, a great New Year, and a great life.

MEMORIAL DAY

58

Audience: general
Message: Let's remember so that others don't have to die.
Tone: respectful
Timing: 2 minutes

Ladies and gentlemen, honored guests.

Commander in Chief of the Grand Army of the Republic, John Logan, issued an order that made May 30, 1868, a day for "decorating the graves of comrades who died in defense of their country in the late rebellion." He was speaking of the Civil War. But subsequently we have kept this Memorial Day to honor all those who have given their lives in all past wars.

Appropriately today, we honor those who have served the cause of freedom in the wars we remember more recently—World Wars I and II, Korea, Vietnam. And the undeclared wars and sometimes unrecognized wars and even accidents in maintaining our peace around the world. These heroes have given the ultimate sacrifice that many of us here today have never been asked to give.

All of us have been touched by the cruel necessities of war; some of us are numbed by the loss. A spouse, brother or sister, or friend.

Perhaps some of you have suffered loss yourself in serving your country. Particularly, we thank you men and women seated among us who have served on the battlefields alongside those fallen comrades.

In our own humble way, those of us who have not been called on to serve and sacrifice in such a way feel gratitude that cannot be overly expressed. The sacrifice of a few served to ensure our freedom of speech, trial, education, representation, travel, talent—even our very destiny.

Let's never forget, nor let our children forget, the cost of war so they will never again have to pay the price for neglect or naivete. We are gathered together today to say a heartfelt "thank you" to those of you in the audience who feel a personal loss from your own service or that of a loved one. We owe more than mere words can repay. Our lives have never been the same since you and your loved ones served. We again pledge to you—friends and families—that we will remember and celebrate that spirit. Thank you.

THANKSGIVING

59

Audience: general
Message: We are grateful.
Tone: sentimental
Timing: 2 minutes

You find what you're looking for. The Pilgrims were looking for a new world and new freedom. They found it on our shores. You find what you're looking for.

Despite what you read in the newspaper or see on the evening news, never forget that there is much good and right in our world today. You find what you're looking for.

The cynics see hunger. The grateful hearts know that many orphans will be fed tonight through donations of those who share.

The cynics see poverty. The grateful have their real needs met.

The cynics fear the mugger. The grateful appreciate police officers dedicated to their jobs.

The cynics loath a drug-infested world. The grateful focus on prevention.

The cynics denounce greed. The grateful notice corporations and individuals working for charitable causes.

The cynics see pollution. The grateful take advantage of a democracy where we can vote to change policies.

The cynics see problems. The grateful grasp opportunities.

You find what you're looking for. The proud person rarely feels gratitude because he thinks he deserves every good thing that comes his way. The humble man knows better.

Most of us live a life far removed from real want. Few of us daily encounter muggers, miss a meal out of necessity, have the greedy and corrupt snatch our savings from us. Certainly, most of us can be thankful for the necessities of life. Health . . . Freedom . . . Time to enjoy our loved ones . . . A fall day.

And if we can't be thankful for what we *have*, we can be thankful for what we *don't have*.   Disease . . . Economic ruin . . . Isolation . . . Tragedy.

Let's celebrate. Eat. Love. Laugh. Work. Share. We have the Lord's blessings and we have each other.

Introductions

GENERAL GUIDELINES

- Mention the individual's accomplishments and why he/she is qualified to speak on the subject or handle an assignment: business acumen, results achieved, honors bestowed, educational attainment, diversified experience.
- Highlight the individual's personal qualities: Modesty? Enthusiasm? Wit? Integrity? Can-do attitude? Dedication?
- Add a personal touch if you're introducing the individual or program from your personal acquaintance. But don't take the opportunity to spend time talking about yourself rather than the individual to be introduced.
- Be specific with your praise. If you're introducing a program, state one or two key questions, issues, or topics that have been most helpful to those who've heard the program before. Or, if the individual is "widely published," cite a few of his/her books or articles.
- Be credible. Establish credibility by sharing what others think of the individual and mentioning accomplishments, but don't go overboard with flowery comments that embarrass the individual and sound insincere.
- Overview the topic to be discussed or question to be answered (unless the speaker plans to do so), emphasizing its importance to the audience and your anticipation of what's to follow.
- Give any necessary directions/explanations about the presentation, such as a question-and-answer period to follow.

- State the individual's name again as you close your comments and invite the audience to participate in the welcoming applause.
- Be brief. The audience came to hear the individual or program.

GUEST OF HONOR/SPEAKER

60

Audience: business or civic group
Message: This is an unsung hero who deserves recognition.
Tone: informal
Timing: 2 minutes, depending on insertion of details on affiliations and accomplishments.

You've commonly heard it said: "This man needs no introduction." Well, I'm here tonight to say that this man, our speaker, *needs* an introduction. . . . He needs an introduction because he's not the kind of person who flaunts his accomplishments. He won't tell you that, as an executive with (company), he supervises all international operations. He won't tell you that he landed (company)'s biggest account in recent years. He won't tell you that, as an active member of our community, he serves on three nonprofit boards.

He won't even tell you that, as a member of (organization), he contributes about (number) hours a year to collecting funds for that charity. He won't tell you that, as a member of the Big Brothers Organization, he shares many weekends with twelve-year-olds. He won't tell you that [insert other details about affiliations].

Emerson has said that the truly eloquent man is not one who is necessarily a beautiful speaker, but one who is inwardly and desperately drunk with a certain belief. That certainly characterizes (name), who deeply believes that we *are* responsible for the welfare of our fellowman. He deeply believes that each individual *can* make a difference—in business, in the community, in the world.

(Name) won't tell you all about himself and his own efforts.

So to repeat: He *needs* an introduction. He *needs* to know that we appreciate his contributions to make our community a better place.

So, I'll tell you those things tonight. On second thought, I guess I just have. Here's (name).

61

Audience: civic group
Message: This civic-minded individual deserves credit.
Tone: formal
Timing: 2 minutes

Two words come to mind as I think of (name). Involved and determined. Her job entails long hours, frustration, patience, communication skills, and little recognition. In fact, the only time one in (name)'s position hears from the public is when individuals are upset about something—policies, budget, personnel, or whatever they happen to disagree with.

Only someone who is involved in all the many issues that face our city and state and is determined to do the best for all concerned, only someone who is involved in excellent programs and determined to progress, only someone who is involved with her fellowman and determined to serve others—would give so much of herself personally to see that something happens.

And believe me, something has happened since (name) assumed the position of (title) (number) months ago: She has seen the (project) completed and operating efficiently to provide service for residents. She has been instrumental in funding the (project) program to see that the budget allows for spending where it counts the most in our community. Senator (name) and other colleagues credit her with the ability to work with all parties to bring about compromise and progress in the (project). In fact, here's what Senator (name) recently had to say about her involvement with the project: [Insert quote].

Yes, our "woman of the hour" has spent many days and nights and weeks and months and years getting there.

In reminding you of all these accomplishments—those two words keep surfacing—*involved* and *determined*. I know that we all will take pleasure in welcoming our guest of honor, (name), and showing our appreciation of her involvement and determination on our behalf.

62

Audience: professional or civic organization
Message: This person is an expert.
Tone: informal
Timing: 2-3 minutes, depending on insertion of details about accomplishments

Ladies and gentlemen, we're here to profit—that's the bottom line. To profit professionally as we hear our speaker, (name). You've probably heard many speakers who don't have much to say, but you had to listen a long time to find that out. Or, perhaps you've heard a speaker who used a lot of technical mumbo-jumbo because he was afraid that if people knew what he was talking about they would know *he didn't* know what he was talking about.

Well, I want to put your mind at ease. Neither is the case tonight with our speaker. She will be direct to your interest, and she will be clear.

It would be hard to overstate this woman's qualifications to speak to us about (topic). When someone wants to establish credibility for a colleague, you frequently hear them use the cliche, "She wrote the book." Well, literally, our speaker tonight wrote the book. Several in fact. She is the author of (title) and (title). In addition to these, she has published over (number) articles in industry-related journals and magazines sharing her expertise about (topic), (topic), and (topic).

In addition to the writing, she sits on several national boards and committees: [Insert names.]

Here's what others in the industry have had to say about her expertise:

[Read from reviews or other publicity pieces.]

Although I've not had the opportunity to meet and hear (name) before tonight. But from our brief dinner conversation, I can assure you that the enthusiasm you've already seen beaming from her smile is a genuine concern for us to grasp and profit from the ideas she will be sharing.

It is with admiration and great expectation of professional "profit"—specifically, I want to know how to make my million within the next three months—that I introduce to you (name). Please welcome her.

63

Audience: professional or civic group
Message: This individual is a celebrity but approachable.
Tone: formal
Timing: 1 minute

I'll have to begin with a confession: When I was asked to introduce our guest of honor, I was thrilled, yet hesitant. Thrilled by the thought that if I were going to be introducing him, naturally I would have the opportunity to meet him personally beforehand. Yet I was hesitant, too. What original comments can you make to introduce someone of his stature? It's all been said by others far more eloquent than I. You've heard of his wit and warmth and his talent to entertain.

Let me just sum up those comments by agreeing that our world is a better place because of our guest. We are grateful and honored that he has consented to be here with us tonight.

Therefore, thrilled, but no longer hesitant to introduce such a welcome guest, here is (name). [Begin applause.]

64

Audience: professional or civic group
Message: This individual is an expert, yet just "one of the guys."
Tone: informal, light
Timing: 2 minutes

(Name), our featured speaker, is certain to generate some new ideas and motivate you to make some changes in the way you [insert primary application of the speaker's topic].

As one of the industry's leading authorities in sales, (name) is an executive vice president at (corporation). His clients know him to be a thorough, precise, excellent communicator with those who need their products and services. One client has called him "the number-one authority on [insert] of our decade."

(Name) serves as consultant for numerous Fortune 500 companies, trade associations, and governmental agencies. The airlines tell him he's traveled more than (number) miles to (number) countries to tell salespeople how to [insert].

But enough about the titles and travels. Tonight, I want to tell you something a little more personal about (name.) (Name) is experienced in calf roping, whistling, harmonica playing, and commodities trading.

He has lived in Valley Forge, Pennsylvania; Dallas and Pyorrhea, Texas; Asheville, North Carolina; and Billings, Montana. He has been a fisherman, a golfer, a plumber's helper—the real kind—and a third-string quarterback for his losing high-school team.

He has four teenage girls, a mother-in-law, three elderly aunts who show him partiality, and two parrots. He hates taking out the garbage and emptying the dishwasher, and he loves calling his oldest daughter at college and waking her up after midnight as she and her friends so often do to him.

Surely, somewhere in there you can find something to relate to (name) when you have a chance to chat with him after the meeting. For now, please give him a warm welcome from some of us who've "been there." [Lead applause.]

65

Audience: professionals, civic group, social gathering
Message: This individual is a genuine friend—a person of high standards and personal warmth.
Tone: informal, personal
Timing: 2 minutes

Some people succeed by what they know, some by what they do, and a few by what they are. (Name) has succeeded for all three reasons. But I want to talk about the latter reason—who she is personally.

Our guest and I chased boys together. In fact, as high-school co-conspirators against cafeteria food and later as college roommates, we ate late-night pizza together, borrowed each other's clothes, spent holidays begging our parents for more spending money, and even flunked an art class together. Those days of secret conversations and bold assertions of independence are precious in my memory.

But it's been a long time since I've whispered to her how much her friendship has meant to me over the years. Oh, yes, we've stayed in touch as we've raised families, changed our careers, and cared for elderly parents. Through all these years (name) has always known the right words of encouragement when I was down, given me splendid advice on business decisions, and offered emotional support when I needed her presence. But I want to take this opportunity tonight to tell her and you as a group how much I value that friendship and all it entails.

And, yes, she has all the right credentials to speak to you tonight. Her associates and you know her as Dr. (name). Her professional stature in the community is recognized by the media attention to her name and her many invitations to speak to groups such as ours. She knows her subject.

But more than her professional credentials, I wanted you to know tonight that (name) is genuinely the type of person you, too, would want as a friend if you'd had opportunity to know her individually.

Golda Meir once remarked to an acquaintance, "Don't be humble: you're not that great." But I'm here to say that (name) is that great. Personally. A woman of integrity and tact, wisdom and warmth. With pride, I introduce you to my friend, (name).

PROGRAM/EVENT

66

Audience: professional organization
Message: The program is going to be of immediate benefit to you.
Tone: informal, light
Timing: 1-2 minutes

How many of you are here today because you wanted to hide out somewhere until somebody else solved the crises back in your office? I won't ask for a show of hands, but let me just tell you that you lucked out by showing up. This afternoon you're going to walk away with some challenging ideas and immediately applicable how-tos.

As stated in your program, our seminar will focus on key challenges currently facing our industry and ways to successfully turn those problems into opportunities in your local organizations.

We have a panel of experts to share ideas with us. I will be directing questions to each of them, focusing on the following topics: Reducing costs. . . . Improving customer service. . . . Reducing out-of-season inventory. . . . Ensuring quality in the manufacturing process. . . . Developing and motivating a talented staff.

Our speakers have graciously supplied us with journal articles and a bibliographic listing that will be helpful to you as you follow up on their ideas. And we've assembled copies of all these materials in the binders in the back of the room. We ask that you pick those up during the break or as you leave for the day.

Thank you for joining us. I'm eager to get started and have my own pen and notepad poised for pitfalls to avoid and performances to emulate. Out of the maze of challenges or "opportunities" facing us in this decade, I think most would agree that the primary question on the minds of those in the audience is [insert statement, question, or issue].

I'll ask you, Dr. (name) to begin on that issue.

NEW EMPLOYEE

67

Audience: employees
Message: Please appreciate the difficulty of this new manager's job.
Tone: informal
Timing: 2 minutes

What is a manager? She's one who sits behind the desk where the buck stops in her department. But a simpler definition is that a manager manages—paper, . . . deadlines, . . . communication, . . . clients, . . . crises, . . . risks, . . . and relationships. A manager keeps one eye on the future to plan, one eye on the past as a balance, and two hands busy in the interim to keep things moving from one location to the other.

Being in that position, a manager plays many roles. Protector of values. . . . Planner. . . . Delegator. . . . Sounding board. . . . Financial wizard. . . . Architect. . . . Educator. . . . These roles require business acumen, tact, leadership, foresight, courage, inspiration, interpersonal skills—and a great sense of humor.

I don't have to tell you that it's rare to find all those skills in a single individual. But in the opinion of the "powers that be" and my own, (name) exemplifies all these qualities and skills.

You have read (name)'s past titles and associations in the memo announcing her arrival on the scene. Her resume has all the expected past titles and acronyms of one very capable of assuming this position. Some of you may have crossed paths with (name) in other positions in other departments or subsidiaries. Her record has been outstanding, and from our past conversations, she is here to continue her own professional growth and to help us grow along with her.

I'm pleased to introduce (name) to you this morning. Say hello.

68

Audience: subordinates of the new executive
Message: This new executive has all the right credentials—and he's modest.
Tone: informal, light
Timing: 2 minutes

Thank you for taking time out of your schedules to show up to meet our new chief. And yes, I think, he probably knows what a rarity it is for any of you to leave your desk and responsibilities for more than a couple of minutes during the week and how eager you are to get on with your usual challenging, exciting, dynamic, and excellent work. So I'll be brief.

To summarize his resume: (Name) has served as a vice president in two small corporations you may have heard of—Exxon and General Motors. At GM, he was responsible for [insert details of position]. At Exxon, he tried his hand at [insert details]. Trained in his undergraduate work as an engineer, he has toyed with a few technical ideas in his spare time and holds (number) patents. Oh, and along the way, he has managed to get his doctoral thesis published in a Prentice-Hall book entitled (title). A few other editors of technical journals have asked him to share what he's learned with the rest of the industry, so he's published a few hundred articles.

(Name) didn't start at the top, however. Through the ranks at GM and Exxon, he held positions as design engineer, regional and divisional sales manager, and manager of operations. As you can see, he had quite a little difficulty in holding down a job until he got to the top of these organizations.

But from my understanding now, he's here to stay. They say that a good executive is judged by the company he keeps... solvent. (Name), we're placing our bets that you're going to keep us solvent. And I'm very pleased about your decision to join us here. Meet your new chief executive, (name).

69

Audience: colleagues in the immediate department
Message: This new employee is worth getting to know personally.
Tone: informal, light
Timing: 2 minutes

Eleanor Roosevelt observed: "If you approach each new person in a spirit of adventure, you will find yourself endlessly fascinated by the new channels of thought and experience and personality that you encounter."

I agree with her. During the last (number) years as I've worked with all of you, I've come to appreciate what really fine individuals you are. You are talented and creative. . . . You care about the job. . . . You care about each other.

From my brief association with (name), I've already found her to be much like each of you. She is talented and creative and cares about the job. Her former supervisors have commented on these attributes while she held the position of (title) at (corporation); the position of (title) at (corporation); and the position of (title) at (corporation). In our reference checks, one point came through above all the rest: (name) pulls her own weight. She gives 110 percent.

On a more personal note, she has two boys at home, ages (number) and (number), and some of you can identify with the feeding, shopping, consoling, and refereeing that entails. She has a great racquetball backhand and jogs a few miles each week.

I mentioned at the beginning that (name) was like you in that she was talented, creative, and cared about the job. The last quality I noted about each of you—that you care about each other—I'm sure will also come to be true with (name) as we welcome her into the group.

[Turn to the new employee.] (Name), we have about half an hour left, would you give us a brief overview of your life up to this point? No, I'm kidding. We won't put (name) on the spot today, but please make every effort to get to know her one on one and offer your help as you always do.

Rather than applaud, turn your heads her way and give her a big nod. Glad to have you on board, (name).

Motivational

GENERAL GUIDELINES

- Express appreciation for what the audience has already achieved or contributed.

- Focus on one objective, and prefer to make only one primary point in any given speech. Then illustrate that key point with several supporting details, statistics, or anecdotes. It's better to make one point well with several memorable illustrations than to present several key points and have none of them remembered.

- Call for a specific action. Don't leave your audience with the feeling of fluff: "What did he say?" Instead, give them specifics about changes, improvements, or goals to which you want them to aspire.

- Be clear and direct—even about the negatives.

- Use a "we're in this together" approach.

- Be upbeat in your tone; express confidence in the future rather than condemnation for the past.

TO EXPRESS APPRECIATION
FOR WORK DONE

70

Audience: employees, civic associates
Message: Each of you, in your own way, has contributed to our success.
Tone: informal
Timing: 3 minutes

We've finished. . . . The pressure's off. . . . We've been successful. . . . So who gets the glory? I'm here tonight to say, not me. Not management. But you. Each of you.

So how did we motivate you to do such an excellent job? To pull off such a feat? *We* didn't. You motivated yourselves. The difference between ordinary and extraordinary is that little *extra*. And each of you has contributed that little extra to make a big difference. They say that one of the greatest sources of energy is pride in what you're doing. You displayed that extra—that energy, that pride, that commitment.

You can't pay somebody enough for that.

(Name) rescheduled the vacation she'd been planning a full year in order to be here at the crucial decision time. . . . You can't pay someone for that.

(Name) spent (number) weekends out of the last (number) at the office, redesigning plans that we found necessary to change for various phases of [insert details]. . . . You can't pay someone for that.

(Name) dropped out of her night class at the university to devote the extra time it took to get her end of the project started. . . . You can't pay someone for that.

People in the (name) department put in (number) hours of overtime during the last two weeks to complete the paperwork. . . . You can't pay people for that.

(Name) spent days listening to completely unjustified, unreasonable demands from the public. She did it without losing her poise and her perspective. . . . You can't pay someone enough for that.

(Name) postponed surgery to avoid being away from the office during their crucial phase of the project. . . . You just can't pay someone enough for that.

So many of you have made similar sacrifices. You just can't pay people enough for that. So what *do* you do? Well, first you hope these individuals, and others like them, gain an inner satisfaction from a job well done. You hope their coworkers recognize and value their sacrifices and dedication. You hope their families reaffirm their commitment to personal excellence. In short, you hope other people recognize the qualities that make them unique.

Yes, as a management team, we hope that, in some small way, each of you, who has shown such commitment to your job, feels pride in our joint success and in your individual contributions. As British educator and social commentator John Ruskin so aptly observed, "The highest reward for a man's toil is not what he gets for it but what he becomes by it."

But you can't pay someone enough for that kind of attitude, for that kind of hard work, for personal sacrifice of time and emotional energy. We can only say a small "thank you" and hope each of you understands the gratitude we feel. You have our respect.

71

Audience: employees, civic associates
Message: I commend you for your hard work and your success.
Tone: informal
Timing: 5-6 minutes

You may have met a couple like this: The husband and wife have been married for about 40 years, but the wife grows increasingly unhappy. After all her efforts to communicate her feelings to her husband, she finally gives up on resolving the conflict herself. So she persuades her husband to go with her to their minister for counseling. The minister asks the husband what he sees as the problem in the relationship, and he details his wife's growing solitude and grumpiness. Then the minister turns to the wife and asks her what she identifies as the difficulty.

"My husband never tells me he loves me," she answers.

"What do you have to say about that?" the minister probes with the husband. "Are you aware that a woman frequently needs to be told that she's loved?"

The husband looks downright insulted. "I told her I loved her the day we got married. If I ever change my mind, I'll let her know."

Even if you don't identify with that couple in your personal life, you may in your corporate life. After all, when we recruited you here at (company) we told you that you were special. And in your periodic performance appraisals, somebody pats you on the back.

So why tell you again how much we appreciate you? Well, someone put it like this: "Appreciation is like an insurance policy. It has to be renewed occasionally."

Today we want to extend the coverage—for years to come. My purpose is simply to tell you that we think you're doing a maximum job with minimum recognition. The equipment we've been using has not exactly been state of the art. The customer's specifications and instructions are not always what anyone would call lucid. And the potential for profit on this latest project will probably be miniscule.

But you've given it your best—regardless. You've had a great attitude about everything we've asked you to do. You've performed well under pressure deadlines with near perfection. You've accomplished something we can all be proud of. Without you, we'd soon find ourselves without the talent necessary to compete and survive.

As part of our efforts to show you our appreciation, we have begun a company newsletter in which several of you will be highlighted in the coming months. Let us know who's doing what where so we can get our editorial crew out to interview them and share their expertise with the whole company.

You can contact (name and department) to pass on your suggestions for this recognition. With those referrals, you'll be doing the newsletter editor, the spotlighted employee, and the rest of us a service. Great work deserves recognition and emulation.

And we want to continue to receive your input on how we can do a better job for our customers—both internal customers and external customers. You know best what it takes to get your job done and where the wastes are. You can tell us best what changes still need to be made and in what areas you can contribute more. You can tell us best what we need to do more of and what we need to do less of. Your input has a direct impact on our bottom line.

We appreciate your concern in all these ways: your enthusiastic spirit, . . . your creativity, . . . your attention to detail, . . . and the sound business sense needed to make this corporation profitable.

As you help us meet our business goals of profitability, we can in turn help you meet your personal and family goals of job stability, . . . good salaries, . . . and a satisfying sense of accomplishment.

Although I won't play the part of the out-of-touch husband, I am sincere when I say that you as individuals are uniquely important to us. You've worked hard with great results and we appreciate it. Keep up the good work.

TO INCREASE PRODUCTIVITY

72

Audience: employees, civic associates
Message: We need to do more at a lower cost with fewer people.
Tone: motivational, informal
Timing: 18-20 minutes

Asking me to talk about productivity is like asking third-world countries to apply for a loan; persuasion just isn't part of the picture. I preach the subject with the fervor of a tent revivalist. It's *practicing* the message, however, that's the hard part. But practice it, we must.

I want to begin by raising a few questions, and then outlining a few answers we've stumbled onto. Perhaps—and we're really hoping on this one—you can add to our answer list.

First the questions: What's happened to our capitalistic system here in the U.S.? It's still suffering from a bad hangover after years of celebrating technological superiority. Granted, our businesses have not ordered their burial plots, but neither are they well enough to do calisthenics.

What has changed—that we Americans now have to concern ourselves with productivity and quality?

I remember Saturday afternoon shopping sprees in the local variety stores as a child. I'd sidle up to my mother and show her my selection for the dollar she'd given me for being "good." She'd look carefully at what I'd picked out. . . . And if she turned the label over and saw "Made in Japan," the verdict was always, "Put it back. That's no good. It'll tear up before we get home with it." Today, the reaction of mothers is just the opposite. "Made in the USA" has meant shoddy while the Japanese have surpassed us in everything from radios to microchips.

Why did it all happen?

For one thing, bureaucracy buried flexibility. Policies and procedures took precedence over ideas. Assumptions about our technological superiority smothered creativity and technological advancement. In other words, smugness settled in for smartness.

Then there was the energy crisis. . . . Then the recession. . . . Then inflation. . . . Then scandal in high places. . . . Then our drug war. . . . Then our literacy problem. . . . While we were and are fighting these fires, the Japanese have been outworking us. Their products have cut into our profit in most of our basic industries.

But the tide has been turning.

We're a competitive group as Americans. You've heard it said that people always root for the underdog. Well, we ourselves have become the underdog in the economic competition around the world. And American workers have started rooting for themselves. To put it succinctly: We were up against the ropes, but we didn't go down for the count. In fact, we're responding well to the challenges.

Now here's where you come in.

All of us individually have the power to produce. You, as well as I, know that there's a difference between working every day and simply having a perfect attendance record. We want to find those people who are giving it their all—day after day after day. We want to reward them and promote them. We want each of you to get excited about carving out a future here—not just whittling away the time.

You are our economic advantage in winning this competition. You have much to contribute in making this a better, safer country. The question is: How badly do you want to win? How much do you want to find a way to do your job better? Can you find a way to do it cheaper? Can you come up with an idea that's both better *and* cheaper?

Our pledge to you is to give you an environment that will make you comfortable in reaching your highest potential. We want to do everything possible to eliminate any obstacles to team effort and spirit. We want you to understand that the only long-term security for any of us in American business is innovation and cost-effectiveness.

We want to attract, retain, and reward people who are sold out to excellence in every way. And, in turn, we'll provide you with security and any retraining you need to climb to your highest potential. We guarantee you that if you work yourself out of a job, we'll find you another, better place. One more in line with your creative talents. In other words, we not only want your good ideas, . . . we expect them.

You are our biggest asset. Although we can't go to the bank and borrow against you, you will show up on our balance sheet. In the years ahead, you'll be the difference between profit and loss. And we want to ensure your personal ownership in the success you foster.

So, together, how do we get the job done?

Well, productivity simply means working smarter, not harder. It means completing a task with fewer ergs of energy. . . . Or less raw material. . . . Or less machine time. . . . Or less paperwork. . . . Or fewer worker hours. . . . In other words, we need you, our extraordinary people, to find ways to make extraordinary tasks just ordinary after all. I'm finding a lot of people around here capable of doing just that.

Work smarter, not harder. We're starting to do that again in America. As Ann Landers would say, "We woke up and smelled the coffee." We're once again inventing new products and new processes that will continue to raise our whole standard of living.

Specifically, here's what we're asking you to do to work smarter, not harder.

1. We want you to use our technology to its fullest. What products and processes can we improve with our know-how?

2. We want to reduce the number of people it takes to do a job. That's a sensitive issue, of course, and our plan is to cut our workforce through attrition rather than layoffs. But believe me, you don't have to put off thinking until someone voluntarily leaves or retires. If you work yourself out of a job, there'll be a better one waiting for you, one that can fully use your talents and expertise.

3. We want you to help us redesign our products to make them easier and faster to ship out the door. And even more importantly, to make them exactly what the customers want to buy at a price they want to pay.

4. We want you to become motivated to give it all you've got—to do more work in less time so that you receive the personal benefit of a higher paycheck based on higher profits.

Let's translate these into a more specific to-do list:

We have to talk to each other smarter. We need input from all of you—from those of you who service our elevators to those who prepare our annual stockholders report. From those of you who design our (product) to those of you who invoice our (product). We want our vendors to talk to our buyers. We want our engineers to talk to our accountants. We want our sales reps to talk to our service technicians. We want you to share your goals and your obstacles to those goals. It's only with widespread collaboration that we can spark each other's creativity.

We have to measure smarter. Do we know where the waste is? Do we know where to cut? Admiral Joseph Metcalf had this to say upon discovering that some of our largest Navy frigates carried as much as 20 tons of paper and file cabinets. "I find it mind-boggling," he said. "We don't shoot paper at the enemy."

Neither do we here at (corporation) shoot paper at our competitors. But we have enough of it to do some serious damage—to ourselves. We've got to measure what we're doing now against where we're going, so we'll know when we arrive.

For years, management teams have asked ourselves and our workers how much we could save if we bought this or that software. If we accessed this or that database. If we hired this or that consultant. And you know what? We couldn't find out. The savings didn't show up on any radar screen, computer printout, or bank statement. We wanted a PC on everyone's desk, but we didn't know how to pinpoint its impact on the bottom line. And those who hold the purse strings—ultimately our stockholders—keep nagging us with their questions.

Consequently, we have to learn to measure. We need to count how many unnecessary files we keep on employees and projects. We need to count how many invoices we have to prepare before we get the numbers right. We need to know how many times the average monthly project reports have to be rewritten before they're clear. We have to measure everything we do so we know where the waste is.

But the real improvements will come when we can *do* something *about* the waste. When we can cut invoice handling to once rather than twice. When we can write the research report clearly the first time without having to ask an editor to interpret and rewrite for us. In other words, we have to understand that being busy can no longer pass for being productive.

Another to-do on our list, besides talk to each other smarter and measure smarter: We need to market smarter. We need to go to our customers and show them the value they're getting for their dollars. We need to tell them what it costs us to build thus-and-so, and then ask them what feature they don't think is worth the cost. We need to ask them what they want first—then figure out a way to make it better and faster than the competition. We have to do that to hold the line on prices and make our customers profitable in their own businesses. In our narrowing economic circle, we're going to have to hold hands.

Another item on our to-do list: We need to educate ourselves smarter. Once upon a time, we Americans had all the great ideas in the world. Then the rest of the world followed our lead and began to think. They've come up with some good ideas while some of us have taken a long recess. Individually, we have to realize that education never stops. Formally, we are putting our budget where our mouth is and increasing the number of training opportunities open to you through the company.

But individually you can build your own productivity power base by reading magazines, journals, and books. Then those research efforts and those training classes have to be translated to practical processes and products the customers want and need.

Another to-do: We have to dream smarter. You've heard it said that some people entertain ideas while others put them to work. We want you to be in the last category. People are finding new ways to do their jobs every day. We have to continue to look for new ways to do things rather than to settle for "this is the way it's always been done." The best way has to win over the old way.

We have to focus smarter. We have to work with direction and good aim. Our left hand has to know what our right hand is doing. We have to eliminate duplication of effort and research. We have to focus on one task at a time. Step by step, task by task, day by day, and month by month, the little completed tasks turn into big completed projects. The quickest way to do *any* task is to do *only* that task. Productivity is concentration and focus.

We're building quality smarter. Doing it right the first time means doing it faster over the long stretch. If you cut out all the costs of poor quality—the cost to do something over, . . . the scrap and waste, . . . the service cost for things that don't work right, . . . the supplier rejects, . . . the auditors and the inspectors—then you simply have to be increasing productivity.

We have to lead smarter. People of our generation are better educated and informed. They think creatively for themselves. They ask "Why" when told what to do. They want more than a paycheck from our payroll; they want a sense of satisfaction from contribution. So we have to stimulate ourselves to think productively.

We want to give you the freedom to use your intelligence and internal motivation to our advantage in thinking of better, faster, cheaper ways to do things that are assigned. Your smarter thinking means our better production. Your skill, ingenuity, and use of the newest technology will determine how well we hold down costs and raise our quality.

To repeat: We have to talk to each other smarter. To measure smarter. To market smarter. To educate ourselves smarter. To dream smarter. To focus smarter. To build quality smarter. To lead smarter.

As with many new management ideas circling the globe, after all is said and done, . . . much is said and little is done. But this productivity issue I've been discussing is more than a new slogan—more than the latest management fad.

We are in earnest. This way of thinking—increased productivity—has to become part of our company culture. It has to be more than a hobby; it has to be our work lifestyle.

To produce more, we have to see further down the road—to long-term quality and savings. Only as we get that big picture will we cope with tomorrow's challenges and harness its opportunities. Yes, it is hard work out there. But Americans of the past have never been afraid of hard work. Especially when we know what we want and how to get it. As your management team, we're determined. We hope you're ready to climb into the driver's seat with us and take off for the game. Winners eat free.

TO CUT WASTE/EXPENSES

73

Audience: employees
Message: We have to do more with less.
Tone: motivational, instructional
Timing: 12-14 minutes, depending on insertion of expense details

Einstein once said, "My mind is my office." Now, that's low overhead.

There's no doubt that with employees like him on our payroll, we could reduce day-to-day expenses. But don't worry—we're not going to ask you to clear out your desk and work in your mind. Instead, we're going to ask you to clear out your mind and work at your desk—productively.

You've heard a lot in the last two decades about increasing office productivity. I say you've heard a lot about it because you as a group have been doing more with fewer people for several years now. That's the story from the smallest firms in the U.S. to our Fortune 500 colleagues. U.S. companies globally have had to do some belt-tightening to compete with the Japanese.

And I do mean belt-tightening—that's what you do in a recession. In a depression, you have no belt to tighten. And when you have no pants to hold up, that's a panic. Well, we're not in a panic yet; we do still have a belt.

But we want you to be aware of more than one way to get things done—the cheaper way.

The late Malcolm Forbes claimed that the answer to 99 out of 100 questions was money. But maybe not in our case. Maybe productivity is.

In other words, learning how to produce the same quality products and services with less will result in more—more productivity and more profit for the future. That's our goal.

But we can say this for adversity—people stand up to it. That's more than we can say for prosperity. When there's plenty of water in the well, we waste it. When the well goes dry, we learn the real value of water. We build character. We see what kind of employees and managers we really are.

In past difficult times, you've stood up to adversity. You've hung in there with whatever it took to get the job done. That's why we're confident that if you have the right information and a plan of action, you'll continue to improve the way we work.

So, I want to give you the scouting statistics before we get to the game plan. These numbers should give you a framework for understanding our strategy.

[Insert statistics on some of your monthly or annual costs to emphasize the magnitude of the troublesome expenses.]

Now here's the game plan to bring such costs under control.

We are learning to get the work done with fewer people. Through our early-retirement incentives, we've had volunteers to take their bonus payouts and leave. With the fewer people remaining, we've given our managers wider responsibility and control. We're learning to delegate downward. And we're now in the middle of eliminating nonessential tasks and other wasteful expenditures of time, energy, and money.

That's where you come in.

First, we want you to look at the expense of pushing paper. Governmental studies show that we white-collar workers spend 50-70% of our workday on paperwork. Reading it, writing it, analyzing it, responding to it, filing it, maintaining it, and retrieving it.

I encourage you to get rid of the unnecessary paperwork on your desk and mine. Information is power, but information comes in many forms other than paper. We don't need 17 copies of the same information floating around in four different report formats. Get off other people's distribution lists and get them off yours. Experts tell us that we'll never look at 85% of all the paper we stick in our files. We don't need to confirm every telephone conversation in writing. We don't need to write memos to protect ourselves in case somebody down the line fouls up. We don't need to draft a formal cover letter when a Post-It note will do.

Look at those weekly status reports. Those routine trip reports. Those reams of computer printouts. Those two-page forms filled out and filed in triplicate.

Could the work get done without them? What processes could we eliminate? What actions could we cut out of the loop? I challenge you as managers and individual employees to find out what goes where and why in your department. What comes in? What goes out? What would happen if we stopped sending this or that?

The computer was supposed to create the paperless office. Instead, it simply added to the paperwork pile. We can now edit so easily that writing has become a pastime. And with the stroke of a single key, we can send copies to the world, snowing everyone with paper.

Most of our work should get done *in spite of* the paperwork—not *because of* it. Ignore what you can and see if it won't just go away. Paperwork usually begins as a cure for a mild case of forgetfulness or distrust. But quickly the cure becomes worse than the disease. Paperwork threatens to devour our time and our budget.

Eliminate the unnecessary.

Second, we want you to take a hard look at your travel expenses. Before you hop on a plane, consider what you would do in person that you couldn't do by phone or letter or fax. And when you do have to fly, consider the off-peak hours and discount fares. Even with penalties when we have to cancel at the last minute, we usually come out ahead with advance purchases.

And a hidden cost of travel is human "downtime." Here's how you can make travel time more productive: Take along a reading file—all those journals that you've been meaning to get to. Pack your laptop or your dictaphone for those long layovers and missed connections. Do your strategizing and planning processes while you're away from office interruptions.

A third cost we want you to scrutinize is meeting time. Count noses around the conference table and multiply that half-day meeting by the average salary of those in attendance for some idea of how much the meeting is costing in lost productivity. Could you get the information out in another way? If the purpose of the meeting is just to inform, could you write a memo instead? Now, that would be a meaningful, money-saving memo.

Meetings are appropriate for brainstorming and problem-solving with a special goal in mind. Meetings are appropriate for negotiating details and gaining buy-in from your colleagues. But consider eliminating those for the purpose of simply informing.

Fourth, we want you to consider unnecessary telephone expenses. Check your watch before you dial. Could you wait until cheaper hours? Could you leave a complete message so you don't have to play telephone tag? Could you let someone's assistant help you rather than making four call-backs?

Fifth, we want you to consider the use of office supplies. A $2 binder here. A $10 ribbon there. Fourteen highlight pens left open to dry out around the training room. A ream of paper with coffee stains. It's the little things that add up to that astronomical cost of supplies I mentioned earlier, (number) dollars every year.

So there you have our strategy for eliminating the nonessential and performing the essential most effectively: Reduce paperwork. . . . Control travel expenses, using travel "downtime" well. . . . Eliminate unnecessary meetings. . . . Monitor your telephone habits. . . . Make do with less around the supply cabinet.

The tendency in times of cut-backs and belt-tightening is to whine because we've been taught the squeaky wheel gets the grease. But in times of difficulty, it gets the ax. If we can't find a way to do the job with less money, we may find that we can't do the job at all.

We don't want to have to put the ax to anything in its entirety—not our benefits, . . . not our travel, . . . not our training programs, . . . not our jobs. Instead, what we want to do is just prune the whole tree a little so our entire operation will bloom next season.

Our goal is to save everybody's job, yet to be able to turn a profit for our shareholders—and that includes many of you who are participating in our employee stock-purchase plans. You have a double motivation to work lean and mean.

As you well know, there are two ways to put money in your pocket— earn more or save more. We'd like to do both. And in our present industry's downturn, we think it's a lot easier to save more than earn more. We hope you'll agree. And we welcome your ideas on doing more with less.

You will make the difference. When a company faces upturns or downturns, the willingness of its employees to accept the challenge makes the crucial difference. Your attitude will be contagious.

Thank you for your hard work. . . . For your commitment. . . . For your continued confidence and support. Together, we can trim our fat and still enjoy a profitable dessert.

TO COMMUNICATE UP AND DOWN
THE CORPORATE LADDER

74

Audience: employees
Message: Clear communication builds credibility and the bottom line.
Tone: motivational, light
Timing: 14-15 minutes, depending on insertion of details about employee-involvement plans

You ask a teenager who is having problems with his parents to explain the difficulties. He'll respond with something like this: "We just don't communicate."

You ask a professor about why those in his class aren't making the grade and she'll respond, "They just don't communicate well."

You ask a married couple whose marriage is on the skids about the cause of their difficulty. They'll respond with, "We just don't communicate anymore."

My thesis is that the whole world is in a mess because we don't communicate. Students don't listen to the teachers. Politicians don't listen to the taxpayers. Suppliers don't listen to the customers.

We're not communicating. And I can't think of anything more vital to our organizational health than communicating—and communicating well.

A friend of mine tells this story about her elementary-age daughter. The mother came home from work one chilly fall afternoon and found her little girl sitting out on the patio, wrapped up in a big sweater, with her head buried in a library book. She went to the door and called out, "Honey, what are you doing, sitting outside reading when it's so cold?"

The little girl looked up, "Well, my teacher told us that if we wanted to be good students we should do a lot of outside reading."

I'm afraid that's been the story around (company) too often. Between management and employee. . . . Between Engineering and Marketing. . . . Between Service and Sales. . . . We're just not communicating all that well.

So what I want to talk to you about today is your communication style and mine. About what's happening. And how we can improve it. First, here's what I see happening.

We're not talking to each other *at all*. Many of us are retreating into our offices and writing memos about things that could be more clearly communicated and negotiated face to face.

Second, we're ignoring all the formal channels of communication— meetings, face-to-face discussions, internal correspondence—and opting to listen to the grapevine. Not that the grapevine isn't a viable rope—it's just that it's going to hang someone if we're not careful.

And finally, we're building paranoia because we're withholding information that everyone has a right to know. Management has a right to know that we've discovered a better way to get something done. And employees have a right to know the why behind decisions and policies.

That's the problem summary. So what's the solution? Talk more. . . . Listen more. . . . Match behavior to words.

Personally, I used to have a communication style a lot like Calvin Coolidge. One Sunday night after he returned home from church, his wife asked him what the preacher had talked about. The president answered in a word: "Sin."

His wife probed further. "What did he say about it?"

The president thought a minute and then responded, "He's against it."

That used to be my communication style. Not a word to spare. Say what you mean, mean what you say. But I've wised up a little since then. I've realized that the effect of my words alone are minimal in conveying my message.

Communication experts tell us that only 7% of our message comes from the actual words. The other 93% of our impact results from our voice quality and our appearance. In other words, our tone and our body language. That's the personal dynamic of one-on-one communication.

Now consider what I've just said in light of our organization as a whole. Multiply that 93% impact by the number of employees around here to see what's going on. You'll notice that a lot more gets communicated . . . than gets spoken.

How? Just as is the case personally, we as an organization sometimes communicate more by what we *don't* say. We communicate by our selection of what information to pass on and what to hold back. We communicate by what policies we enforce and which we ignore. We communicate our values by what behavior we expect and what behavior we reward on the job.

You've just heard my first point. Communication and the lack of it up and down the corporate ladder involve much more than talking. We communicate by appearances, by actions, by policies.

The second intriguing aspect of communication is that it needs to flow in all directions—upward, downward, and laterally—to be true communication. A one-way flow is a monologue. A two-way flow is a real dialogue.

You'll appreciate this communication dynamic a little more with this illustration used in many communication classes. Instructors often divide the class into two teams and assign some project to both groups, such as building a model with sticks or Lego blocks.

But the two groups play by different rules. One group leader must give all the directions without any feedback from the group. The audience can ask no questions. But the second group leader follows no such restraints. His group is allowed to stop him at any point for a repeat of something he said, for questions, for clarification or illustrations.

Well, no doubt you know how this exercise turns out. The group that gives the leader some feedback—tells him when his instructions are unclear and asks questions—does a much better job at the task. Such exercises are a real eye-opener for participants.

And the exercise pinpoints a major organizational problem. When communication flows only one way, we're in trouble. We're misunderstood. We're ineffective.

People don't make friends, . . . make enemies, . . . make a marriage, . . . or make a living without the effort involved in talking and listening to others. Yet for all its importance, communication doesn't get much formal attention. Perhaps because everybody talks, we assume that communication comes as naturally as breathing. It's not until we get communication hiccups that we decide to pay a little attention to the specifics.

Well, we've got the hiccups at (company) and we're paying attention to the cause. One of our primary goals in this coming year is to open up the ears and mouths of management and employees alike to get messages flowing both ways.

And flowing correctly:

You may have heard about the farmer who stopped by the barn to see how his new roustabout was doing on the job. "Where's the horse I asked you to have shod?" he asked the new employee.

"Did you say 'shod'? I thought you said 'shot.' I just buried it."

Like the farmer and the roustabout, we all can probably recall a few such miscommunications. And the consequences may have been more serious than a dead horse.

Those hurt profitability.

So, in the next few months we intend to improve our communication. We intend to put a process in place that will help you as employees analyze your jobs and suggest improvements to us. We expect to generate more involvement from you. And we intend to make managers better listeners.

Here's how the process will work:

[Insert details about your plans for the employee-involvement program.]

We've learned, however, from other companies' experiences that such an employee-involvement plan won't work if people view it as an empty gesture. As I mentioned earlier when talking about the 7% impact of our words, we won't communicate our earnestness in seeking your solutions with our words only.

We'll communicate our commitment to this program by the priority we give it in allowing on-the-job time for your analysis and follow-up of problems and proposed solutions. We'll communicate our commitment to this program by grabbing excellent ideas generated from the program and acting on them quickly. We'll communicate our commitment to this program by rewarding those good ideas and those people that communicate them.

Having this program printed in a little booklet is easy. Having this program happen on the ground floor is difficult. But we're committed to communicate.

We're going back to our basic assumptions. At (company), we hire the very best people. When you get the job, it's because we assume you have certain talents and abilities. That we can trust your judgment. That you can decide how to carry out your assignments without step-by-step instructions. If we hadn't made these assumptions, we wouldn't have hired you.

So we're going back to our basic assumptions. You are very capable people to whom we're trusting our profits. We want to hear from you. We *need* to hear from you. We're *committed* to communicating with you. And we want that same commitment from you.

In short, we want you on the front line of corporate warfare with our competitors to improve on Silent Cal's style.

Now we know good two-way communication won't happen overnight. It won't happen next month. But it will happen, a few conversations at a time. A few meetings at a time. A few suggestions at a time. And I promise the effort will be worth it to you—in personal satisfaction on the job and in corporate profitability that affects us all.

TO COOPERATE AMONG DEPARTMENTS

75

Audience: employees
Message: We're partners, not opponents.
Tone: motivational
Timing: 14-15 minutes, depending on insertion of details about team-building plan, appraisals, reward systems

Playwright Henrik Ibsen wrote, "A community is like a ship; everyone ought to be prepared to take the helm." My version is: "A *corporation* is like a ship; everyone ought to be prepared to take the helm." Everybody ought to have a compass.

Some of us share an attitude with the cartoon character Snoopy. He and Charlie Brown are standing on top of Snoopy's doghouse when the cat scurries away with Charlie Brown's blanket. "That cat has my blanket," screams Charlie Brown. "How are we going to get it back?" Snoopy looks puzzled, "We?"

For years, American corporations thought that competition was the key to outstanding performance within the doors of the organization. Get everybody to compete for their bonuses, their commissions, and their jobs, and, the theory went, they'll scramble with the ball. They'll get fired up and achieve, achieve, achieve.

But that's not what has happened. That competitive spirit has fostered jealousies and resentment, low morale, and lower productivity.

Harvard professor and author Dr. Rosabeth Moss Kanter has dubbed these competitive environments "cowboy" management. Cowboy management makes competition, rather than cooperation, a virtue. Cowboy managers and employees like to get out there in the wilderness with a few trusty pals and no restraints. They practice survival of the fittest for their product, service, idea, or department. But research has shown that this kind of competitive environment has *not* been effective.

At (company), sure, we want to race against the clock to get the product to market. Sure, we want to go up against our competitors' proposals to our customers. Sure, we want to race against our own track record of performance for increased productivity.

We need to compete against the rising tide of economic troubles. We need to compete with the Japanese and the whole Pacific Rim. We need to compete with (name of competitor's organization).

But what we *don't* need . . . is to compete with each other.

Comedienne Lily Tomlin once quipped, "We're all in this alone." But here at (company), we shouldn't be.

In short, we benefit from a cooperative, not a competitive, attitude between people and departments. And on some occasions, we may not even be aware that we're working against each other.

Let me tell you a little story about (name of marketing manager) and (name of engineering manager). [Be sure to use names of well-known company leaders here who do get along well.]

It seems that (George) was having a horrible time carrying some heavy boxes of books when we moved into the building here. In fact, just as (George) walked by (Mark)'s desk, (George) threw his back out, dropped the box of books he was carrying, and fell to his knees with excruciating back pain.

So (Mark), being such a helpful, compassionate sort of guy, offered to finish moving the boxes while (George) went to the doctor for x-rays. When (George) got back to work, (Mark) ran into him in the front lobby. "I finished moving all the boxes in and have the books all on your bookshelves for you."

(George) smiled. "Thanks. And I appreciate your help. . . . But I was trying to move them out to my car to take them home."

As I said earlier, similar things have been happening too often lately between departments here. Unintentionally, maybe even unknowingly, we are doing or undoing each other's best-laid plans.

If you don't believe we're interdependent, watch what happens to a conference room chair when one leg falls off. Now, the outside world may not know that our conference room chair has a leg missing. And our competitors may not know the chair has a leg missing. But I'll guarantee that the person who tries to sit down in the chair will know there's a leg missing.

When departments around here are vying to see who gets credit for the idea and the results, we'll know it. Because things will get really lopsided. People won't sit in those positions for long. And those around them will be moving away because they don't want to be nearby when the chair falls apart. That's a good picture of what happens when departments don't cooperate. Everybody just stands to the side to see what happens. We have a circus, but nobody's laughing.

Team-building can't be just a program around here. It's got to be a way of life. Of course, everyone pays lip service to teamwork. "He's a team player," we say. Or the referral letter says of the applicant, "She's makes a real contribution to the team." Believing in teamwork is like believing in apple pie and motherhood. We believe in it, but we haven't always practiced it. That practice is not automatic.

Oh, yes, we have processes for teamwork such as profit-sharing, employee stock-purchase plans, and quality circles. These processes and plans *should* foster a team spirit because the reward is based on our pulling together as a team to make a profit—a profit that goes directly into our pockets. The idea is that since we have team ownership, we should jointly feel responsible for our company's problems and profits.

But those processes don't always lead to the team spirit on the job every day. And that's the issue here.

To carry this goal of teamwork day to day, we're changing the way we evaluate what you do. We're no longer going to evaluate and reward on the basis of building a departmental empire. Instead, our performance appraisals and our reward systems are going to rest on a much broader base. We're going to look at the management of complex, interdepartmental tasks and teamwork efforts. We're going to reward those people who mentor and groom their employees to assume more responsibilities elsewhere. We're going to reward those people who spend time on buy-in and compromise rather than ultimatums and stalemates.

We want to sponsor team players, not referees.

Let me ask you mentally to take a scorecard and rate yourself on your team-building skills.

Do you consider people in other departments as your internal customers? And are you as eager to please them as our sales reps are to please our external customers?

Do you value consensus on decisions? Are you willing to take the time to gain buy-in from those who must contribute and make your idea work?

How are you at listening? Do you evaluate and act on feedback from other groups?

Do you look for ways to communicate your goals and problems to those in other departments who can help?

Do you fear that offering suggestions across department lines will foster resentment rather than resolutions?

How did you do on that quiz? . . . Teamwork isn't easy. Ask any member of Congress. Ask any pro ball team.

So we want to offer some coaching help—some goalposts and a game plan to get the ball between them.

Here is (name) to give you the details of that new plan:

[Call on the responsible person to speak, or you yourself incorporate details of training programs for team-building skills or new appraisal or reward systems that foster teamwork. Then conclude the other individual's talk or your own with the following comments.]

According to author Robert Allen in his book, *The Challenge*, "A network saves legwork." We need a network of people who talk to each other and who help each other, who solve problems together and who produce together.

And it's up to us as management to give you the framework and the systems to become a real team. You've heard our plans. We're eager to put them to work. We think you're the players we need to take us to the bowl game. We're betting our paychecks on it.

TO CHANGE OR TAKE RISKS

76

Audience: employees
Message: We must accept change and take risks. Failure will not be punished.
Tone: motivational
Timing: 13-14 minutes, depending on insertion of anecdotes about past risk-takers in the organization

Most of us grow up asking ourselves, "Am I normal? Can I run as fast as the other kindergarteners?" In high school, the question becomes, "Am I normal? Can I get a steady date?" In college, the question becomes,

"Am I normal? Can I make the grades?" In the corporate world, the question becomes, "Am I normal? Can I get the job and do the job?"

Well, let me answer all the questions at once: To *change* is normal. To take risks is *not*. We've heard the old saying that nothing is constant except change. Our interest rates change. . . . Our clothes change. . . . Our cars change. . . . The face of our workforce changes. . . . Our politics change. . . . Our philosophies change. . . . Even our cultures change.

Change has become the status quo. Think of that. Change is the only thing that's the same. That's normal.

But to take risks, . . . well, that's . . . risky.

It's risky to get too enthusiastic about new ideas. Someone has observed: "We have never learned to support the things we support . . . with the enthusiasm with which we oppose the things we oppose."

We're vocal about the status quo. It works—at least to some degree. But we're much more vocal about new ideas that we count as risky. After all, risky can mean wrong.

You've heard it said that two wrongs don't make a right. Well, that may be true when you're talking ethics. But in matters of productivity and quality, two wrongs may very well lead us to right. We need people who are not afraid to be wrong occasionally . . . in order to increase our chances of being right most of the time—when it counts.

I repeat: What's normal? The normal reaction to a new idea is to think of reasons it won't work. But we can't afford that normal reaction. The greatest risk of all is to take *no* risks.

But risks require courage. It takes courage to think creatively about what if. . . . It takes courage to break through barriers. Frederick Wilcox put it like this: "Progress always involves risk; you can't steal second base and keep your foot on first."

We have some great examples of risk-taking in the corporate world. CEO Roberto Goizueta risked changing Coke's formula to increase market share. Allen Neuharth risked profits and reputation to start *USA Today*, because he believed there was a market for a new type of newspaper.

We've had our own risk-takers here at (company). Our founder was a risk-taker, for example, when

[Insert details about how the company's founder began the business.]

But our first CEO and president wasn't the only risk-taker. There have been others blazing risky trails.

[Insert anecdotes of other company figures who have taken risks in organizational decisions—with new product lines, new plant openings or closings, changes in packaging or polices, and so forth.]

If you study our company's past record, I think you'll agree that risk-takers have always been around—our own variety of movers and shakers.

Try your hand at this rhyme or brain-teaser from former Citibank Chairman Walter Wriston: "If wages come from work, . . . rent from real estate,. . . . and interest from savings, . . . where do profits come from? . . . The answer is that profits come from risks."

We agree. And we intend to set a climate for constructive change and risk-taking. We intend to applaud, not undercut, risk-takers. We intend to provide recognition and reward rather than rules and reins.

So here are our principles for dealing with change and taking risks. We want you to see change not as an obstacle but as an opportunity:

One, do your homework—collect the available information and analyze it. Notice I said "available information." No one will ever take a step if we wait for *all* the information to come in. It never does. Waiting for all the market studies, . . . waiting for all the reports, . . . waiting for all the numbers, . . . is simply delayed decision-making. The risk-taker uses the numbers that are available, . . . analyzes them, . . . and then acts.

Two, recognize that inaction in staying with the status quo can be as risky as action in trying something new. The concept is as old as the Bible and the parable of the Ten Talents. The landlord gave three servants money for investing while he was away in the far country. The man with the ten talents risked them by investing and returned them with ten additional talents upon his master's return. The one given the five talents did the same. But the third man feared the risk. He buried his money in the ground and then simply returned the sum upon the landlord's return. Was he commended for his security-conscious action? Hardly. The angry landlord took away what he'd protected so well and gave it to the ten-talent servant who had proved he knew how to take a calculated risk.

To repeat: Maintaining the status quo can be a costly mistake.

Three, take action. You may find that you can't get all the sign-offs you need before the opportunity has passed. You may find that the market has moved on before the research has been completed. But if you've collected the available information and weighed the risk of the status quo against the change, act. We'll support you. We don't punish mistakes.

Four, admit mistakes. This is not contradictory to what I just said. Taking risks doesn't always result in profit. Never mind that.

Admitting mistakes has to be a way of life as much as risk-taking. It took Coke about 78 days to bring back its old formula as Coca-Cola Classic. But admit their mistake they did, rather than further anger their loyal customer base and lose more market share. Admitting mistakes and then going to work to reverse them is a natural part of risk-taking.

Let me list these steps again: One, do your homework—collect the available information and analyze it. Two, calculate the risk of maintaining the status quo against changing something. Three, take action. Four, admit mistakes. That's what we're *encouraging* you to do.

No, more than *encouraging*. We *expect* you to take risks.

And in response to that risk-taking attitude we're encouraging and expecting, our policy is going to be . . . explain, . . . train, . . . and then refrain. We're going to *explain* what our goals are. We're going to *train* you to do your job. Then we're going to *refrain* from controls that make you fit the norm.

In other words, we're going to change the meaning of normal. To us, normal won't mean "conformity." Normal will mean "different."

Today's environment—as fast-changing as it is—requires risk-taking. Companies large and small, new and old—companies like ours—have to risk to grow. Businesses do not win by letting marketing research studies, short-term profit reports, and fearful employees dictate the future.

CEO of Phillips Petroleum C.J. Silas has summed it up this way: "We've exchanged *free* enterprise for *frightened* enterprise. Some people fear being unprofitable. Some fear going to court. Some fear embarrassment. Some fear rejection."

But we don't. At least here at (company), we fear inaction and stagnation more.

Yes, it takes courage to change, to risk. Taking risks means moving forward while others are waiting for better times. Taking risks means moving forward while others are waiting for proven results. Taking risks means moving forward while others are waiting for applause on their past performance.

Yes, it takes courage to change, to risk. But then we have never aimed to hire the normal employee. We hire only the abnormal, . . . the extraordinary, . . . the excellent.

TO IMPROVE QUALITY

77

Audience: employees

Message: Here's what quality means specifically at our company. We need your commitment to build quality in, not add it on.

Tone: motivational

Timing: 23-24 minutes, depending on insertion of anecdotes and details about quality-control issues at your company

I want to talk to you for a few minutes about quality and elephants. Someone has said, "An elephant is a mouse built to government specifications." We've built a few elephants around here over the history of our company, and not necessarily for the government. Some of the specifications were ours. And, to give you the bottom line on this subject, I guess you could say we've found building elephants to be an unprofitable product line.

According to Aristotle, "Quality is not an act. It is a habit." Although we're not staging a hanging for our few acts of omission or commission—our mistakes—we are determined to ingrain the quality habit. It's no longer enough to make the *most* products or the *greatest* array of products; we have to make the *best* products.

And quality doesn't just have to do with products.

Here's the way we define it at (company). Improving quality involves all our activities: Products and services. . . . Customer relations. . . . Management style. . . . Human-resource policies. . . . Community-involvement projects.

Quality is nothing but . . . continued attention. Continued attention to everything. Every nut and bolt. Every product packaging and coat of paint. Every process and policy. Attention to detail.

In fact, that's the nature of business in general, says John L. McCaffrey:

> The mechanics of running a business are really not very complicated
> when you get down to the essentials. You have to make some stuff
> and sell it to somebody for more than it cost you. That's about all
> there is to it, . . . except for a few million details.

Those details are in your hands. As someone has said, "Every job is a self-portrait of the person who did it. Autograph your work with excellence." You are our quality control. Individually and collectively. Attention to detail will produce profit or put us out of the market.

What kind of detail? Let's translate all this talk about quality into specifics. To some people, quality means "being American" or "using common sense" or "being ethical." Vague generalities.

Although quality is easy to talk about in generalities, it's difficult to define in specifics.

Think for a minute about what the term quality means to you: The lonely Maytag repairman? Exxon's "quality you can count on"? AT&T phones that don't fall apart?

Or maybe you think of what it is *not*: Like "guaranteed" hotel reservations and airplane seats that are not? The full-service gasoline station that isn't? Department-store clerks who answer "I don't know—that's not my department"? Or, maybe "The computer's down again—we can't give you that information"? Or how about the bank teller's "You'll have to get at the back of the line, sir"? Quality can't always be measured in widgets per hour or durability alone.

So let's define it specifically and broadly:

With internal policies, quality means: Are our employees happy with their work environment and benefits? How many people do they have to talk to when they need to get a problem straightened out? How much paperwork do they have to shuffle to get their insurance claims filed and paid? How many forms do they have to fill out before they can arrange for a payroll deduction? Can they come to work in a pleasant, comfortable environment? Do we make it easy for them to handle their family responsibilities as well as their job responsibilities?

With regard to management style, quality means: Does your manager tell you what the department's goals are? Does he or she give you feedback about how you're contributing to those goals? Does the manager set realistic deadlines on projects? Does your manager provide you with the necessary training to do your job? Does the manager follow through on promises? Do you get rewarded for your contributions?

With community involvement projects, quality means: How many of our employees contribute their talent and time to community efforts? How many hours do they devote? Does the community view us as a willing corporate citizen or one that has to be cajoled into contributing? What projects have we participated in and with what success?

With our internal customers—say, the people in Public Affairs—here's what we mean by quality: Do they get the information they need from Data Processing on time? Does it make sense? How many times do they have to ask for an interpretation of the computer printout? Does the VP— the internal customer—get the results of an internal audit in a form that he or she can read? Is it timely information?

These are the definitions of quality with internal customers.

In customer relations, here's what we mean by quality: How many times does the phone ring before we answer it? How long does the customer have to wait on the phone or in person to talk to one of our reps? How many people does the customer have to tell his or her story to in order to get some action? Are we courteous? Are we reliable when we say we'll do something? How easy is it for the customer to buy from us? How often do we make billing mistakes? Do we ship fast enough to meet the customer's expectations? Do the products arrive in good condition?

With products, we're talking about these quality issues: Does the product work as the instructions say it will? How often does it break down? How many times does the customer have to call us to ask an operational question? How long will the product last?

Journalist Russell Baker has classified things into three scientific categories: Those that don't work to begin with, those that break down, and those that get lost. We plan to eliminate all three categories from our product line.

These are some pointed, difficult questions to ask ourselves. But ask we must. All of these are the essence of the vague term "quality." The specifics. ... The details that we need to handle effectively to be productive and profitable.

No matter how vague we may think the term "quality," our customers don't. They define it specifically, but subjectively: To one, quality may mean, "It won't break when I drop it on the floor." To another, it means,

"It doesn't fade when it has been sitting in the sun." To another, it means, "It will print faster than anything else on the market." To still another, it means, "It will impress my colleagues and friends."

However they define quality, customers are "hopping mad," as my grandmother used to say, when they don't get it. Here's a letter to the editor published in *Newsweek* from Michael J. Cohen, New York:

> Don't you get it—you big cheese, decision makers, production whiz kids? We consumers are not fools. We want fine design, good quality and long-lasting products. Foreign—read Japanese—products are designed, produced and marketed to respond to those wants. Until American manufacturers wake up to the fact that we consumers are entitled to the very best, we have every right to use our good taste and shopping skills.

Whatever the customer's subjective definition, we have to define quality to mean all those things I've just mentioned.

Quality goes in after the necessary and practical features are already assumed as part of the design.

Someone has been laughing at the customer's expense. Have you heard this riddle? How can the competition make money selling their products so cheaply? Answer: They make their profits repairing those products.

When I first read that quip, I laughed. Later it wasn't so funny. That's been the story in the U.S. at too many companies over the last 20 years. As a consumer, it hurts me to think about the broken gadgets and widgets that I've trashed after a few uses because to get them repaired was more trouble or expense than to buy a new one. There's got to be something unethical in all that—not to mention unprofitable in the long-term.

In fact, there's a big connection between quality and productivity—that's why so many industry journal articles lump them together. David Kearns, chairman and CEO of Xerox, believes that "one-fourth of all work in American industry is done to correct errors." Now, that's expensive.

You've heard the question before: "If you don't have time to do it right the first time, how will you ever find time to do it over?" Another pertinent question might be, "If you can't afford to build in quality the first-time around, how can you pay someone to add it on later?"

Here is William A. Foster's definition of quality, written almost a century ago: "Quality is never an accident; it is always the result of high intention, sincere effort, intelligent direction and skillful execution; it represents the wise choice of many alternatives."

Foreign competition has shown that low cost and high quality are not mutually exclusive terms. Making things right the first time eliminates waste and increases productivity over the long haul.

A recent survey by the American Electronics Association revealed that although 85 percent of respondents had undertaken a quality-improvement effort, fewer than one-third could document significant improvements in quality and productivity.

But these studies showed something else. Most of these quality programs had been designed for "after-the-fact" quality. Finding and correcting errors in things that had already been made. That's expensive. That's
why we're aiming to build the quality in up front—not add it on.

I want to outline our framework for building quality in. Within the
next few weeks and months, you'll be hearing a great deal about these
quality-assurance programs:

[Insert an overview of the new programs you plan to implement.]

In other words, the quality race is a marathon—not a 50-yard dash
to the finish line.

The Strategic Planning Institute's research on 3,000 businesses has shown
that as quality increases, so does productivity, . . . market share, . . . customer
satisfaction, . . . profitability. To put it simply: Quality pays its own way.

Someone has said, "It's better to deserve honors and not have them
than to have them and not deserve them." We may not have won any
worldwide titles for our products—I don't know that there are any except
for the bottom-line title. But we ourselves will know the quality's there.
And our customers will know—that's what really counts.

Well, you may be saying, we do pretty well. We already handle 99.9
percent of the details well. Isn't that enough? That's a good question.
Here's how quality consultant Jeff Dewar of QCI International would answer that. He argues for a goal of zero errors or defects with a few analogies.
If we accept 99.9 percent perfect as our goal, we'd have to accept the
following conditions:

- 2 unsafe plane landings per day at Chicago's O'Hare Airport
- 16,000 pieces of mail lost by the U.S. Postal Service every hour
- 22,000 checks deducted from the wrong bank account every hour
- 20,000 incorrect drug prescriptions each year
- 32,000 missed heartbeats per person per year

That puts our total quality goal in perspective. Our aim is perfection
in every way every day. We don't want to build more elephants.

We can't let ourselves work in circles. We hit the market with a new
product—like our (name of product). It's successful. That builds pride and
confidence. That confidence and pride relaxes our attention to detail. That
let-up in attention to detail produces problems. Those new problems in quality
destroy our confidence. It can become a circle—a circle that we want to break.

You may have known some people who don't want it good—they
just want it Tuesday. We've got to break that line of thinking.

Quality is everyone's responsibility. That's not a new statement or
idea, but one worth repeating often. There is no job so simple that it
cannot be done wrong. I don't know about you, but some mornings I have

problems tying my shoelaces so that they stay tied. But we don't want to let the simple things trip us up. Simple things such as how we

[Insert details about a few specific, "small" things that need to be done right in your organization.]

In other words, we need to question ourselves on every task—just like the second-grader who questioned her teacher while they were on a class trip to an art museum. They stopped in front of an abstract sculpture. And the second-grader asked, "What's that?"

The teacher answered, "It's supposed to be a galloping horse."

"Well, why isn't it?" the second-grader wanted to know.

We need to be asking ourselves similar questions about our tasks and products. Why aren't they what they're supposed to be?

Customers see a big difference between almost right and right, between good and best, between so-so and superior. That difference is what we want to manufacture around here.

Journalist Sydney J. Harris has observed: "An idealist believes the short run doesn't count. . . . A cynic believes the long run doesn't matter. . . . A realist believes that what is done or left undone in the short run determines the long run."

I'm a realist. Quality in the short run determines our long-term profit. Customers often forget how little we *charge* to do the job. But they remember how *well* we do the job.

I'm not a prophet, but I have a prediction. In the years ahead, technology won't win the war. Even those companies who are the first to develop certain technologies will lose their advantage in time. Everybody will follow the leader and eventually develop the same products. The competitive difference will be the people who attend to the quality.

That's you. You will be our decision makers on quality. Every day. With every detail.

TO IMPROVE CUSTOMER SERVICE

78

Audience: employees
Message: You each represent our company to the customer; you have the power to win or lose customers for us.
Tone: motivational, light
Timing: 23-25 minutes

You may have seen this advertisement used by a training consulting firm: Two colleagues are talking about a particular company and one says,

"Their product is fine, but their customer service is a joke." The second person responds, "Oh. Well, then, who would you recommend?"

The implication? Good product is not enough. Customer service is what people are buying. And anyone who thinks customers aren't important should try doing without them for a period of 90 days. When someone says to you that pleasing a customer is hard, ask them, "Compared to what?" To having to find new ones? Believe me, it's a lot harder to get new customers than to treat the ones we have right.

And we've all read a lot about that lately. From Tom Peters, from Lee Iacocca, from Buck Rogers. But let me get a little more personal. I want to tell you a true story about two friends of mine who recently moved. A rather long story. But I think you'll identify with it.

Like the proverbial average family which moves every five years, Mike and Marsha got the itch to mow a new lawn. Finding the house of their dreams, they applied for a loan with Mortgage Company X, which guaranteed in-house loan approval within 30-45 days.

"Will I need a CPA-prepared financial-worth statement since I'm self-employed?" Mike asked. "If so, I want to get it now rather than slow up the process somewhere down the line."

"No problem," the loan officer answered. "If you keep your own books, your statement is good enough."

A few days later, the loan officer called to say she had lost the VA eligibility certificate. Could Mike and Marsha supply another? They did. A few days later the loan officer phoned to say that they would, after all, need their CPA to prepare a statement. He did. Mike and Marsha waited.

Finally approval came. But two hours before closing, their realtor called to say there would be no closing. Without notice, the mortgage company had decided to reneg on their interest-rate commitments not yet in writing and "to relieve from duty" all loan officers at that location. Others were flying in shortly from headquarters to hear customer complaints. But no one there thought to call Mike and Marsha to let them know the closing had been cancelled. A couple of days later they "permitted" Mike and Marsha to quietly take their loan package to another institution. They ran.

But that was just the beginning of their experience with customer service—or lack of it. They pulled out the home-furnishings catalogs. Custom window covering came from Department Store A. The master bedroom woven-wood was two inches too short and two inches too narrow. Someone didn't measure or record the dimensions correctly. Would Marsha mind if the designer just sprayed a chemical treatment and "yanked" the window covering down? Mike and Marsha agreed. It didn't work. The department store refunded the money and my friends were only out the four-week delay.

They called Store B. Humming to herself while the installer hung the second woven woods, Marsha dreamed of privacy in the bedroom. But

the installer came down the hall shaking his head. "You wanted a dou-
ble-pull wood, Ma'am? I'm afraid the factory made a mistake. Or someone
copied down your order wrong. I'm going to have to send this back."

On Store B's second delivery, Marsha was afraid to look. "Ma'am,"
the installer said, "you're not going to believe this, but they made the
same mistake. It's the same one we sent back." They got the correct window
covering six weeks later.

Store C delivered a brass bed for their daughter's room. One hole
for the frame was drilled higher than the other. "But it is a $34 special,"
the salesclerk reminded Mike on the phone. Mike drilled a lower hole.

The master bedroom brass headboard, a more expensive variety, Mike
and Marsha didn't dare leave for a delivery truck. The salesman promised
to send it to Package Pickup while they pulled the car around. He did
and they did. In the bedroom light, after Mike and Marsha had unloaded
the headboard with (literally) gloved hands, they saw the scratches. Headboard to footboard. Yes, the salesman said on the phone, they could return
it if they brought it back immediately. The sales clerk "had a feeling"
Package Pickup would be careless with it. "They do it all the time," the
clerk assured them. It was the only headboard of its kind in stock.

The following Saturday Store D delivered the new washer; the old
one, in its 12th year, had washed its last load a week earlier. On its first
spin cycle, a smoky scent filled the house. The repairman said it couldn't
possibly have a burned-out motor. It did.

After only two tries, Store E delivered the fireplace screen (without the
screws) and a dinette. They had delivered both to the old billing address
rather than the one carefully printed on the contract under "Deliver To."

"Be glad to give you a refund on the fireplace screen if you want to
bring it back," the clerk said. Was it worth the 45-minute trip across town?
Mike found the screws at the corner hardware store and made do.

The garage-door opener they bought as an unassembled do-it-yourself
kit. After installation the remote controls didn't control. The store owner
promised to have the manufacturer send new ones. They came ten days
later, COD for $62. After refusing the delivery, Mike phoned the store
again. Ownership had changed hands, and the assistant office manager
"didn't know" about honoring the old guarantee. Old guarantee? Eleven
days? Mike took the opener off the garage door and returned it anyway.
How could they refuse eyeball to eyeball? They did.

"If you'll come back tomorrow when the repairman will be around
to see that you haven't damaged the controls when you installed it, we'll
see about a replacement," the new owner offered. After they made a second
45-mile trip the following day, the repairman verified that the remote
controls never controlled. Their refund was uncheerfully given.

Now you're asking: Had my friends been singled out for this perse-
cution? Believe me, they'd begun to wonder. Was the rest of the world

faring any better? Not even their daily newspaper could tell them; the assistant who took the address change by phone argued that their street was nonexistent. Four days and two lengthy direction sessions later, they got a paper at their new address.

So much for the outside world. But could they make contact? Now, Mike and Marsha had always been ones to get mail. But the second week after their move when mail dwindled to "Dear Occupant" circulars, a trip to the old address produced approximately an eight-inch stack of first-class mail.

Yes, various clerks responded, the Post Office did still have the change-of-address notice on file. But frequently a sub was on the route and possibly nobody had told him to forward the mail. The supervisor promised to "take care of it personally." Four months and numerous phone calls later, Mike resorted to removing the mailbox from the pole.

But anticipating such "disruption of service," they had planned early phone installation: One month before M-Day, they called to have telephone service transferred and asked for a cost estimate. A "marketing specialist" promised to call back because their order was quite "complicated." After hearing nothing for two weeks, Marsha phoned again. The representative apologized for the delay and promised to give the order "her personal attention." Marsha asked if the phone rep could give them an assigned number. Which she did, insisting, of course, that the number couldn't be guaranteed until installation. Relying on the "96 percent chance" that the number would work, Mike used the number in a national ad for his consulting business. The next day, the phone rep called back to explain that she'd made a mistake in assigning the number and figuring the charges. So much for an ad that reached the public.

Four weeks later, the installer phoned. He wanted to know where Marsha was. The installer was at the new residence to hook up the phone and the house was empty. Marsha told him about the reschedule due to Mortgage Company X's shenanigans, giving him name, date and hour of rescheduling. The installer had never gotten the word, he insisted. According to his assessment of the situation, "Somebody" fouled up. Marsha rescheduled installation for a week later.

Marsha waited in the new, cold, empty house for the installer to arrive between 8 a.m. and 5 p.m. At 4:55, he showed up. The phone worked, but the answering service would take another five days. Thank goodness for at least one inefficiency; the phone company had failed to put the transfer tape on their old number. We, in the outside world, could still contact them.

Fifty-four days after their original order request, my friends had a working telephone. Rejoicing, they phoned us with the correct new number. But when Mike tried to dial the downtown library, he couldn't. Had the phone company done what he suspected? Yes. The operator verified that they had indeed installed a limited suburban line instead of the metro service Marsha had ordered.

Two days later, the phone bill arrived for one month's service. Since the phone had been working for only 46 hours, Mike called to complain. "Not to worry," the assistant told him. She would adjust the bill and send a corrected copy.

A week later Customer Relations called to ask about "the manner in which their recent order had been handled." Was it worth 15 minutes to tell her? Marsha decided that it was, giving the Customer Relations rep names and dates. "This is my job," she gushed, "to catch problems like this. I'm going to give this to my supervisor for his personal attention and he'll get back to you immediately."

A disruption-of-service notice arrived. Marsha phoned to say that she had never received a corrected bill. "We'll make a note not to disconnect, then," the representative promised, "so don't worry." They did.

Two days later, the phone wasn't working; their line was crossed with another number. The phone company corrected that problem 12 days later.

And no one ever called back from Customer Relations. . . .

You're smiling. No, I take that back. Some of you are crying. It's all too familiar, isn't it? The frustration of getting products that don't work, . . . of getting poor service, . . . of telling people who don't listen, . . . of telling companies that don't care.

And in most cases, the *problem* is not the problem. It's one's *attitude* about the problem. Well, whatever it takes to make the customer happy, our attitude at (company) is going to be to get it done.

We don't want to be one of those companies Mike and Marsha dealt with. We've got to learn from the mistakes of others—we can't stay in business long enough to make them all ourselves.

We're *not* going to be one of those companies that think selling is enough.

Starting today, (date), I want to go on record with my number-one priority: customer service.

We don't want a customer to walk out of here mumbling: "This isn't really the color I wanted." Or: "This really will be difficult to use." Or: "I wonder if that sales rep's going to be here if I have to return this thing." Or: "I paid enough for this (product); you'd think they could at least help me get it to the car." Or: "The salesperson didn't have the foggiest idea how this works."

Never do we want to hear our customers mumble something like that. Or even *think* it.

So how can we achieve that goal? I can't. Oh, I'll do my part by setting policy that supports you all the way. But the key to our success will be you. Each of you individually.

In the moving fiasco of my friends, any one employee who cared could have turned the tide.

What if the loan officer had gotten around to putting the interest rate in writing, as she'd promised? Or had bothered to phone to say that the house closing had been cancelled?

What if the drapery designer had taken correct measurements?

What if the rep in Package Pickup hadn't banged the brass headboard around?

What if the inspector had noticed the fireplace screen was missing screws?

What if the new manager where they bought the garage door opener had gladly offered a refund without Mike having to make two trips across town to prove his point?

What if the newspaper rep who handled new subscribers had asked for directions?

What if the mail carrier had cared enough to check out a situation where mail remained in a residence box for four months?

What if the telephone installer had double-checked his installation orders and given the customer a clue about when he would arrive?

What if the customer service supervisor had cared enough to follow up when the rep discovered Mike and Marsha's phone horror stories?

What if . . .?

What if . . .?

What if businesses saw themselves as the candidate and saw the customers as the voters? In a real sense, that's the situation. Customers vote with their dollars.

Mike and Marsha shouldn't have had to go through a nightmare to move into their dream house.

Our customers shouldn't have to be hassled to get what they need when they phone us or walk into our place of business.

You are on the front lines. You see fiascoes like Mike and Marsha's waiting to happen. Today, I'm asking you to become the customer's advocate. You, as a (company) employee, practice the golden rule: If you wouldn't want it done to you, don't do it to our customers. Take the initiative; go the second mile. If that means making an extra phone call or two, do it. If that means replacing the product, do it. If that means working overtime, do it.

Customer service is an idea whose time has come. Customer service keeps us in business. Our attitude isn't going to be the problem. Your attitude—those of you who are on the front lines with customer contact—your attitude toward the customer will be our key to success. That's what our market is buying. That's what we're selling.

You know, as John McCaffrey observed, "The mechanics of running a business are really not very complicated when you get down to the essentials. You have to make some stuff and sell it to somebody for more than it cost you. That's about all there is to it, except for a few million details."

Those "few million details" are in your hands.

TO REACH GOALS

79

Audience: business, civic, or social groups
Message: You need personal and career goals to become successful.
Tone: motivational, instructional
Timing: 13-14 minutes

You've heard it said that the road to hell is paved with good intentions. Let me twist that a bit: The road to *achievement* is paved with good intentions. We call them goals.

If you don't know where you're going, any road will get you there. So it's not enough just to "start out" in your career; you have to know where *you're* going personally and where *we're* going as a company.

"There's no point in carrying the ball until you learn where the goal is." At (company), we tell new hires right from the beginning that they have to let their managers know what their career aspirations are. Do they want to get into management? Do they want to stay in a technical field? Do they want to be a specialist? Or do they want to be a generalist? We have to know where their goal line is—and they have to know ours—so that we know who to give the ball to and when.

But then talk is cheap. Everybody talks about goal-setting. We have corporate mission statements and objectives. Department goals. Sales quotas. But really what's their value? An old proverb from India sums it up like this: "No one was ever lost on a straight road." And you'll have to admit it, some companies have gotten lost in the global race for quality products.

Something like 90 percent of all products launched in the U.S. are failures. Our success rate at (company) is (number) percent—better than the average. And we're always looking for ways to improve those odds.

So why don't *people* set goals as methodically and frequently as corporations? Fear. Not having goals covers up for failure. We don't have to face failure if we have no yardstick. If we don't do much, nobody—including ourselves—knows. People without goals drift.

The most important thing about a goal is to have one. Goals focus our attention.

I like the story about the old man who was trying to lead a contrary donkey down the road. A passer-by stopped him and commented on the way the donkey was behaving. "Oh, I can make him do anything I want him to with just a kind word," the owner said.

"Doesn't look like it to me," the other sneered.

"Sure, I can," the owner said. Whereupon he climbed off the donkey, picked up a two-by-four beside the road, and clobbered the animal on the head, then explained to the onlooker. "I simply have to get his attention first."

Goals get our attention. Losers stay busy doing things. Winners concentrate on planning before they ever make a move. For people who don't give attention to long-term goals, the future is any time after tomorrow. But the future has a habit of suddenly becoming the present. And some 40-, 50-, and 60-year-olds are still asking themselves what they want to be when they grow up. To repeat: Goals make us focus.

So what are the characteristics of good goals?

Well, first, good goals are set by decision, not default. You have to set the long-term goal early on in any project. Have you ever started out for a Sunday afternoon drive with a friend without a particular destination in mind? And after a mile or two the conversation began to go like this:

> "Where do you want to go?"
>
> "I don't know—where do you want to go?"
>
> "How about to Tony's for dinner?"
>
> "Well, we already passed that highway."
>
> "Okay, how about a game of golf?"
>
> "The best golf course is all the way across town."
>
> "Well, then how about a movie?"
>
> "Hmmm. It's 2:45—everything's already started now."

I can tell by the nods, you've had some of those Sunday afternoons. John R. Noe, in his book *Peak Performance Principles for High Achievers*, sums up the experience like this: "By the time we are ready to make the big decisions, the options have been narrowed by our little choices along the way. If we do not focus our goals, our lives will be controlled by haphazard decisions."

You've heard it said that not deciding . . . is deciding. In goal-setting, the same is true. Late goal-setting is not really goal-setting—it's recapping after the fact.

The second characteristic of a good goal is that it's a big goal—one worthy of your efforts. Someone has said that if you intend to succeed beyond your wildest expectations, you have to have some wild expectations. A few people wake up every day to go out and slay dragons. Most are satisfied to chase lizards.

If you're an "average" performer, don't set your sights on "above average." Look at "excellent." Whatever the average, look at what your colleagues would term a "reasonable" goal and then double it. That would be worth working for. That would be worth achieving. Consciously or unconsciously, you always get what you expect. So the secret to success, it seems to me, is to raise your expectations, to set goals worthy of your effort.

And don't let fear that you won't reach big goals keep you from setting them. Here's what author and management consultant Peter Drucker has to say about that fear:

> Objectives are not fate; they're direction. They are not commands; they are commitments. They do not determine the future; they are means to mobilize the resources and energies of the business for making of the future.

Oliver Wendell Holmes agreed: "The greatest thing in this world is not so much where we are, but in what direction we are moving." Unless you set big, worthwhile goals, you'll never move beyond your current abilities.

The third characteristic of a good goal is that it has a completion date. Goals are dreams with deadlines. Always put a deadline on your goals, because deadlines wake you from your dreams to bring you to the reality of achieving them. Sleepwalkers don't get around very well—at least not without a lot of bumps on the shins.

When talking to the authors of the bestseller *Thriving on Chaos*, Fred Brooks, a System 360 Chief Designer at IBM, had this to say about the lack of setting corporate goals: "How does a project get to be a year behind schedule? . . . One day at a time."

Set five-year goals. Ten-year goals. Six-month goals. Without deadlines for their achievements, goals are simply "pie-in-the-sky" plans.

A fourth characteristic of good goals is that they are followed up by a plan of action. The how. Will Rogers quipped, "Even if you're on the right track, you'll get run over if you just sit there." You've got to put the how-to to the goal. If you plan to switch careers, what new training will you need? Where can you get it? What college or corporate course?

If you plan to raise funds for a civic memorial, how? Which contributors do you want to reach—individuals or corporations? Do you want to use a direct-mail campaign or a fund-raising dinner? Or both? Goals are no good without plans of action to bring them into reality.

Successful companies have elaborate plans. You wouldn't dare to go to work for them if they didn't. "Buy low, sell high. Collect early, and pay late," says educator and author Dick Levin. Sounds good in theory, but we'd be in trouble if we depended on a paycheck from companies that didn't have a more complete game plan than that. Without plans, the only way businesses run is downhill. The same is true for individuals and organizations such as ours. We need specifics to be successful.

A fifth characteristic of good goals is that they can be broken into specific short-term steps and completion dates. Maximum achievements are the result of minimum steps. A big house is built with one little nail at a time. A suit is sewn one seam at a time. A business is built one employee at a time.

Next, good goals are written goals. Committing them to writing makes them real for you. You can review them. Modify them. Commit their accomplishment to others. They're constant reminders of where you've decided you want to be at what point in your life.

Finally, good goals generate excitement. The late Malcolm Forbes said, "Men who never get carried away should be." Don't be afraid to show your commitment—some might even call it fanaticism—about reaching a goal. If you're kicking and screaming about reaching or not reaching a goal, at least we all know you're alive.

Let me run those by you once again. How to set good goals:

- Set them by decision, not default.
- Set big goals.
- Add a completion date.
- Develop a plan of action.
- Set short-term steps and interim completion dates.
- Write them down.
- Get excited about them.

Norman Vincent Peale may have oversimplified it, but I don't think so. He said, "Plan your work for today and every day, then work your plan."

If you don't start, it's certain you won't arrive.

TO BE ETHICAL

80

Audience: employees
Message: We want every thing you decide to do in this company to be ethical.
Tone: motivational, instructional
Timing: 8-10 minutes, depending on insertion of details on policies

My topic this morning is ethics. Just how far our society has come on business ethics was brought home to me recently in reflecting on this incident about a neighborhood teenager looking for a part-time job. He was asked to take one of those integrity tests before the supermarket would hire him to sack groceries. At dinner he confided to his parents: "I'm kind of worried about that test they had me take today. They had questions like: Have you ever taken drugs? Have you ever cheated in school? Have you ever stolen money from your parents? Have you ever stolen anything from a schoolmate or an employer? When I started answering 'no' to all those questions, I started worrying that they'd think I was lying because I sounded too good to be true."

The student got the job. But where have we gotten to when our teenagers feel uneasy about being too honest to get a job!

Unfortunately, too many businesses grab today's headlines for the wrong reasons—their unethical behavior rather than their new technology. Executive extravagance at the expense of shareholders. . . . Insider trading scandals. . . . Corporate espionage involving trade secrets. . . . Overcharges and kickbacks on contracts. . . . Price-fixing. . . . Illegal disposal of chemicals. . . . Patent infringements. . . . Warranties that aren't.

Of course, these are not typical of *all* businesses—not typical of even the *majority* of businesses. But the point is—they *are* typical.

Allen I. Young, general counsel at Price Waterhouse, points out in their *Price Waterhouse Review* the fraud and dangers in what is termed "cute accounting" or "loopholing." If caught, the people who lie in these ways can always point out a chapter and verse in accounting literature that, they claim, led them to such erroneous thinking. Their rationalizations, however, rarely wash with the IRS because they know they are following only the letter of the law rather than the substance.

Why do we have to pass policies and establish procedures on ethics? Isn't just plain old-fashioned honesty in vogue any more? It hasn't been for quite some time. According to Winston Churchill, "A lie can run around the world before the truth can get its boots on."

But besides an inner code of morality, there's a bottom-line reason for our interest in ethics. In the experience of most CEOs—or at least among those who voice their experience to others—unethical behavior sparks a failure mode that runs throughout the entire company. All the way to the bottom line, given enough time.

The Greek poet Sophocles admonished: "Rather fail with honor than succeed by fraud." And the Greek sage Chilon put it like this: "Prefer loss to a dishonest gain; the one brings pain at the moment, the other for all time."

So there are two overriding reasons for our concern with ethics: A basic moral code that we value and subscribe to. And a common-sense law of business—credibility with our customers and long-term profitability.

This morning, I want to highlight some of the key areas where we have concerns:

[Insert details about specific policies and procedures that have ethical implications.]

Speaking of ethics in general, C. J. Silas, CEO of Phillips Petroleum, says, "Improving our corporate credibility is something that merits a strong effort. It will take substantive, structural work—not just a quick paint job."

In our lifetime, we've come to some fuzzy thinking where ethics have been concerned. The philosophy in the highest political offices in the country today seems to be, "Do whatever you have to; just don't tell me about it." With this message, these leaders have removed themselves from responsibility, should the questionable conduct be discovered.

Such bury-your-head-in-the-sand management sounds much like the widow who was talked into a shady real estate deal by a fly-by-night developer. After she calculated her losses at over $50,000 from her life savings, she contacted the Better Business Bureau to file a complaint.

The Bureau representative chastened her a bit: "Well, it sounded fishy right from the start. Why didn't you come to us before you invested your money? Didn't you know about our services?"

"Oh, I did," she answered. "But I was afraid that if I called you, you'd tell me not to do it."

I assure you that that's not our thinking here at (company). We don't want to have our heads in the wastebasket—or in the sand.

We ask that you make those individual decisions that involve an ethical matter based on our general guidelines. But when you find yourself in a situation that you feel needs clarification, ask. Don't keep quiet. What we as management don't know *will* hurt us—eventually.

As Andrew Jackson said, "One man with courage is a majority." We want you to be the individual with courage to make the ethical decision. We're committed to making sure the ethical decision becomes the majority position here at (company).

Yes, we have tried to write company policies that dictate ethical behavior. For the corporation as a whole, we intend that ethical behavior overshadow profit. And it's our intention that these policies and procedures I've outlined color in those gray situations for you.

But you as our representative write the final line. You are the company's signature. To the general public and to our customers, you are (company). And all the policies in the world won't do much good if you, as our front-line representatives, make the wrong decisions day to day. Our ethics are embodied in you.

If you want to verify that you're in step with the organization, honesty and integrity are of value here. We want those to be the primary considerations in all personal or professional decisions.

In short, we don't want you to bend the rules; we want you to brace them. Mark Twain once said, "Always do right. This will gratify some people and astonish the rest." Either way, we win.

Public Relations

GENERAL GUIDELINES

(To address positive news coverage)

- Prefer modesty and goodwill as you agree with the positive news coverage of your organization.
- Let the facts and events tell the story for you, without embellishment and arrogant rhetoric.
- Avoid the temptation to say "See there" to your competitors; instead show tolerance and goodwill.
- Take a low-key approach about your successes and the causes in order to profit from all goodwill this coverage can provide.

(To address negative news coverage)

- Be open, direct, and swift to acknowledge bad news.
- Summarize the situation and your opinion/response succinctly.
- Elaborate with examples, statistics, or illustrations.
- Restate your key summary message.

(To create employee awareness of public image)

- Generate enough excitement to catch the audience's attention.
- Explain specifically what you want the audience to do or not to do to create a favorable image.

- Give personal, as well as corporate, benefits for positive participation in your public-awareness campaign.
- Call the audience to action.

(To react to a crisis)

- Acknowledge the situation with a brief and candid statement about the actions you've taken to manage the crisis. It is not enough to state the facts of a situation and give a conclusion such as "there should be no more concern for public safety" without giving the details of *how* you came to that conclusion.
- Give all information in language clearly understandable to a lay audience. Avoid technical jargon.
- Express concern for employees, stockholders, and the general public who may be affected by the crisis.
- Assure the audience that you will continue to inform them of further details and actions.
- Aim for "headline" messages—clear, succinct statements that give your entire message in a well-thought-out phrase.
- Say what you want to say and then stop; don't let reporters' microphones "rattle" you.
- Avoid an impatient or testy tone with a reporter.
- Remember that a "no comment" or other evasive answer implies guilt and a cover-up to many people.
- Use these crisis opportunities to build credibility for your company's trustworthiness, truthfulness, and responsible actions.

TO ADDRESS MEDIA COVERAGE

81

Audience: your own employees
Message: We're finally getting the attention we deserve. Let's enjoy it together.
Tone: informal
Timing: 5-6 minutes, depending on the insertion of details of media coverage

Good afternoon. . . . We should have asked you all to enter the auditorium backward. We want to pat you on the back. In case you haven't read the newspapers recently, our company has just been cited as (citation or media mention).

The (name of newspaper) had this to say in a recent issue: "[Insert quote.]"

Others of the print media have joined the chorus singing our praises. Here are a few of the lyrics they've used:

[Insert quotes from other papers and journal articles.]

One school bulletin board had this truth posted: "Laugh and the class laughs with you, . . . but you stay after school alone." That's a fairly true commentary on the state of the average person's response to business difficulties. If our company had been responsible for a nuclear mishap or had spilled oil offshore, we'd be hanging alone in a very nasty breeze.

I dare say that 98 percent of the businesses in this country are well-managed companies made up of honest, hard-working employees. But it's usually the other 2 percent that get the coverage.

Not this time, however. It's positive news. And we're pleased that the press and the public are celebrating with us. The media have done a valuable service in bringing to light the nature of [insert details of the issue]. Our customers have a right to expect such, and we've given them that possibility.

[Insert details about the situation/research/changes/products that have produced such positive attention.]

We as a company can celebrate. But in essence that means you. You are (corporation). You contribute creative ideas, . . . develop them, . . . plan for their implementation, . . . and then carry them to their logical outcomes—the products and services we now offer and plan to provide in the near future. You are the people behind the machines. You are the people behind the policies. You are the people behind the customer counters. You are the people making the service calls.

In short, you are the reason we are celebrating.

Take this bit of good news and swallow it. Enthusiasm goes down much easier than medicine and will go a long way in reducing fatigue and generating energy. In fact, we encourage you to share it with your neighbors and professional associates. The more other people understand of what we do and its significance to their daily work lives, the more they like us.

Our sincere thanks to each of you for your conscientious dedication to every detail of your job. And thank you for coming and basking in the limelight with us this afternoon. We'd like to get a good tan before this is all over.

TO CREATE EMPLOYEE AWARENESS OF PUBLIC IMAGE

82

Audience: your own employees
Message: Let's change the image the public has of us.
Tone: informal
Timing: 10-12 minutes

What you will be doing in the next year is critically important to us—important to our stockholders, important to our customers, and important to the press. I don't want to leave the room until I get that point across.

You are critical to our success, and we appreciate how well you have been doing your jobs. You have built and are running what we believe to be the best (type) business in our industry. We know that.

But the public doesn't. And that's the issue today. That's why you're critically important to us. We need you to talk to the right people with the right message.

We as management speakers talk about you often—just like family. Obviously, we want to share your achievements because they make us look good. We talk to securities analysts, investment managers, and the press. Our objective is to let them know what a great group of capable employees you are.

But we also need you to start acting like grandparents. That is, we need you to pull out the wallet photos and start bragging. We need you to talk about every member of the family. To tell them we're well managed. To tell them the financial facts of life. To tell them you're eager to provide good customer service.

Grandparenting in the vein I've just described is usually easy. Grandparents can tell total strangers that grandson Johnny who lives in Kalamazoo is a darling, and nobody will argue. First, because nobody knows Johnny personally. Second, because others don't care all that much.

But grandparenting for our company can be a little more tricky. First, because the public *thinks* they know our industry pretty well. Second, because they *do* care. What we do affects their everyday life.

My point is this: Convincing the public of the facts is sometimes not an easy job. And we're asking you to take on this "bragging" task in addition to your regular assignments. We're asking that you preach our message from your desk every day when you talk to visitors and telephone callers.

And we're even asking that you take it "on the road." We'll be asking for volunteers to undergo special training to become official spokespersons in the local community. We'll ask you to speak to large audiences and small. To friendly audiences and maybe a few unfriendly ones. Nothing has such an impact as face-to-face, question-and-answer, in-person explanations about what we do and why we do it.

Misinformation and outright distortions are spread one to one. And that's exactly the way we have to correct the misinformation—one to one, face to face. Yes, the media can compound the problem with their own misinterpretations. And they can correct misunderstandings with accurate, fair reporting. But they'll never be as vital to our efforts as *you* are—individually, one on one. In the next year, several of you will be called upon to receive this special training and special briefings on our internal workings—finances and future plans for products and services. You will learn the complex problems that face us. And you'll learn how to explain those problems in lay terms so that everybody understands. Those in your local professional organizations. . . . And those standing around the bus stop in your local neighborhood.

Most people accept a clear statement for a true statement. That's what we're counting on. We want to help you as our employees to learn the facts about the complex issues that face us and then be able to pass on those facts clearly to others.

You are a valuable resource, and your efforts become more vital to us daily.

Who else can tell our story better than you? You deal with our customers every day. You are (corporation) to them. You are the eyes, ears, hands, and feet that make this company work. You create the impression of competence or incompetence. . . . Of poor quality or excellent quality. . . . Of an efficiently run system or a lavish, inefficient system of perks and mismanagement.

You are the grandparent who knows us very well. So what do we want you as flesh-and-blood embodiments of (corporation) to tell people? We want you to explain how our products contribute to their everyday life. We want you to tell them how we operate internally to cut costs and then pass those savings on to them. And finally, we want you to tell them the realities of our cost to operate—increasing suppliers' costs and the cost of maintaining the quality of service we provide.

So why do we need you to take on the extra responsibility usually assumed by a PR department? Well, grandparents brag about their offspring out of sheer love. But we'll present you with a more reasonable reason.

Here's why we need you to talk to your customers:

Ignorance generates suspicion and fear. Knowledge brings trust and favor.

And how did we come to that conclusion? A random telephone survey of (number) customers told us what the public's perceptions were. Of those polled, (number) percent said they felt they knew our company very well; (number) percent claimed they knew little about our company, although they did business with us from time to time. Of those who claimed to know our company's products and services well, a large majority—(number) percent to be exact—held a favorable impression of us. But wait until you hear the last half of the story: Of those who claimed they knew little about our company, a whopping mass—(number) percent—rated our company with a negative tag.

To put it in a sentence: The better they know us the better they like us.

So to correct the image problem, we first have to get the facts out. We have to show them we're interested in making a reasonable profit for our stockholders and we're equally interested in providing quality products and services to the public.

But here comes the more difficult part in your telling our story to our customers. People aren't rational. They don't always just listen to the facts and come to logical conclusions.

Instead, like grandparents, they are emotional. Grandparents can brag on Johnny's well-mannered behavior, his wit, and his intelligence without a single fact to back them up. Why? Are they being deceptive to the strangers who might listen to them? No, grandparents are simply emotional. They love Johnny; therefore, Johnny must be intelligent, witty, and well behaved.

That's why I'm saying you can't just give the facts and persuade the public of the truth. We could publish facts in the newspaper. No, instead you have to make them *feel* the truth. They have to *sense* emotion. They have to *see* service in your eyes. They have to *feel* quality when they walk in the door.

In short, we need your words and your emotions to convey the message to everybody you come in contact with as a representative of this company.

What's in it for you when you take on this PR job? Well, many of you are stockowners through our employee-savings plan. You will benefit directly through your dividends. But you also can picture those other stockholders out there—men and women, families just like you and yours—who depend on a reasonable return for their investment.

And possibly even more directly, you will benefit from a healthy company image through your regular paychecks—salary, benefits, bonuses, raises.

As I said earlier, *we* know you're doing a good job. *You* know you're doing a good job. Our new job is to make sure the *public* knows we're doing a good job. An excellent one. They have to understand that we are an efficiently run operation that makes a reasonable return for our stockholders and provides products and services they must have to maintain their quality of life.

Let's tell that story like grandparents—clearly, . . . emotionally, . . . repeatedly.

TO REACT TO A CRISIS

83

Audience: employees

Message: We regret what's happened. We are working to control the situation and plan to keep you fully informed.

Tone: formal

Timing: 10-12 minutes, depending on insertion of crisis details

Hello. We've asked you to lay aside your work for a few moments to attend this meeting today under very disturbing circumstances.

I've been reading a lot of Charles Schulz's Peanuts cartoon strips—not necessarily for laughs but for some poignant insights on the human condition. To express exactly how I feel and how I know some of you feel today, I want to share four cartoon strips collected over the years that bear directly on our situation here.

The first strip shows Lucy with baseball cap and glove in center field, waiting, . . . calling for a fly ball. She's yelling, "I've got it. I've got it. I've got it." But then the balls drops to the ground a few feet behind here. She stalks off the field with, "I've been wrong a lot lately."

That's my sentiment exactly. We've been wrong lately. We thought we had taken care of the problem of . . .

[Insert overview of the troublesome situation or issue.]

The second cartoon is Snoopy sitting on top of his doghouse peering into space. An airplane approaches and then passes overhead. "He hates me," thinks Snoopy. Someone asks, "How do you know he hates you?" Snoopy sighs, "I can tell."

The last frame shows the rooftop of his doghouse riddled with bullet holes.

Likewise, we have no doubt about what the public sentiment is with regard to us and this crisis situation.

The third cartoon shows Linus and Lucy. Linus tells Lucy, "I just talked with Charlie Brown's mom. He's not any better."

Lucy screams back, "He's not any better? That's crazy! He's got to get better.!! What's wrong with a world where someone like Charlie Brown can get sick and then not get any better?" Lucy finally stalks off with, "I need somebody to hit!!"

The public, like Lucy, needs somebody to hit for this situation. And we're a likely target. And frankly, I could use a punching bag or two myself about now.

The final strip shows Sally talking to herself about a school homework assignment. She says, "This is my report. . . . I sat up all night working on it. . . . Well, actually, I didn't sit up all night working on it. . . . What I did was I sat up all night worrying about it. . . . There is a big difference!"

Like Sally, we know the difference between worrying and working, but there's little we can do about the damage at this point.

To sum up: We took all the precautions that could be expected against something like this. Obviously, the precautions weren't enough. A lot of somebodies out there don't like us a lot right now. They and we need to hit somebody. We're worrying and we're working—and we do know the difference.

We've called you together to give you the facts as best we know them. The facts are these:

[Insert the details of the incident/accident/situation, including the facts about who, when, where, why, how, and how much.]

To paraphrase newspaper publisher and Congressman William Randolph Hearst: "[We've tried] to be conspicuously accurate in everything. . . . Truth is not only stranger than fiction, it's more interesting." As incredible as the details may seem, to the best of our abilities to investigate, this is what has happened.

We regret the situation. More than concern with the profitability of our company, we're concerned about the long-term effects on you, our employees, and on the public. We know there will be specific concern about

[Insert details that show you understand the impact of the problem.]

We do think that we have the immediate problem under control. I want to outline the steps we've taken to date and what actions we're considering and investigating to try to prevent a recurrence:

[Insert details of immediate actions and plans under consideration.]

We know of no stronger action to take in this situation. We think you'll agree that we took precautions against all the possibilities that we could foresee, . . . that we have acted responsibly in response to the crisis, . . . and that we have the welfare of you, our stockholders, and the general public in mind as we plan our future course.

We know that you as employees will personally feel the brunt of some of the public's reaction. And we regret that. We simply ask that in dealing with any outrage from those you come in contact with—our customers, suppliers, other staff—you remember that they feel a lot like Lucy. They just need somebody to hit.

But we encourage you to talk back. We've presented the facts to you in a very straightforward manner today. First, because as employees, you have every right to know that your management has acted responsibly.

And second, we've given you the facts so that you can pass them on to those business associates and neighbors who ask questions of you.

I assure you that as other details become available, we will pass them on—either with memos, internal reports, or press releases. We will keep you informed every step of the way as we resolve the immediate crisis and then develop preventative procedures.

Feel free to direct any questions to (contact name and phone number), who will be the most informed person in our organization. We simply ask that you be patient as she and her staff try to research and respond to your questions.

Last, I just want to say how much we will count on your help and how much we already appreciate your support in this difficult time.

Retirement

(To the retireee)

- Express appreciation for your association together.
- Expand on pleasant personality traits, contributions to the group or you individually, and successes on the job.
- Comment on future plans, if they are not too personal.
- Wish the person well.
- Be sincere, avoiding flowery, overblown sentiment.
- Avoid remarks about age, conflict, ill health, or future finances, remembering that retirement may not be something the individual is looking forward to.

(From the retiree)

- Thank the group for their contributions to your career successes and personal growth.
- Comment on future plans in a positive, upbeat manner.
- Wish the group well on any ongoing plans or projects.

TO THE RETIREE

84

Audience: associates in the immediate department or larger group
Message: You have made a valuable contribution; best wishes in your retirement.
Tone: informal
Timing: 2-3 minutes

Samuel Johnson wryly observed: "Don't think of retiring from the world until the world will be sorry that you retire. I hate a fellow whom pride or cowardice or laziness drives into a corner, and who does nothing when he is there but sit and growl. Let him come out as I do, and bark."

Well, the world—at least ours here at (company)—is sorry to see (name) retire. And not that he's been barking. But rather that he's been leading the pack.

(Name), we're going to miss that leadership. You've been vocal about policies that needed to be changed; management has changed them. You've been vocal about quality manufacturing; we've set up new quality-control procedures. You've been vocal about teamwork rather than turf divisions; we're still working on that. But I think we've come a long way.

Because you have "been there," been in the battle wholeheartedly, the demands of the job have been do-able and our motivation has been replenished with your enthusiasm, . . . your insight, . . . and your dedication.

That's not to say, of course, that we have always agreed. We haven't. But always, (name) has stood up for what he thought was right and best for all concerned, often in the face of heavy opposition. We agonized over delays and decisions and deadlines. We fought budget defeat, equipment deficiencies, and computer downtime. He has worked hard and long to bridge whatever gap there happened to be. There were even times we considered other careers—both of us. But the work was enjoyable because, ultimately, we were always on the same side—quality service to our customers.

I could go on to compliment (name)'s competence and his results. But then those have been obvious to everyone who has had opportunity to work with him. He has handled his work with admirable efficiency and expertise. As a result, we can say to our colleagues in the industry that our company is one to model.

Let me just sum up by saying, we as a company and as individuals will feel a great loss from your absence, (name). You command our attention and our respect.

We understand that you plan to remain in this area and continue your volunteer work with (project or organization). It's good that you have a plan.

Let me just add a few other suggestions for these golden years: Continue to sound off in public about what our community and world needs to change. Influence our young people to apply themselves. Exercise every day. And spend your children's inheritance!

Our best as you do so. Your rest and relaxation is well deserved.

85

Audience: associates in immediate department or larger group

Message: We will miss your friendship; best wishes in your retirement.

Tone: informal, light

Timing: 2-3 minutes

Set up a filing system for bills and canceled checks. Repot the ivy. Wallpaper the hallway. Oh, excuse me, that's *my* list of honey-do's, not yours. Oh, well, I'm sure yours will be similar—and longer. After all, you'll have more time.

But, (name), look at it this way: Retirement has cured many a businessman's ulcer—and given his wife one! So at the conclusion of this get-together, we are going to proceed with a very moving ceremony. We plan to bronze your coffee cup and send it home to (wife's name). She'll need it now.

Seriously, we know she and the rest of your family are looking forward to having you available to them more often. Their gain is our loss here at the office. Truly.

You've had a brilliant career, spanning (number) years. First at (company), then at (company), and finally at (company). And there may even be a few other places you've hung around while deciding what you wanted to be when you grew up.

This is both a sad and happy time. Happy because (name) is going to have time to enjoy himself. Sad because we hate to say good-bye to a dear friend. He's proven that many times over. Whenever we've needed him, he's been there through triumphs and tears. Our minor problems required only band-aids; our major problems often required crutches. He's supplied both and always knew which to use on what occasion.

He has encouraged us loudly and encouraged us quietly. With our successes, he has given us personal attention and company-wide attention. With our failures, he has given us solace and direction for the future. He's been there to explain—sometimes two or three times—to answer, to guide. That's how he's interacted with me and that's how I've heard and seen him interact with many of you.

He knows that work is more than a desk, a pile of paperwork, and some customers. By his listening and sharing of his own wisdom gained through life's experiences, he has demonstrated a realization that work is, after all, people rather than paperwork.

Our retirement wish for you, (name), is that you enjoy what's ahead to its fullest. Enjoy your travel, your golfing, your church work. We know your retirement will be filled with all those returned kindnesses—those listening ears, unexpected favors, care and concern coming back to you.

You're a dear friend and a real winner. We love you. God bless.

86

Audience: associates in immediate department or larger group
Message: You have done a fine job; best wishes in your retirement.
Tone: formal
Timing: 2-3 minutes, depending on insertion of career details

I'm pleased to have the opportunity to help you mark your retirement and move into the golden years you've earned. To you, I'm sure the years have seemed to go by quickly. And, in fact, the time does pass quickly when you're breaking industry records and piling up awards for yourself and the company.

Just to remind the group of a few:

[Insert several awards and career accomplishments.]

With all sincerity, we can say that in a disorganized world, (name) has conquered confusion. In a troubled industry, she has conquered obstacles of competition. In a difficult job position, she has conquered complacency.

And while gaining these awards for herself and making such contributions to the company, (name) has not lost sight of the opportunities for involvement in making our lives better outside the office. She has given her time on committees that contemplate the extracurricular around here at (company) and in the larger community.

Specifically, I'm thinking of her work on the (type) programs and the annual (charity) drive. On both professional and personal problems that have needed a push off dead-center, she has offered insight and lent a hand with her network of contacts in the industry. Her uncollected favors from community leaders and her extensive files that seem to encompass anything of value that's transpired in the past 30 years also have come in handy.

As I understand it, (name) is ready to mark the next 30 years as efficiently by beginning her own part-time consulting service. Let me say that if you offer the same quality of expertise we've been able to take advantage of during your career here, you're going to be equally a success with that effort. When (name) walks out our front door, she'll take our admiration with her. And she'll leave memories of a competent, yet caring, individual. We're the better for knowing and working with you, (name).

On this your retirement, I offer congratulations on a very successful career—one many of us hope to emulate. Your energy and vitality will undergird years of happiness, hobbies, and whatever hopes you have. Enjoy your leisure, your family, and your friends. Godspeed in the years ahead.

FROM THE RETIREE

87

Audience: associates in immediate department or larger group
Message: Thank you for your contributions to my life; I hope I've contributed to yours.
Tone: formal
Timing: 3 minutes

A long time ago, someone asked me: "Why are you hurrying through life? Are you trying to get to the end?" That statement, or admonition, has taken on much more meaning as the years have passed.

Over (number) years ago, I walked out of the college corridors ready to conquer the world. With all the arrogance and confidence that college graduates possess before life has taken them on for a few rounds. But as I've despaired in some economic hard times and have lived high in better times, I've come to appreciate the uncertainty of tomorrow . . . and the happiness of the present.

I ran into some good advice about half way through my career, back during the time when I thought 14-hours days were normal, . . . when I thought all missed deadlines would doom me to career disaster, . . . when I thought paper could replace people. . . . James Burgh, the Scottish author, advised: " . . .It is necessary that you have a mind so composed by prudence, reason, and religion, that it may bear being looked into. . . ."

In other words, he cautioned that I'd never enjoy retirement until I prepared for it.

So how does one prepare for it? Well, I'm not sure I've discovered that completely. But what the thought meant to me was to slow down and develop some other interests in my life. So I've done that. I decided that when they wrote the last chapter of my life, I didn't want to be disappointed to find out it was only a short story. Or worse, a book in a narrow specialty market—business only.

So, to prepare, I've spent more time with my family on family outings and projects. I've spent more time with some hobbies I enjoy, even taking a course or two just for fun through the years. And finally, I've spent more time learning to care about those people around me—people like you.

And time will eventually tell if I've prepared well. But at the moment, I look forward to the years ahead to expand all the opportunities. I'm grateful for good health, a supportive family, and a free country to live in as I please.

I didn't have to wait for retirement for the full pay-off, however. During my years here, each of you has shown me many facets of life and laughter. I've enjoyed our Monday morning quarterbacking, . . . our celebration luncheons and dinners, . . . and just our routine, everyday work together.

Working with people like you means someone cares when you triumph. It means someone cares when your son has come in from a school event too late the night before. It means someone cares when an elderly parent is lying in a hospital bed across the country. It means simply sharing a cup of coffee on a cold, dreary Monday morning. You have contributed to my life, and I hope in some small way I've contributed to yours.

Thank you for the kind words today and for coming to celebrate with me. I will miss you.

88

Audience: associates in immediate department or larger group
Message: You are my friends, and I will miss you.
Tone: informal, light
Timing: 2-3 minutes, depending on insertion of personal anecdotes

Next week, I'm going to be a neophyte again. . . . You're wondering how anyone at my age could be new at anything? The new task will be readjusting to more than six hours' sleep and honestly listening to my wife when she talks. Why is it that some companies—when you retire and time is no longer so important—give you a watch?

I see good news and bad news in all that. The good news is that I'm going to be spending a lot more time on the lake. The bad news is that I'm going to be spending a lot of time missing you guys.

But one of the joys of retirement is that I can look back at you younger guys and be thankful I don't have to go through all that pain of uncertainty again. Will I get the job, or won't I? Will I meet the deadline, or won't I? Will I get through traffic to my appointment, or won't I?

Sitting on my boat, I'm sure to recall times like when

[Insert one or two personal anecdotes.]

Although I have plans to travel and to delve into several hobbies such as woodworking and stained glass, I will think often of you. Your laughter. . . . Your concern. . . . Your support in the emergencies. . . . You have added immeasurably to my professional success and to my personal well-being.

Thank you for the good times. I plan to stay in touch.

89

Audience: associates in immediate department or larger group
Message: I will miss you, but I'm eager to get on with life.
Tone: informal, light
Timing: 1-2 minutes

Thomas Edison once remarked, "I start where the last man left off." Although I'm certainly not comparing my successes to Edison's, I do feel his modesty about those achievements you've mentioned in your earlier comments tonight.

Whatever I've been able to accomplish in these (number) years at (company) has been due in great part to the team spirit we have here. I've never considered myself to be a lone ranger. Whatever the project, there was always someone around—many of you in the audience. To give advice. . . . To lend support. . . . To bend the budget. . . . To approve the exceptions. . . . To applaud the results. That team spirit is what makes success sweet.

Thank you for making me look good on the projects and in the positions others have mentioned today.

Despite the enjoyment in working with you, I do not approach retirement with reluctance and regret. I'm looking forward to relaxing without fear that a customer will phone and catch me daydreaming. To eating a big lunch and not caring whether it makes me sleepy in the afternoon. To traveling without having to type up a trip report when I get off the plane. Although—I *will* probably miss those airfare and hotel reimbursements on my paycheck stub.

And I will miss (name)'s weekly football statistics and predictions. . . . Sincerely, I will miss you all individually—your wit, your warmth, your willingness to help me out whenever I've called on you.

Keep up the good work here. You've been a wonderful team to work with. God bless.

Sales/Marketing

GENERAL GUIDELINES

- Offer congratulations on past achievements, being as specific as possible.
- State any plan of action.
- Generate enthusiasm with tangible or intangible incentives.
- Challenge the audience to emulate the results of the most successful among them.
- Express confidence in the audience's future successes.
- Motivate your listeners to take action immediately.
- Keep the tone upbeat and informal.

(Introduction of a new product or service)

- Overview the benefits of the new product or service.
- Tell how it differs from what else is on the market.
- Prepare the sales reps to answer any objections from customers.
- Explain ways customers can investigate, sample, or see the product or service demonstrated.
- Mention any sales aids (such as ads, displays, samples, articles, research information or other literature) that management can provide to support their individual efforts.

GENERAL MOTIVATIONAL

90

Audience: sales reps
Message: Your enthusiasm and passion to win can boost your sales.
Tone: motivational
Timing: 5-6 minutes

"Desire creates the power," says Raymond Holliwell. I'm picking up enough vibes in this room to know there has to be power here somewhere. If not electrical, then it must be coming from you in the audience. Anyone in here has the power to dream.

Writer Bernard Edmonds said it this way:

> To dream anything that you want to dream. That's the beauty of the *human mind*. To do anything that you want to do. That is the strength of the human will. *To trust yourself to test your limits.* That is the *courage to succeed*.

In belief, there is power. Our eyes are opened to opportunities. Our mind lays out the plan. Our courage commits us to that plan. High expectations breed high performance.

Your primary enemy will never be the competitor and his or her product. Your enemy on the road to selling success will more likely be complacency, lack of vision, lack of commitment.

No, I'm not minimizing competition. In our free-enterprise system, there's competition in every endeavor. But rather than worry about the competitor's (product) or (product), let's make the competitor worry about us! We don't want to fuel ourselves by memories of the past, but rather by visions of the future.

If desire is the power, enthusiasm and sincerity are the channels that allow it to flow.

Good salesmanship, then, is simply transferring that belief to the buyer through your sincere enthusiasm. I once had a sales associate so enthusiastic about his product that he sold two milking machines to a farmer with only one cow . . . and took the cow as down payment.

Enthusiasm is your investment in your customers. If you don't feel comfortable in investing in them, how can they feel comfortable in investing in your product? Enthusiasm is contagious. And unfortunately, so is the lack of it.

Billionaire H. Ross Perot, talking about the people he liked to hire, has said, "I'm looking for people who love to win. If I run out of those, I want people who hate to lose."

Whatever the source of your passion—whether you love to win or hate to lose— you have power in enthusiasm.

And don't be afraid to show your customers that your power and enthusiasm have made you successful. Everyone wants to be part of a success. If you don't believe it, see how many employees grab for the annual reports or monthly sales reports as soon as they're released. You hear the buzz in the cafeteria and on the elevator—"Earnings are up; looks like we had another good quarter. *We* had another good year."

As I said, everyone—your customers especially—want to be part of a successful organization. So the more successful we look and act, the more we sell. People don't want to throw good money after bad people. They choose enthusiastic, successful people.

Sincerity also counts. Have you ever wondered how much more successful TV commercials would be if viewers knew the celebrities really used the products they touted? All the paid celebrity commercials in the world can't outsell a shot of the President of the United States or a pro quarterback using the product in real life.

Sincerity counts. That's why the telephone marketer who sounds as though she's reading a script is often met with a click and the dial tone.

Sincerity counts. Persuasive people practice what they preach. They use what they sell. They *love* what they sell. They tell the *truth* about what they sell.

How could anything be more fun in life than to love what you do and to do something that matters? Our products matter. And I'm having fun—sincerely. How about you?

91

Audience: sales reps and managers
Message: Set some specific, long- and short-term goals.
Tone: motivational
Timing: 8-9 minutes

"The best way to predict the future is to create it," says Alan Kay, director of research at Apple Computer. Any one of you can create your future around here—by deciding where you want to set the goal posts . . . and then developing a specific plan to get there.

In today's competitive marketplace, it's not enough to build a better mousetrap; the world *won't* beat a path to your door. You have to build them a superhighway. The need for an overall marketing plan is acute.

And that plan has to have three parts: Research your market. . . . Position yourself against your competitors. . . . Then develop a promotional plan to tell about your uniqueness.

Like any road map, that plan needs to be on paper to take you through important decisions to your destination. That's our part—as management. We've designed the overall marketing plan.

But you have to have your own map to come along with us.

That means you need goals. But then that's nothing new. We salespeople are notorious for goals—monthly quotas, quarterly quotas, annual quotas. But our superhighway goals—or maps—are inadequate by themselves. All the little farm-to-market roads are left off.

That's the way it usually is with less-effective salespeople. They have very high goals and can articulate them well. But they never achieve great feats. Why? Because they don't have a detailed map—one with all the farm-to-market roads—to get them to their destination.

You're familiar with those maps you get at the rental car agencies. They have a blow-up of the immediate area and the rental car agency is marked with a "You are here" arrow. The problem with those maps is that they don't tell you "how to get there from here." You may know the finish line, the destination, but if you're driving from Los Angeles to New York, you'll need a few other state maps before you pull out the little blow-up of the local area.

Big goals and little, intermediate goals. You need both kinds for the complete trip.

Screenwriter Mark Caine said it this way: "There are those who travel . . . and those who are going somewhere." You've seen the difference in the airport traveler's face. That big-picture direction—or lack of it—in a salesperson's face is a dead giveaway to customers. The blow-up of the end destination will help you travel. But the intermediate road maps will get you where you want to be.

My point is simply this: If you want to become the top salesperson, you have to set intermediate goals for making those daily sales calls.

And you have to put a time frame around those goals. When will you finish the market research on those five new companies in your area? By when will you develop a standard proposal as a model? By when will you send out that direct-mail piece to 16 new prospects?

Some people *fear* to set such specific goals with actions and deadlines. Because then they're committed. And what's more scary is to commit those specific goals to someone who can check up on you. So some people just never get specific about their plans.

Don't let yourself get away with that. Sure, if you set such specific goals you'll run into obstacles. The manufacturer may keep the price that you wanted to include in your direct-mail piece in limbo for two months. Or, you get caught up on the lengthy proposal for the big sale and make only ten of your 22 planned calls. Never mind those exceptions or "interruptions."

Obstacles are always part of the picture. If you find a path with no obstacles, then it probably doesn't lead anywhere.

Don't be afraid to be specific with your goals and timetables. And don't hesitate to commit those specifics to yourself and to others.

And don't be afraid to think big. Ralph Charell put it this way: "Nobody succeeds beyond his or her wildest expectations . . . unless he or she begins with some wild expectations."

Set your goals high. Imagine the results you want. Then make it happen for yourself. Never wait on "the big opportunity," the big once-in-a-lifetime chance. That's another reason sales reps fail to get anywhere—waiting for luck. Rather than going out to look for customers, they're out in the backyard, looking for four-leaf clovers.

Set specific goals—commit yourself with specific activities and deadlines. Accept obstacles when they come. Think big. Make your own opportunities.

And here's a final consideration for goal-setting: Set risky goals. Your goals this year may be more than simply selling $X worth of product. Experienced, exceptional salespeople eventually get their egos out of the way and work to make the business *as a whole* more profitable. That is, they're not afraid to try something new. To risk. . . . To bring back to management an unfavorable customer comment on a product or service. . . . To encourage an improvement in the product. In other words, they even take risks in their selling. They're not just satisfied to turn in acceptable numbers. They set goals to go after the hard sell. In short, they act like management.

These salespeople see selling as a creative experience. They learn from failure. They're true team players and understand business success from the whole team's point of view.

Whatever your long-term goal—whether it's in terms of volume or in terms of creativity with high-risk customers—you *will* fail on occasion. Challenging, specific goals always dictate a few failures.

But so what? So what if you misjudged a customer's walk-away point? So what if you're wrong from time to time? We're not going to march you out to the parking lot and shoot you.

Selling isn't only a numbers game; it's an intellectual game: Shutting your competitors out and locking your customers in.

The surest way *not* to fail is to determine to succeed—with specific goals ahead. If not you, then who? If not now, then when?

Envision the target destination. Plan how you'll get there—every day, little by little. Then strike out on a steady, straight path.

92

Audience: sales reps
Message: Sales success is a matter of good time management.
Tone: motivational, instructional
Timing: 12-13 minutes, depending on insertion of details about paperwork

Somebody once said that a motivational speech is like a Saturday night bath—the effects wear off quickly. My favorite saying about motivation is that it energizes incompetence. At best, there are limitations with only motivational pep talks. They tend to create immediate peaks and long valleys.

Even though I get motivated when I watch Jane Fonda do her workouts, that doesn't necessarily help me peel off my own flab. That's why I plan to be more instructional today than purely motivational.

I don't mean to leave the impression that motivation isn't important. Even though the effects quickly wear off, you do keep bathing. And even though motivational quickies wear off, we need them. We need to energize our can-do spirit.

But I want to offer you something more than motivation. I want to leave you with some concrete techniques you can use tomorrow morning. We're beyond hit-and-run selling.

Used to be, all you had to worry about was finding a map of your territory and then making calls. But being state of the art in sales now means that you have to become your own general manager.

Competitive companies like ours are now asking that you be responsible not just for sales volume, but also for seeing that that volume makes us profitable. We are expecting you to sell *internally* to get the support you need. To work with the delivery people, . . . the installers, . . . the service people. We expect you to negotiate effectively with the customer within the ranges we outline.

And often, we expect you to develop your own marketing plan. Those of you who've been most successful find that you're conducting product seminars for your customers, coordinating direct-mail, and even designing your own advertising campaigns. And, of course, you've always had to learn to balance your high-activity accounts against the time and yield of low-volume accounts.

So what does this "state of the sales industry" address mean to your daily schedule? You're beyond the techniques that made you successful as a hit-and-run salesperson. You have the same hours in the day, but you have to use them more efficiently.

The sales cycle used to be about 30 days from presentation to close. Today it's about (number) months. You often have the technical buyer, the user buyer, the economic buyer, and the coach buyer. Four different people or groups you have to make your pitch to. That means it takes much more time to earn the same dollars.

That means that no matter how new the "state of the art" in selling, we are still back to the basics of selling: Time is your best tool; you have to use it to your advantage.

Although time-management tools aren't new to you, they get lost in the garage on occasion. May I remind you of a few:

First, set priorities. We keep telling you to add value to the products. To be there when customers need answers to their problems—to offer more and more consulting services. But you may be feeling frustration. "If my day is already full," you may be wondering, "how am I going to add value?"

Focus on the 80/20 rule again. Eighty percent of your results comes from 20 percent of your activity, from 20 percent of your clients. So list all your activities and set some priorities. What activities bring in the most revenue? What things could an assistant do to free you up for those top selling activities? Could you pay a $20,000 assistant to increase your commissions by $50,000? What activities could you *stop* doing to give yourself more time to concentrate on those profit-making priorities?

You've heard it said: "You win some; you lose some, but you've gotta get dressed for them all." Maybe. But that doesn't mean you have to take the time to rent a tux and get a haircut just to go out for a Big Mac. Some sales efforts call for blue jeans. Only the most profitable demand time to rent a tux.

Second, determine the right mix between reach and frequency. You always have to balance these two: Do I spend my time and budget reaching more people with our message? Or spend my time contacting the people who buy more frequently? Generally, it's more important for your potential customer to get your message more often . . . than for a large base who may or may not be potential customers to hear your message sporadically.

Third, learn to give CPR by phone.Telemarketers are having great success with what telemarketing expert George Walther calls CPR. Consult. . . . Personalize. . . . Recommend. . . . Consult by asking questions of the customer about his or her needs. Personalize by explaining the benefits of your product in terms of the needs the customer has just expressed to you. You've asked the right questions. You've intelligently related your answers to the customers' needs. Then at that point, you're in a position to recommend what the customer needs to buy from you.

With the cost of our average sales call now topping $X, we've got to get off the plane and on the phone. Nobody said the telephone has to be impersonal. Just remember, not the same pitch to everyone. CPR. Consult. . . . Personalize. . . . Recommend. . . .

Fifth, use letter-writing as a pro-active sales strategy. Instead of those three-hour, goodwill-building visits, write a "thinking-of-you" letter or note.

Such as "Saw a great article that answers some of the questions you raised last month. I'm enclosing a copy."

Such as "Harry Smith ran into me at the convention last week and asked about you. You may want his new address and phone number, which I'm enclosing."

Such as "I'm wondering how your new (product) is working out for you. Do you need a (product) to go with it?"

Letter-writing, once you get a collection of models for your customers, can be a sales strategy unto itself. A side benefit is that it builds goodwill in less time than a half-hour phone conversation or a two-hour trip to the customer site.

Fifth, *stop* putting *everything* in writing. Get rid of those ubiquitous transmittal letters that say, "Here it is." That habit ties up your sales correspondence in the word-processing pool for days. Just put your business card or a handwritten note on the literature, the price list, the specs and put them in the mail. Underline the answers to their questions in the sales lit. A handwritten note says to the customer that you're personalizing your pitch, . . . that you listened to their needs, . . . that you preferred a speedy response to a formal typewritten transmittal.

Just decide how formal the paperwork has to be. If a note will get the job done, why send a 20-page report or proposal?

[Insert details about which paperwork you as a group can eliminate or do more efficiently.]

Sixth, get rid of the clutter. On the plane this week, I saw a sales rep who probably thought he was being efficient. No sooner had we gotten off the runway than he had his briefcase out, trying to fill out his expense report. The problem was that he spent half an hour listing his expenses on half a page because he couldn't find anything. A receipt in this pocket. A receipt in that pocket. A blank form—somewhere. Now, where did he lose that pen? Clutter is not the sign of hard work. It's the hallmark of the disorganized and the inefficient. Get organized.

Abraham Lincoln quipped: "Things may come to those who wait, but only the things left by those who hustle." Ask yourself at the end of the day tomorrow, at the end of next week, are you *using* your time or *losing* your time?

If you're losing it, set priorities. Determine the right mix between reach and frequency. Give CPR by phone. Adopt a pro-active letter-writing strategy. Stop the unnecessary paperwork. Get rid of the clutter.

In sales, well done is better than well said.

93

Audience: sales reps
Message: Sales success means persistence.
Tone: motivational
Timing: 6-8 minutes

Common terminology aside, there's no such thing as "hard sell" and "soft sell." According to CEO Charles Brower, There's only "smart sell" and "stupid sell."

Pig-headed persistence is not what I'm getting to. *Planned* persistence is.

I'm not suggesting the method of the bachelor who suddenly decided he wanted to get married. He proposed to his current sweetheart, and she turned him down. Disheartened, he was sharing his frustration with a friend who advised him not to despair but to be persistent. . . . So the next day, he stood on the street corner and proposed to every woman who passed.

You'll agree that that was "stupid sell." Persistence involves being persistent at the right things.

It involves identifying those prospects and current customers who need your products and then keeping your face . . . or phone number . . . or fax number . . . or friendly letter in front of them consistently. Persistently.

Even when they send mixed messages. I knew a man who checked in for a flight at the airport and purchased a million dollars of life insurance from the automatic machine. Then being one to play with gadgets, while waiting for his flight, he wandered over to one of those scales that gives out a fortune card. His card read, "A recent investment is going to pay a big dividend."

Like he was, you may feel a little ambivalent and disheartened from time to time with customers who string you along. When they ask you to "drop by" and you have to invest a little more time with them, you may not always be sure that's good news.

But persistence—planned persistence—does pay. It simply takes patience.

And when I think of patience, I think of fishing. In my way of thinking, nothing takes more persistence than sitting in a boat out in the middle of the water for hours on end with nothing to stare at but that little bobbing on the surface or tug on the line.

Like fishermen, persistent salespeople need these five qualities: Trust . . . Vision . . . Commitment . . . Courage . . . Accountability. Let's take them one at a time.

You have to trust that your persistent effort will pay off. The vacation-only fishermen often have the fish or cut-bait philosophy. But those who do it for a living trust their skill and know-how to pay the bills.

Persistent salespeople have to envision the pay-off. You can't keep taking snapshots of the day-to-day still-life. You have to take movies of the whole party—the long-term plan. You as successful sales reps have to motivate yourselves by envisioning the reality of reeling in the big one. You envision the kind of fish you want to catch, then you choose the appropriate place and lure.

Persistent salespeople have to commit to their long-term plan. You can't get the big fish if you row out only so far, decide the fish aren't biting, and then head back for shore. Staying in the deep water takes commitment to the whole trip. Once in the appropriate, promising fishing hole, you as successful sales reps develop a network inside your client's organization. You look for new internal clients if your first contact isn't biting.

And when someone bites and you make the sale, persistence means a call back. You ask for referrals and personal recommendations. You always think leverage. How can I use this open door? Who else can benefit here if I get the word to them?

And once you get the door open, keep it open. Studies show that within 10 years, 81 of every 100 customers just drift away. Persistence means keeping them on the line—for good.

Persistent salespeople have to have courage when motorboats and skiers dash around them. The tendency is to look for a new fishing hole. If you do your homework up front and know the prospect has a need, why change holes? Keep your line in the water. You may even have to add another pole or two to discourage the skiers from coming too close and getting tangled up in your business.

Finally, like fishermen, persistent salespeople are accountable. People who fish for a living don't return to shore after half an hour with, "The lake's too big and the fish aren't biting." They figure out how to make them bite.

Successful sales reps like you know that progress comes from a detailed plan. You don't look to someone else to feed you all your leads. You don't blame the support people for lack of service. You don't complain about the sales literature not being helpful. You are accountable. You feel responsible for the plan, you will be responsible for the results, you deserve the credit.

About persistence and consistency, Vince Lombardi said it best:

> Winning is not a sometime thing; it's an all time thing. You don't win once in a while, you don't do things right once in a while, you do them right all the time. Winning is a habit. . . . Unfortunately, so is losing.

Success is getting up before dawn one more time. For the fisherman, success is trusting your skill and your reel. Success is an insight about where the fish will most likely bite. Success is commitment to stay in the boat, the courage to reel in the big one, and the accountability for the results when returning to shore.

To the sales rep, likewise. Success is long hours. . . . Trust in your skills and knowledge. . . . Vision to prospect. . . . Commitment to persist. . . . Courage to leverage for other sales, higher volume, better referrals. . . . Accountability to us, your families, and yourself for your success.

94

Audience: sales reps
Message: Sales success means knowing your customer.
Tone: motivational, instructional
Timing: 8-9 minutes

The days of the one-night stand are over. Today's selling relationship is a marriage; both partners must commit to it. Less-effective salespeople are still selling products . . . while customers are buying relationships.

Second, the days of mass-marketing are gone. Everyone needs a custom solution. The competition is still busy making red soda-straws and doesn't want to change. But our customers are asking why they can't have striped and plaid ones.

Nothing fails like success . . . success that has become stagnant. To stay in the market today, we've had to listen to our customers and make some changes. Not one-time changes. But daily, monthly changes.

So I guess what I'm saying to you is this: Get to know your customer as well as you do your marriage partner. Develop intimacy.

In marriage, that intimacy is developed by talking. By sharing self-knowledge. It's the same with your customers. They want intimacy. They want to hear what you know about your company's service, technology, products, future plans. What can you do for them specifically now? What plans do you have to meet their needs tomorrow and during the next decade?

We've come full circle. The days of chomping at the bit while sitting in new-product orientation sessions, I hope, are over. Just such knowledge is what the customer demands when you get to her door. Educate your prospects. Given a choice between a low-priced, no-frills, what-you-see-is-what-you-get product and a higher-priced product that comes complete with a knowledgeable salesperson to act as a consultant, today's customer is choosing the knowledge base. The more your customers know about your products, the more likely they are to buy.

If you don't know your product, you're being irresponsible in the relationship.

But intimacy requires more than self-talk. To get intimate with your customers, you have to help them disclose self-knowledge.

Never stop asking questions. It's amazing what a few minutes spent with your customers will tell you about what needs they have. Know what benefits motivate them. Charles Revson once said about his marketing of Revlon products: "In the factory, we make cosmetics. In the store we sell hope." Find out what motivates your customer—the benefits they want, not just the features.

That's valuable knowledge to us as management. To stay competitive, we're going to have to turn your customer's wants-and-needs list into next year's products and services. You can help us do that. Lead your customer to disclose self-knowledge. Then pass it on to us.

Although I'll add a side note: Here's where the marriage analogy breaks down. My advice is *not* to disclose your spouse's snoring or spending habits to friends or neighbors. But such customer knowledge *is* valuable to us here at (company).

Selling, like marriage, also involves changing. The newlywed husband who expects to have a gourmet meal set before him every night promptly at seven is in for a surprise. His expectations are going to need to be changed. Likewise, with your customers.

You may have to change their expectations to build volume. Under normal conditions, customers call a real estate agent, expecting to buy one house. But what if they learned that most customers buy two houses—one to live in and one to rent out as an investment? You'd have to change their expectations if you wanted to sell them two houses.

If your customers expect to order only six-months' supply from you, you've got to lead them to expect to need a two-year supply. If they expect only a product—one your competitor also offers—you've got to lead them to expect that they will need training to use that product. And guess who is the only provider of that now-expected training?

Another facet of the marriage relationship is protection. Happily married people protect each other physically—or at least try to. They protect each other's health by the right kind of diet and insistence on more rest and less stress. They protect each other's reputation. They protect each other's best interests in general. Likewise, with the sales relationship.

You have to protect your prospects. Big-ticket items represent a risk—customers have to risk their money on something you claim is worth the price. You have to reduce their perception of risk by offering guarantees. By making it easy for them to believe you. By encouraging them to talk to satisfied users. Let them taste it, feel it, see it. Tell them about our buy-back policies. Assure them you'll be there to hold their hand through the birth.

And what would marriage be if partners couldn't count on each other to "be there" for them? That's your role, too, with your customer.

When there's a problem, be there to add value. If you're present, ready to help when problems surface, customers will remember you forever. They will fall in love.

And, as in all marriages, there are the all-night sessions. The arguments, the tears, the truth-telling. You need that—especially with prospects, . . . and with customers you lose and must win back.

Ask prospects why you failed—sincerely. Was the product not suited to them? Did you really not understand their needs? Is the customer afraid the value won't be perceived by the rest of the work family, especially higher-ups? Did you just not communicate well? Was your proposal off target? Were you unresponsive when they had questions and wanted answers?

At worst, with such specific questions, you may get some good feedback. At best, the prospect might change her mind.

I challenge you to look for a marriage relationship out there tomorrow. Make a date and tell customers about who we are—and keep telling.

Encourage them to tell you about their wildest dreams.

Protect them; reduce their risk so they can make that buying decision.

Add value by "being there" for them when there's a problem.

When you don't get the second date, ask why? What can you do differently when you court the next prospect or customer?

I want to leave you with one last comment from an acquaintance of mine: "A sales job is easy. I just keep reminding myself these are *not really people*—they're only *customers*." That observation comes from supersalesman, J.K. Duff. [Start to walk away from the podium; then turn and add the last word.] Unemployed.

95

Audience: sales reps
Message: Don't ever forget the selling basics.
Tone: motivational, instructional
Timing: 6-7 minutes

Opportunity is an open door. But before you get hit smack between the eyes trying to enter, remember that the door swings on four hinges: Product and customer knowledge. . . . Initiative. . . . Hard work. . . . And integrity. . . . I want to take these basics one at a time this morning. We'll call it a refresher course, just like the college campus—with two exceptions. Our tuition here is a lot cheaper and the schedule always fits yours.

Mathematics professor John Freund has concluded: "Marketing is simply sales with a college education." Now, I don't doubt that there's a lot more we all could learn about marketing. But I feel much like the member of the congregation who didn't show much enthusiasm when the minister announced a new, in-depth Bible study class. The minister probed, "You mean you don't think the deeper truths and doctrines are important?"

The member responded, "Well, I suppose. But it's the part that I *already* understand that I haven't mastered yet."

To repeat: I'm not denigrating all the sophisticated market-research tools at our disposal. But I am suggesting that we may have gotten away from the basic, simple but successful techniques that produce sales.

You'll pardon me if I don't get as theoretical as you remember your college profs to be. I think in down-to-earth terms. In dos and don'ts. Here we go:

Product and customer knowledge. There's a journal or magazine story printed every day that educates your customer. That tells the customer what his needs are and what he should expect from a supplier. How can we afford to know less about our products than our customers do?

We're committed to you to provide product training and product literature. It's up to you as individuals to read, to attend training classes—to digest it all. Of course, they say overeating is a major cause of indigestion. That being so, you'll have to take your chances because there's a lot of technology out there to digest.

Customers also expect you to know as much about *them* as you do about your own products. They're willing to talk if you're willing to ask questions.

Talk to everybody concerned—the technical buyers who can screen you out with a simple, "I don't think it can cut 23 widget strings a minute." Talk to them and be ready to show them the specs.

Talk to the users. What they want and what they think they want are often two different things, as you well know. Find out what their needs are on the job and then tell them how we can meet those needs. They don't give a hoot about the specs on the 23 widget strings. They want to know that if they use our (product), they'll get the task done quicker.

Talk to the guy who's got the pocketbook. He's the one that you have to make business sense to. If they install the (product), how much will that investment return on his balance sheet?

There's simply no fad that will replace the need for product and customer knowledge.

Second, we need to get back to the basics of initiative. The days when selling meant simply taking orders are ancient history. We've got to take the initiative in keeping our products in front of the customer. We've got faxes, phones, and first-rate software to network. Customer loyalty is there only if we take great pains to build it day by day.

The third basic is simply hard work. The sun comes up about (time) and it goes down about (time). Can you afford to be far behind it? They keep telling us to work smarter, not harder. But in my experience, smarter is harder. It takes a plan. . . . It takes conscientious follow-through. . . . It takes phone calls. . . . It takes letter writing and proposals. . . . It takes personal visits. . . . And those add up to hours. Look at it this way, at least you as sales reps can set your own hours. We don't care if you want to sleep in the day and work in the dark. But hard work is part of the plan.

Finally, the fourth basic is integrity. The French magistrate, Nicolas de Latena, observed: "One may be better than his reputation, but never better than his principles." They go hand in hand. In our business, your reputation rests on your principles. Pardon me, I did get a little philo-sophical there. But I'll translate.

If you quote a price, honor it. If you tell them we'll ship, see that it's shipped. If it's broken, fix it. If you say you will mail it, see that it gets out the door. If the customer isn't satisfied, take it back. If our product can't do the job, say so. We're not looking for a one-time sale—we're looking for a long-time customer.

The basics: Product and customer knowledge. . . . Initiative. . . . Hard work. . . . Integrity. . . . We can't work on the passing plays until we have the blocking and tackling down pat.

By the way, this has been a pass/fail refresher course. If you passed, let's see your scores next month!

COMMENDATION/AWARD ON SALES RECORD (See also "Awards.")

96

Audience: sales reps
Message: In spite of the odds, you have been successful.
Tone: tongue-in-cheek, motivational
Timing: 2 minutes

You have officially done it. In total defiance of adverse market studies and published media surveys of public awareness, . . . using all means available, . . . you have planted, watered, tilled, and harvested a new crop of buyers. Your defiance has resulted in the shipment, as of the close of business Friday, of (number) (product).

I suppose no one told you that it couldn't be done. Obviously, you were unaware that the design was defective—that the (feature of product) was too large and that the (feature of product) was awkward. You didn't know that the colors were too obtrusive for such an impressive status symbol.

Furthermore, you obviously didn't do enough reading about the prod-uct—reading from the national media, that is. Somewhere you must have missed the publications that insisted the marketplace wasn't ready for this technology—and would even fear it. How did you guys handle the shrieks of terror from the faint-hearted who asked to see your demonstrations?

And obviously no one told you that the price of $X would meet with major customer objections. I say that's obvious because the bulk of these orders sure showed that $X was the sales price you negotiated on 98% of the orders. I guess you know you're in the same danger as that frontier judge in Texas. He was about to hang an outlaw for his heinous crimes, and so he asked him if he had any last words.

The outlaw said, "Judge, I'm aware of the fact that you have a great reputation in this town. They think you're fair. Honest. You're compassionate when necessary. Everybody thinks you're wonderful. But I gotta be honest, Judge. You done went and ruined your reputation with *me!*"

All I can say, group, is that you done ruined your reputation with us here at (company).

You're a defiant bunch of sales reps that need to be educated about what we can't sell. The media have suggested that we smarten up. So we're planning a strategy meeting—some time next decade. In the meantime, stay away from the newspapers.

97

Audience: sales reps
Message: You have broken records. Congratulations.
Tone: informal, motivational
Timing: 2-3 minutes

They tell us that old salespeople never die—they just get out of commission. If that's the case, you people are as young as ever because I saw some hefty commission checks leave our offices this past quarter. To paraphrase General George Patton: You have accepted the challenge, and you are feeling the exhilaration of victory.

You have broken all past records, but let me see if I can put the puzzle pieces back together long enough for you to taste the victory. In the first quarter of last year, you sold $X of (product). In the last quarter of last year, we shipped $X of (product). That's more like a race record set by tortoises than hares. Then in the first quarter of this year, our benchmark was $X in gross sales. Second quarter, we shipped $X out the door. By third quarter, we had racked up a respectable figure of $X. Then somebody put the accelerator to the floor in the last quarter. You can congratulate yourselves for selling $X worth of the best (product) in the nation.

And I'm left trying to figure out how you did it—where the momentum developed.

For starters, you had some specific goals for each model in the line.

Second, you had increased advertising in (title of print media).

But most of all, I think what took you to victory was your own growing awareness of what the product can do for our customers. And once you yourselves became sold, you had little trouble communicating that confidence to your customers who had taken a wait-and-see position.

There's one thing to be learned here for future situations: Enthusiasm doesn't have to be assigned to the newest item on your order form. Some of you may decide to go back through your bags of goodies and see what staple products you may have overlooked. This (product) line may not have been the "firstest with the mostest." But it certainly has been the bulk of our bottom line this past quarter.

Enthusiasm is the fuel that drives a lot of engines. This product line was simply a little more sluggish at the start. You got the lead out and the commissions started to roll in. We appreciate your efforts.

98

Audience: sales reps

Message: We appreciate your hard work to make us successful; we're drowning the competition.

Tone: informal, sincere

Timing: 5-6 minutes, depending on the insertion of details of sales records set by various groups

"Never murder a man when he's busy committing suicide," Woodrow Wilson advised. Our competition is doing just that—self-destructing. In a period of recession, instead of putting forth more effort, it seems that they have decided the game has been rained out.

You, on the other hand, have continued to meet and exceed your quotas. You have outsold both of our major competitors—combined. I'm delighted to report that (year) was a dynamic year for us at (company). We have set several records. Let me mention who, where, when:

[Insert details of the sales records set by various groups and divisions.]

Why the continuing success when our competition is lagging so far behind? You know as well as I do that it takes more than superior products to make a successful sale. It takes superior people. Like you.

As impressive as our records are for this year, they're history the day after they're recorded on the balance sheets. Our history and our future as a company rest with you, our sales team.

As impressive as our team record is, we can be *more*. More productive. We can budget our time better and knock on more doors. Our training programs to be offered this coming year are opportunities for you to polish your time-management skills and get more hours in your week. You can learn to set priorities, favoring large-volume customers, . . . and to plan a strategy for add-on sales.

As impressive as our record is, we can be *more*. More alert to new prospects that our marketing research turns up. From the most recent advertising campaigns, we already have fat databases of prospects awaiting our attention.

As impressive as our record is, we can be *more*. More diligent to ask our satisfied customers for referrals to their associates who can make use of our products and services. Most will be more than happy to help us help their colleagues reach their own goals. They want their associates to get the same kind of performance they've been getting from our products.

As impressive as our record is, we can be *more*. More knowledgeable about our customers' needs. We can continually probe to find new needs to pass on to our engineering and research staff. Today's unfilled needs are tomorrow's innovative products.

As impressive as our record is, we can be *more*. More appreciative. And this one's addressed clearly to us in management positions. We can be more appreciative of your efforts—of what it takes to sell in today's market.

Let me say it more clearly: We are impressed with you. . . . Your hard work. . . . Your knowledge. . . . Your skill. . . . Your drive.

History tells us that we have the competitive edge—a superior sales team that goes out every day to "make it happen." That's history. And we have every confidence that it'll be the future, thanks to each of you.

INTRODUCTION OF NEW PRODUCT OR SERVICE

99

Audience: sales reps

Message: This product will sell itself.

Tone: motivational, informational

Timing: will vary greatly, depending on insertion of product benefits and facts

Enthusiasm is a good driver, but it needs intelligence for fuel. That's why we're here—to give you that intelligence. We want to outline the key benefits of a new product line, the (name of line).

It's the first product on the market to [overview the unique benefit or feature].

The competition can offer only products that will [insert standard benefits or features].

Ours are also more sophisticated in that they can [overview other feature that has been improved].

Here are other key customer benefits:

[List the most important ones.]

Preliminary market tests have generated lots of *enthusiasm* but not much *information* about why our customers are buying. It's not that we plan to argue with these early buyers or refuse to ship them our (product).

But we do want you to have a few facts at your disposal before you start to write up the orders.

[Insert other key product information.]

Now that you know the facts, we want to help your customers know them. We are making available to you (number) machines to lend your best customers on a trial basis. For lower-volume customers, we plan to offer demonstrations and answer questions by conducting specially arranged seminars here at our site.

(Name) will tell you later about details for enrolling customers in those seminars.

To interest your customers in taking a look—at their site or ours—you need to create awareness and provide print info. We have both.

Beginning (date), we will have ads appearing in (publication), (publication), and (publication).

And to stuff your travel case, we have three brochures—each designed for a different buyer.

[Insert details on the available printed literature.]

Well, that should complete the process—add the necessary intelligence to your usual enthusiasm. Let's give 'em the facts and the product will get up and walk out of here.

100

Audience: sales reps
Message: This product won't sell itself.
Tone: informal, motivational
Timing: 5-6 minutes

"Maybe I will and maybe I won't" we said to the neighborhood bully who was trying to get our cooperation on his mischievous plan for something like sabotaging the cafeteria food.

That less-than-positive stance is what we're feeling about our newest product line we want to introduce to you tonight: Maybe it will and maybe it won't. That is, maybe it will and maybe it won't sell itself.

That's not to say it's not an excellent product. It is to say that it probably won't sell *itself*, because our marketplace doesn't yet know it has a need. Our advertising people are working on creating that need. But, as always, that's where your real sales skills come into play.

How is this product going to do in the market? If I were going to paint you a picture of last month's sales, it would be a still life.

But one of my philosophies is that there's no failure—just feedback. And our feedback from last month is that the market's not beating our door down for this product at the current moment.

Now why am I telling you all this? Our usual introduction is to tell you how the product will break all records on its first time around the track.

Well, we're just as enthusiastic about the *eventual* sales of this new product. But we're more knowledgeable about the realities of how to present it to your customers. First of all, they will be unaware of the need to [overview the unrecognized customer need].

Second, they will not have heard about the process for [overview new process].

And finally, they will have trouble convincing their bosses to approve the money for the initial investment of equipment.

So we've prepared literature to help you explain these benefits and to overcome these issues.

[Insert highlights of the relevant ideas you plan to provide on the literature.]

The bottom line is that this product *won't* sell itself as many of our other products do. With our older products such as the (product): customer see, customer buy. Not so in this case. We simply want you to be prepared to present this product with your feet on the ground while your customer's head is still in the clouds on these issues.

We can't *promise* you a *quick* sale. But we can *predict* a *big* sale—once you are prepared to invest the time in analyzing the customer's situation and savings with this product. In other words, you'll have to do your homework.

But let me remind you of the experience of Joe Namath: "When you win, nothing hurts." You *will* eventually win with this product—and that paycheck will take the sting out of your struggle.

INTRODUCTION OF NEW SALES CAMPAIGN

101

Audience: sales reps and their managers
Message: Here's how we plan to reward and support your efforts.
Tone: informal
Timing: will vary greatly, depending on the insertion of details about the sales campaign

I'm the one the others who have gone before me on the program have kept predicting was coming. The one with the details to tell you how to make your first—or second, or third—million. Here's the plan to make *you* rich and to make *us* profitable. PULITZERS FOR PROFIT. That's our slogan for the new sales campaign.

Meaning? The original Pulitzer Prize was established in 1917 by Joseph Pulitzer to recognize excellence in journalism, literature, and music. But on the outside chance that our sales literature will be omitted for consideration for the traditional Pulitzer Prize, we have decided to establish our own Pulitzer. We've changed the selection criteria but have kept the prizes as part of the package. Here are our own Pulitzer Prizes for winning sales reps:

[Announce monetary awards and prizes such as trips, tickets, and so forth that will be presented to salespeople who excel in this new campaign.]

Do these sound worth the struggle for recognition? If so, here are the Pulitzer details:

[Insert the goals and the rules of the competition.]

No great prize—particularly the Pulitzer—is won without great sacrifice. You'll be sacrificing chitchat with friends and a laid-back lifestyle for the next three months. But in return your Pulitzer will win the admiration of colleagues, . . . new business from old customers, . . . new business from prospective customers, . . . and ultimately Pulitzer profit for your pocket.

Don't forget to pick up your Pulitzer sales literature at the back of the room. You'll find the texts of TV and print ads, the additional 800 telephone coverage to take your orders, and samples of dealer displays to underscore your efforts. Let's go for the Pulitzer prizes and profits.

Stockholders Meetings

GENERAL GUIDELINES

- Welcome stockholders by making them feel a part of the company.
- Present a state-of-the-company summary, including your financial position, new product or service information, marketing issues, ongoing research, pending legislation that will affect you, pending litigation, management and staffing changes. Also include comments on the negatives, particularly responding to press coverage and downturns in the economy.
- Overview your plans for the future.
- Invite the stockholders to ask questions or offer suggestions about the organization's operations.

102

Audience: stockholders, members of the press
Message: Our steady growth continues.
Tone: formal
Timing: will vary greatly, depending on the insertion of financial, managerial, and legal details

It's my pleasure to welcome you today to our (number) annual meeting of (company) stockholders. Your copy of this year's annual report should now be in your hands—a report that reviews our (number) years of continued growth.

Last year can certainly be tagged as one of the most turbulent in the history of our industry. Negative impacts ranged from a troubled world economy to declining [insert specific problem faced during the year], to increasing costs for [insert details]. Yet we weathered those challenges. We made substantial progress on a number of fronts.

Although the year started off like a bad joke, the punch line has been this: We achieved sales of $X and revenues of $X—setting a record for the (number) year in a row. Our earnings totaled $X, a record surpassed in only (number) years since we opened the doors. We saw new investments of $X in the future growth of the company, our total assets being $X. The price of our shares has risen from $X to $X during this past 12 months—a direct reflection of our steady plodding even in troubled times.

Of that total investment, we funded [type] programs. Additionally, we joined other groups in participating in [type] activities.

[Insert details about new product lines and services.]

Our involvement in all these areas looks promising. Specifically, we're excited about our ongoing research into the field of [type]. Never before have the possibilities been so ripe for plucking.

[Insert research details and practical applications.]

Now that we know what the potential here is, we owe it to the public and to you to continue to move ahead with our quest into this new technology. What's taking place in our laboratories today will create a healthier, happier, safer world tomorrow.

Congress has made great strides in correcting the problem of [type]. We are encouraged by recent tax legislation to [overview purpose of legislation].

If our timetables are accurate, we should see an impact from these new programs and tax changes in the last quarter of the year. We are resolved to succeed in keeping our rates competitive and accomplishing a smooth transition in current programs.

We want you to know of some current field-testing in the area of [type]. The results of these field-tests should prove valuable in assessing [purpose of the testing].

We are also pleased to report that we have no litigation pending at this time. That's a welcome change. For the past few years, I've listened to our legal staff and the opponents argue versions of the childhood chant: "Did." "Did not." "Did." "Did not." Thank goodness, we're now at peace with our neighbors and colleagues. Our patent infringement suit filed against (competitive company) was settled in our favor in (month, year). With the $X we were awarded, we plan to [overview plans for funds].

We do have some discouraging news, however. Our foray into the (type) market has not been promising. We've learned several things. First, [insert details]. Second, [insert details]. Our plans to turn this around next year include [insert details].

In the end, all of us understand that it isn't enough to run every program and then immediately define its success or failure only with the short-term numbers. All I can say is that we're going to keep it under the microscope.

As you can see, this was a year of steady operation and consistent growth, as well as one of new direction. Our financing program was improved by an additional upgrading of the company's debt and preferred stock rating: a vote of confidence from the financial community.

The fortunes of the company have improved dramatically since our beginning, (number) years ago. The price of our stock has gone from a (year) low of $X to this year's high of $X, an accumulative return of (number) percent.

Fundamentally, we are a sound company. We have a substantial net worth of more than $X. We are a broad-based enterprise with a recognized diversity and worldwide presence.

(Company)'s performance during (year) demonstrated a sound financial foundation and an efficient operation. We expect to continue that situation. And we have every confidence that our (number) years' experience in the (type) industry and our pioneering spirit will take us in new directions... at the most appropriate junctures.

So what are our most important goals? Making your corporation more competitive globally. Our primary objective continues to be to enhance the value of your shares over the longterm and maintain or improve your dividend. The (year) actions we've planned to meet this objective include

[Insert details of key goals for the upcoming year.]

I'm sure those goals have brought some issues to the forefront of your mind. What questions do you now have?

[Take questions and answers.]

Thank you for coming today. It's been very pleasant for me to be here among new and former friends. And, I might add, it's also been nice to report to you on our continuing successes and our optimistic future.

I've done my best to use this time to give you a detailed snapshot of how I see our company. An impressive picture, we think. And our research reflects great things to come. We plan to continue our growth and repay your initial and ongoing confidence.
In short, we plan to rekindle your excitement.

103

Audience: stockholders, members of the press
Message: We're slowly turning the company around now in a difficult environment.
Tone: formal
Timing: will vary, depending on insertion of financial, managerial, and legal details

Good evening, ladies and gentlemen. I am (name), president and chief executive officer of (company). With pleasure, I welcome each of you to the company's (number) annual shareholders meeting. Let me first introduce our Board of Directors.

[Introduce members.]

These people have served with dedication, integrity, and indisputable expertise. And as you know, they stand today for re-election to another one-year term.
Our corporate secretary will now take the podium to describe the steps necessary to officially convene today's meeting and observe our legal requirements. Then I'll update you on our progress this year.

[Insert details of opening the meeting, election of board members, and collection of proxy votes for any matters before the shareholders.]

With those details out of the way, let's review the year. We began in the wake of the biggest downturn in our industry in recent history. To say the least, as management, we were uncertain what the year would bring. Investors were cautious, keeping our shares at $X for almost (number) months. Although we faced a difficult environment, (company) became stronger despite these difficulties. There's an old saying that "adversity builds character." Certainly, we built character this year.

Despite the environment and discouraging start, we reached several milestones. We've started and finished a solid foundation for our future. Let me get specific about what we've done in four areas: international marketing, customer service, new product development, expense cutbacks.

[Insert details in each of these areas.]

To spearhead these efforts I've just outlined, we have a superb new management team in place. (Name) and (name) you already know for their past excellent performance: (first name) in the area of (position) and (first name) in the area of (position).

I'm also pleased to introduce some new management team players who've joined us this year and who have already made some impressive decisions that resulted in dramatic turnaround results.

[Insert names of new management team members.]

This new team is a welcome addition. They are all outstanding professionals with the skills and knowledge to strengthen the areas we identified in past years as strategic to our growth.

But to get specific about these dramatic changes I'm referring to: First, at a time when others in the industry have been forced to *cut back* on [insert detail], we have *expanded* our services in the area of [type].

Another of our strategic accomplishments has been to [continue with accomplishment details].

In the area of internal controls, we've added to the training plans for our key personnel and gained control of hiring and compensation practices. We've attracted many new star performers in key slots and our turnover of staff has fallen sharply—roughly by (number) percent.

In (month), we expanded our participation in [overview program].

In the areas of communication—telephone and data processing—we have made tremendous strides. You could say we've gone from quill and ink to lasers and modems. Thus, our state-of-the-art equipment has provided us with the opportunity to concentrate on customer services and quality... rather than on shuffling internal paperwork.

Additionally, we think we have put our ear a little lower to the ground to hear what the market is telling us in the area of [type of problem]. During the last six months, we have conducted a market-research study with our own staff to learn to what extent [insert details]. The response has given us immediate insight into new ideas for services and products.

[Insert new product and service plans.]

Public awareness is another area we've tackled. We found that the public is almost totally ignorant of (number) percent of what we really do here. So, education of the consumer has been a major goal. To improve awareness, we've participated in and sponsored several events in the local community and in the larger industry arena.

[Insert details about increasing public and consumer awareness.]

These are just a few of the ways we've been working to strengthen our relationship with the (industry) community and local citizens. We plan to continue our promotional efforts by [insert details].

Of course, we will not see positive results of these last promotional efforts until next year.

Turning our attention to management of our finances, we've made these areas our priority for investing our reserve cash.

[Insert details about investments.]

Our primary aim is to generate consistent above-average return through traditional forms of investment management. With so many capital needs for personnel, equipment, and marketing, you may be wondering why we didn't aim for home runs rather than dabbling with singles and doubles. In our opinion, the philosophy of a consistent foundation played a critical role in providing the return we needed for expansion.

In each of these areas I've outlined—public awareness and promotion, new product and service ideas, recruiting—we've made progress in a difficult environment. Our competitors have seen almost a (number) percent decline in gross revenues. On the other hand, our gross revenues totaled $X, with a net income of $X. Our share prices have maintained their value at $X.

Yes, it's been a rough year. But these cyclical downturns are nothing new to people in the industry. History has shown that with a game plan in hand, the situation will improve. It is, in fact, turning around. Until that about-face is complete, we have reorganized to survive and even grow in these circumstances.

We've pared expenses and increased efficiency.

We've added services for our customers and quality to our products.

We've changed our management team's philosophy from "wait and see" to "go and tell."

We've let the community know who we are and have built stronger relationships in the process.

Without a doubt, our (year) achievements directly reflect the expertise and dedication of our employees, and I want to publicly thank them for their outstanding work.

We have a game plan. We're committed. We're stronger. And, I hope, we have your continued confidence and support. The strength we've built makes us a tough competitor when its our turn to bat.

May I take your questions now?

[Call for questions and answers.]

[Convey the results of any earlier voting.]

In closing, I want to point out that virtually all lasting structures require foundations. And frequently that foundation is the most difficult, time-consuming part of the construction. We have laid the foundation.

We have learned from the past, and the present is our platform for the future. This year we plan to continue and complete the projects that will make us strong. I'm convinced that we have the management and staff, the enthusiasm, the pride, and the skills for the opportunities that lie ahead.

Toasts

GENERAL GUIDELINES

- Express your affection and good wishes for the individual.
- Focus on the other person rather than yourself.
- Be brief.

BIRTHDAY

Audience: mixed groups
Message: Happy birthday; we appreciate you.
Tone: both serious and light
Timing: 10-30 seconds

104

People say you don't look like 40. Obviously, they mean that as a compliment. But I'd like to say you're *exactly* what 40 looks like these days—beautiful, poised, self-assured, intelligent. Here's to at least 40 more.

105

When someone is as special as you've been . . . and still are, he deserves a birthday wish without foolishness, or jokes, or insults. But I can't bring myself to say anything sentimental and serious about such a funny guy. So I'll just leave the jokes to you and make it a straightforward "Happy birthday."

106

Here's to a woman who deserves a birthday that's the happiest by far. Hope you'll have the kind of day and year that bring all life's best and finest. You're a favorite. Happy birthday.

107

May everything about your day be just the way you want. Have a happy and wonderful birthday and life.

108

There are some people who pass through your life like a butterfly. They rarely make contact and then are quickly gone. There are those who pass through your life like fellow travelers. They sit and talk for awhile on the airplane, but upon touchdown, they drift away toward their own destinations. Then there are people who pass through your life and decide to set up camp. They work with you, share with you, borrow from you, care about you. These are the kind that give meaning to life. (Name) falls in that latter category. To my dear friend, I wish a happy birthday and an exciting rest of her life.

109

Someone has said that a friend is someone who understands your past, believes in your future, and accepts you today just the way you are. (Name) has been just that kind of person. That's why his birthday is as special to me as my very own. Happy birthday to a very special person.

110

Birthdays are a time to celebrate—the memories of days gone by, the joys of the moment, and the dreams of tomorrow. We're celebrating with you and you deserve a big parade.

111

Have a happy birthday and try not to dwell on the real number you are. Remember that you're only as old as you are.

112

With much respect and admiration, I offer you our best wishes for a great year. Happy birthday.

113

Maybe it's true that life begins at 40. . . . But everything else starts to wear out. So in case you're in need of spare parts, we've got a useful collection in this circle of comrades. Happy birthday.

114

A Swedish proverb says, "Fear less, hope more; eat less, chew more; whine less, breathe more; talk less, say more; hate less, love more; and all good things are yours." More or less . . . we think you deserve a great birthday. Enjoy without a worry.

115

There's a time to be born and a time to die, and what happens to us in the interval in between is of great importance. (Name), of all the people I know, you've made the most of that interval. Just think of this birthday as a green light on the road to your dreams. Happiness to you.

116

In many ways, (name), you've been like a daughter to me—pouty, arrogant, disrespectful. Seriously, I'd be awfully proud to have a daughter just like you. Here's a to a happy, happy birthday.

117

Just remember that when you get over the hill, you pick up speed on the downside. But you have no cause to worry. The faster you go, the better you get. Here's to a great, fast birthday.

ENGAGEMENT/WEDDING

Audience: business friends and family
Message: We wish you happiness on your marriage.
Tone: both serious and light
Timing: 10-30 seconds

118

Here's hoping that your life together is all that you want it to be and that your marriage brings you much happiness and long-lasting joy.

119

My wish is that your life never gets back to normal—whatever that is. May it always be a special sea of high sailing.

120

Some people have such special ways—an infectious smile, a genuine caring, a magic touch, a sixth sense of good business savvy. You're one of those special people, and you deserve a life of happiness with someone you love. May you cherish each other forever. Happiness to you both.

121

Our love, pride, and best wishes as you begin your lives together. May God walk close to you and continue to be your source of strength as you achieve the goals you've set for your lives. We wish you direction and days of joy.

122

On your wedding day, may God add His blessings to the sacred vows you take. We wish for you a long life together, and may you experience the best miracle of all—the miracle of love. Congratulations.

123

Congratulations on finding each other. Many people search for years and decades for that one special person that will complete their joy. You're so fortunate to have found each other so early in life. Here's to complete happiness now and forever.

124

We wish you happiness that grows and love that deepens and peace that endures. Our very best on your life together.

125

Marriage is a celebration of love. . . . Of life. . . . Of joy. . . . Of contentment. . . . As you walk through life, hold hands and never let go.

126

When two hearts are joined by true love, they both grow and mature into a miracle greater than either could be alone. Remember that always. Two hearts are bigger and better than one.

127

Water your marriage with friendship and faith and favor. And then watch it grow. You deserve a garden of love.

128

As you join your lives as one, we hope the special days and years ahead for you have just begun. Congratulations on a lifetime of happiness with each other.

129

Since God brought the two of you to meet and to marry, may you love and live life's fullest. Here's to a wonderful life together—one day at a time.

130

May your life be blessed with love's rewards—friendship, giving, intimacy, understanding, and contentment. A fantastic life lies ahead for you. Enjoy.

131

It's wonderful to see your happiness and to know that you've found in each other that special friend, partner, and lover for life. Congratulations on the beauty of a new life together.

132

May real joy fill your days, warm your nights, and overflow your hearts forever. Our best to both of you on finding each other.

133

Marriage is a commitment to life. To the best two people can give to themselves and to each other. Marriage deepens and enriches every detail of living. Fun is more thrilling. Happiness is fuller. Compassion is stronger. Forgiveness is faster. Laughter is richer. Sharing is deeper. Marriage has more potential than any other relationship for bringing out the best in ourselves and living life to its fullest. May your marriage bind you closer than any other relationship on earth.

134

Marriage is a constant journey of understanding, fun, sorrow, forgiveness, laughter, sharing. In short, it is a journey of love. With respect and every good wish for a journey filled with joy.

135

Wishing you fun and excitement for today, . . . goals and dreams for tomorrow, . . . and love and happiness forever.

136

As you commit your caring, pledge your love, and join your lives, may you discover life's best together. Our best now and always.

137

We're excited to know that you two have so much happiness to bask in now, tomorrow, and forever. Here's to looking forward to your living and loving together.

138

Marriage of two mature adults such as you is really a meeting of the minds, of two hearts, of two souls . . . and of three cars, four blenders, five bedrooms, and six kids. It'll be a crowd of fun.

139

To date, (name), I suspect your greatest two pleasures in life have been getting organized and reading financial statements. From this time until forever, I also suspect your two greatest pleasures will be . . . loving and sharing. Congrats!

140

Goethe once wrote that we are shaped and fashioned by what we love. Well, in my estimation, if you are both fashioned by the one you love, you'll be in good shape for life. Best wishes to both of you for much happiness as you grow together.

FAREWELLS

Audience: business friends and family
Message: We will miss you; best wishes as you go.
Tone: both serious and light
Timing: 10-30 seconds

141

(Name), as you go, may the warmth of the moment and the goodwill of the group leave you with lingering memories of some wonderful times together here. All our best wishes for your future happiness.

142

"Thanks" seems like such a short, simple word. It's not much to describe our appreciation of everything you've contributed here. Our appreciation of your upbeat attitude. Our dependency on your advice-giving—from career goals to caterers. Our notice of your listening nature during the times we shared the good and the bad. Yes, as short, simple, and inadequate as "thanks" sounds, I want to say it anyway from the bottom of my heart—thanks. Our best as you go.

143

I want to take this opportunity to make an announcement that will confirm what we've all heard through the grapevine. Here's the formal announcement: See Jane. See Mark. She Jane and Mark see each other. See Jane and Mark get married. See Jane and Mark go to work in different cities. See Jane wave bye-bye. As you may have noticed, I'm not exactly eloquent on sentimental occasions. So I'll just wrap it up with this: We will miss Jane and Mark. Jane and Mark, have fun.

144

Robert Louis Stevenson defined a friend as a present we give ourselves. Well, (name)'s smile, his genuinely teachable attitude, and his creative thinking have all been a part of the present we've given ourselves during the (number) years he's been around. (Name), you've been a great present that we intend to keep on enjoying through the years, whenever your name comes up in conversations around the water cooler. Thanks for contributing to our lives. We'll miss you.

145

Those people who, when you ask them how they are, say "can't complain" just aren't trying hard enough. Well, I've *been* one of those people, but I've started to complain—the day I heard (name) was leaving us. (Name), we're going to miss your talent, your savvy, and your comedy routines. Which of those can you leave behind? Seriously, we're going to miss you more than you know. Our best, but remember we're still going to complain about your leaving from time to time.

146

Rarely will there be so few who have changed the lives of so many! You are one of the few. Thank you for your committed caring, your genuine spirit, and your practical, hard work. You came into our department at a most difficult time, and your contribution was priceless. We will miss you.

147

The feelings that go deepest are the most difficult to express. And, for that very reason, I can only hope you'll hear "between the lines" of this toast. You have meant a great deal to us here, and we will remember you often in special times of fun and also in meaningful moments of hard-won victories and jobs done well. May your future work and relationships bring you as much happiness as you've supplied around here. Our best.

148

Thank you for what you've added to our work and to our personal lives here. You've added thoughtfulness and fun and lots of excellent work. In exchange, we want you to take a little of us with you—our admiration and genuine goodwill.

PROMOTIONS

Audience: business associates
Message: Congratulations on your promotion.
Tone: both formal and informal
Timing: 10-30 seconds

149

(Name), you're an all-around nice person, who grows more talented and giving as the years go by. You're someone to count on when things get demanding. Someone to turn to for help and understanding. Someone to have fun with when we get together. Someone who deserves every good thing that comes to him. Congratulations. We're all behind you for the long haul.

150

They say that success is getting what you want, and that happiness is wanting what you get. . . . You've already made it to my definition of success. My wish is that you'll have all the happiness you expect and deserve in your new job.

151

Friendship cannot be bought but must be paid for—in installments. (Name) has been paying installments for years in this department. That's why there's no hesitation at all to go beyond the usual comments about hard work and talent. Although those same things could be said, our friendship is paid in full. Friends to friend, we offer our congratulations and support.

152

As someone once said, "Here's champagne to your real friends and real pain to your sham friends." This toast to thank you for being real friends through some real pain. These past few years together in the department have been some of the toughest. But you've been superb in your support and your expertise. My congratulations to you on your promotion.

153

When you row another person across the stream, you get to the other side yourself. That's what (name) has been doing for a lot of people in this company—rowing them to other departments and raises and promotions. It's about time somebody caught him on the other side and recognized his talent for [insert]. Congratulations to a super skipper.

154

The world has a habit of making room for a man who knows where he's going. You've got the talent and the determination to get anywhere you want to go. We're just glad they made room for you here. Good luck as you move up.

155

Someone has said that those who bring sunshine to the lives of others cannot keep it from themselves. That's obviously very true in your life. You've brought us several rays of glory during your assignment here, and some of that light is now reflecting on you. You deserve the limelight and the sunshine and whatever else good that comes your way in this new job. Here's to your success.

156

They say that true friendship comes when silence between two people is comfortable. Well, it's certainly been silent around here lately—we've all been working too hard and too fast to look up. But the silence has been comfortable because we know you will always come through. We expect no less from you in your new job—friendship, hard work, and continued support. Best wishes to you in your new corner of the world.

157

A friend of mine has said that parents should hope to give their children roots and wings. Although we're certainly not in a parent-offspring role, I hope we've helped to give you the same things as you take over your new job—roots and wings. Roots of good business savvy and decision making and wings to soar to the top of our industry. Best wishes as you get airborne.

SEASONS GREETINGS

Audience: business friends and family
Message: Have an enjoyable, meaningful holiday.
Tone: both serious and light
Timing: 10-30 seconds

158

Here's to a beautiful holiday season and a year full of peace and happiness for you and those you care about.

159

This is a superb time to let you in on a little secret: I've appreciated your friendship and goodwill and hard work the whole year through. I hope you'll find happiness and success in this season and in all of them.

160

Since I'm rather old-fashioned, I want to offer an old-fashioned holiday toast. To you my friends, it's good health and good fortune in the coming year.

161

Well, at this time of year my thoughts turn to you as friends. I value your confidence, your commitment, and your concern. My sincerest thanks. Happy holidays.

162

May your holidays be filled with all that brings you happiness. You deserve it.

163

I wish for each of you a holiday season filled with merry moments, heartwarming togetherness, meaningful traditions, and joyful contentment.

164

Here's to an EST Christmas—the merri*est*, happi*est*, warm*est*, saf*est* holiday of all.

165

I suggest that we drink a toast to an ideal—that we keep the peace and love and compassion of Christmas in our hearts and minds throughout the New Year. We as a group have enough peace, love, and compassion to share with the world. Let's do it.

166

It's a special time for me to get to wish you a great holiday season. You're a special group of people, who've added immeasurably to my life. The best to you all.

167

I have a projection to make about the New Year. From previous reports from confidential sources, I've every reason to believe . . . that you will realize prosperity, good health, and happiness now and in the future. Happy New Year.

168

May the gift of love and light live in your life, heart, and home forever. You are special. The happiest of holidays.

169

Very good wishes for a happy and healthy New Year.

170

I sincerely wish each of you all the peace and joy of the season. We have something very special in our department—genuine caring, a congenial work relationship, and a meaningful mission. What more could any of us ask? My best to you and your families during the holiday season and throughout the New Year.

171

Here's to all the best in (year). May the Good Lord bless you and keep you and shower blessings on you like a thunderstorm.

172

Let's drink to the best of holidays and the brightest of futures. Where you guys are concerned, I welcome more of the same. You're the greatest.

173

May the serenity of the season and the warmest of holiday welcomes be yours as we slide into the New Year. The best is yet ahead.

174

I want to take this moment to thank you for your goodwill, . . . your good cheer, . . . your loving loyalty, . . . and your caring commitment throughout the year. May the happiness and peace of the season be yours throughout the upcoming year.

Welcomes
to Families

(See also "Holidays.")

GENERAL GUIDELINES

- Focus on employees as individuals; make them feel the event is for them individually, not for the company's well-being.
- Overview the program or details of the event.
- Encourage employees to get to know each other and the families of their colleagues.
- Express warm wishes for the season or event.

COMPANY PICNIC/SPORTS EVENT

175

Audience: employees and families at company picnic
Message: We appreciate you and your family's support of the organization.
Tone: informal
Timing: 2 minutes

Mothers and dads, tots and teens, welcome to our annual picnic. Once a year we parade the ants out of town, order warm weather and blue skies, and nominate a few "undiscovered" coaches to organize games, and then we're under way with the picnic.

As you arrived on the scene, I hope you found something of interest—the volleyball nets, the shuffleboard courts, the swing sets, or at least the food. Of food, there's an abundance prepared by the (name) caterers, who've done such an excellent job for us over the years.

Other than these few plans, the day is up to you. You'll find sign-up sheets and our volunteer "coaches" and organizers in various locations to help you show off your athletic prowess and assess the competition. Parents, we ask that you particularly make your children feel welcome and help them discover activities designed for them.

We want you families to know how much we appreciate the mom or dad, brother or sister, aunt or uncle who works here with us every day. We play in the same way we work—with honor, . . . sportsmanship, . . . a team spirit, . . . appreciation of each other, . . . and lots of good fun thrown in.

We also encourage each of you as employees to get to know those around you. Maybe you recognize names but not faces. And as you introduce yourselves, you'll discover the person who phones you every week with that sales figure you need. And to those employees you work with on a daily basis, take your family in tow and use this opportunity to let them see how cute Susie's French braid is and how warm and fun-loving that spouse can be. Here's your chance to do some serious bragging about those you love.

Mix and mingle and make the day a good one. We're pleased you and your family came to party and picnic.

176

Audience: employees and their families at a sports event
Message: Please accept these tickets as a token of appreciation for you.
Tone: informal, light
Timing: 2-3 minutes

What would work be without friendships with our coworkers? And what better way to build friendships than getting to know each other away from the phones and the paperwork? In a relaxing and enjoyable atmosphere where there's time to chat informally about outside interests? Please take advantage of tonight's opportunity to do just that.

Before the game gets under way, I also want to thank you for bringing your families and for letting us get to know them a little better.

Families, a few words to you: Your husband or wife . . . or parent . . . or whichever family member works here . . . represents the most important reason our company exists. Certainly, we operate to make a profit. But in earning a profit, we never want to lose sight of the specific individuals that make that profit meaningful. People who make work "play" in a sense. People who help us grow as a company and as individuals.

And, families, we want you to know that we see you as an important part of our extended employee family. You see, you make it easy for your loved ones to contribute on the job. By your interest in their careers—your listening, your advice, your questions. By your patience with the sometimes long hours and schedule juggling. By your understanding about short deadlines or crises. By your concern and help as they learn and practice new skills.

In all these ways, you offer support. These attitudes say to them and to us as an organization that you care.

Your emotional support—the kind you've demonstrated by coming to events like this tonight—make them happier, more productive people on the job. That makes you a special person to us, too. I'm sure they, as we do, appreciate your active participation in their work lives.

So thank you.

That said, let's play ball.

CHRISTMAS PARTY

177

Audience: employees and their families at a Christmas program
Message: We appreciate you and wish you a happy holiday.
Tone: informal
Timing: 2 minutes

We appreciate your coming tonight to enjoy the holidays for a brief few moments with us. And the effort, I understand, hasn't been minimal. Nothing seems to destroy the Christmas spirit faster . . . than looking for a place to park—particularly tonight with such a crowd. The positive side to all that parking confusion, of course, is that we are growing and prospering as individuals and as a company.

This year we've added our new product line, the (name of line). Our customers have given every indication of loving its new design, the benefits, and its low price tag. So the Christmas spirit around here began early in the year.

But nothing—least of all an organization such as ours—thrives without men and women who care about their jobs all year long. You are those employees. I want to take this opportunity to tell you how much you mean to the company. The Christmas spirit that goes out with the dried up Christmas tree is just as worthless as the company that does not respect the dignity of each individual who contributes to its success. Each of you is unique. And you make a valuable contribution to our total effort.

Someone has said that the best Christmas or Chanukah gift of all is the presence of a happy family all wrapped up with one another. That's probably true.

And I would add: The next best thing is our program tonight. We hope you'll agree. We have music, a story for our children, and a visit from Santa maybe later in the evening.

So put that overdue project out of your mind, along with the unwrapped presents. Relax and enjoy. We think the program will put a smile on your face, a lilt in your voice, and a song in your heart.

May the joy of the season make the holiday especially nice this year for you and your family.

178

Audience: employees and their families at a Christmas program
Message: Let's keep the holiday spirit all year.
Tone: formal
Timing: 7-8 minutes

Good evening, everyone. Thank you for coming. A special welcome to members of our board. And we do so appreciate the program of holiday hymns and other seasonal songs. For those of you who aren't familiar with this group before you—these choir members are our own. They volunteer to stay after work for rehearsals. And from time to time, they present programs such as this for us. I understand the auditions are tough, but the rewards and camaraderie among the group are worth it. Thank you, choir, for adding to our enjoyment this evening.

When I think of Christmas, I think of change, the unusual. Certainly, it wouldn't be Christmas without tinsel and neckties, . . . without music and merriment, . . . without peppermint and presents. But in January the tinsel is stuffed back in the cardboard box and returned to the attic. The neckties are worn or returned. The music and merriment fades. The peppermint turns to calories and pounds. The presents are used or broken. Everything is back to normal. January dawns with dull routine.

But think of it. For almost a full month—from Thanksgiving through the New Year's celebration—everything changes. Our homes, our hearts, our hopes.

Our *homes* change. We string up the lights. Put candles in the window. Decorate a tree. We have wrapping paper in the bottom of the closet. Fudge in the refrigerator. Greeting cards on the table. Even our schedules change. Susie isn't home for dinner because she's out shopping late. On Saturday afternoon Dad suddenly decides to turn off the ball game and head for the mall. Mikie has grandmother sewing his reindeer costume until the wee morning hours. We miss a few meals together. In fact, we get down-right secretive when we used to share the day's events.

Not only do our homes change, but our hearts change. Have you noticed how that happens?

The young person who was once in a hurry stops now to hold the door open for the elderly man as he pushes his shopping cart through.

Parents grow a little more patient with toddlers who can't sleep for excitement.

Grandparents call more often to see how everyone's getting along.

People are more generous with their gifts to charity.

The churches boast their best attendance for worship.

Those who are feuding grow mellower and more forgiving.

The rebellious suddenly feel nostalgic pangs of home and hearth and pick up the phone or drop a line just to say "I'm okay."

We even wish total strangers health, happiness, and prosperity at this time of the year.

In addition to the change in our homes and hearts, we gradually realize our *hopes* change. We seem to take on a longer view of life. We hope that the hungry are fed, that wars cease, that mankind conquers disease, that relationships reign supreme in our lives.

So is all this change during the holiday season for the better or the worse?

On all counts—except the popcorn and peppermint—I'd say the changes are for the better. Change gives us time for reflection, for thought. Change makes us see the meaning of our lives more directly and more clearly. Change makes us re-evaluate our direction.

That's certainly the case in our corporate life this year. Our company has changed in a great many ways. We've added (number) new employees. We've opened new plants in (city) and (city). We've established more quality-control procedures to ensure that we more than meet customers' needs and expectations.

We've even changed our "home" here at headquarters. There's new decor everywhere you look as you stroll through the buildings—and we do encourage you to take your families around the grounds to show them where you spend your most productive hours.

I think we've even had a change of heart here at work. A new team spirit. There's a positive, can-do attitude, a new energy and commitment.

We as a company even have new hopes. We've become more aware of the world around us. As the map of the world continues to change, . . . and the globe shrinks each year, . . . our hopes for peace and prosperity for more of the world's peoples are becoming a reality.

So I ask you to contemplate these changes we see and feel at the holiday season—changes in homes, hearts, and hopes. This is a time for reflection and commitment. Commitment to improvements for individuals and corporations.

I want to leave you with a challenge this evening. I don't know about you, but I like the changes we see at this time of year. I like the smiles, . . . the sentiments, . . . the successes celebrated.

The challenge is this: Don't let the cold wind of January hit you like a hammer and pound you back into the routine. Let's commit to each other as employees and to each other as families to offer loving support and a positive attitude year round.

May you and your loved ones have a joyous season that always keeps life from becoming "routine."

Homes, hearts, hopes. Let's keep those happy changes alive throughout (year). Happy holidays.

Openings

GENERAL ICEBREAKERS

Good evening. Thank you for inviting me and putting me on the program in such a favorable time slot. At this early stage in this game, you are still alert and expectant of great things to come. We're 15 seconds into the program now. So far, so good.

□

Thank you very much. No, I know that most speakers say "thank you" to the audience at the end of their speech, but since I'm sort of a backward person anyway, I thought I'd start out that way. Thank you—I want you to hear that right up front so you don't miss it. I appreciate very much your efforts in . . .

□

Hello. My name is _____, and I'll be your emcee tonight. Maybe I'd better define that role before I fill it. You do know what emcee normally stands for, don't you? Master of circuitous tripe. That is, in between the speakers, they usually apologize for the boring ones and exaggerate about the upcoming ones. Well, I'm not going to have to fill that role tonight because the speakers we have need no apologies and no exaggerations. You'll come to your own conclusion that they are all superb.

□

After being hit on the head by a mugger, a traveler found himself wandering the streets of (city) completely addled. He approached a passer-by, "Sir, excuse me, but could you tell me where I am?"
"Sure, you're right in front of a McDonald's playground."

"Oh," the traveler responded, "You must be a senior executive in a large corporation."

Flattered, the man nodded. "How did you know that?"

"Well, your information is typical—accurate but rather useless."

I'll do better for you today. I want to give you some useful how-to's on . . .

◘

When I asked (name of meeting planner) how long I should talk, she said for me to take as long as I wanted—but that you would leave at 8:00. If that's the case—and obviously it must be, from the looks on some of your faces—I think I'll get started right away. I'd hate for you to stop listening before I finish speaking.

◘

As I began to prepare what I wanted to say tonight, I started to jot down some key ideas about [insert details about speaking topic]. But then the list got pretty long, so I decided to leave off the "nice to know" things and just concentrate on the "must know" things.

But then the list was still a little long, so I started thinking about your frame of mind at this time in the program and what would really be essential information after a week of meetings, several airline hassles, jostling around on the expo floor, and lots of spicy food.

So trying to keep all that in mind, I decided that the thing you would most like to hear is about ten minutes. No more than ten minutes of anything. So here goes . . .

◘

The old proverb that states, "Blessed is he who has nothing to say and who refrains from saying it" does not apply to me on this occasion. I have something of utmost importance to say. I just hope to say it well. I'll be straightforward. My message is simply this: . . .

◘

Very late the other night I was having trouble with a particular software program for my home computer and called the support hotline. And the person who answered "Hello" was only the night security guard.

I explained my whole problem to him: "I need a quick answer before this software drives me crazy. After I get the NET screen, I get a "bad command" message. I don't need a special mag card for that utility, do I?"

There was dead silence on the phone. And I mean I was frustrated. I think I probably shouted back into the phone to him, "Don't you know anything about your own software?"

"Listen," the guard said to me. "I just told you all I know about computers when I said 'hello.'"

Well, that's exactly how I felt when your program chairman called me to tell me your program theme this year. So I'll dispense with an attempt to seem literate on the subject of X, and I'll go to something I do have a little expertise on. And that's . . .

RECOGNITION OF DISTINGUISHED GUESTS (See also "Introductions.")

Chairman _____. Members of _____. Family members. Honored attendees. Friends.

◻

Welcome and thank you for coming. It's great to stand before such a distinguished and beautiful audience. And rarely do I get to say that, not having the privilege of speaking to predominantly female groups. And looking out over this crowd, I can say one thing for sure. Anybody who says this is a man's world is probably not too bright about other things either.

◻

I want to recognize one especially distinguished guest tonight. In this industry, his name has truly become a household word. He has been the catalyst and converter for [insert]. The (type) industry owes him its future. (Name), would you please stand and accept our gratitude.

◻

(Name) is with us tonight. Were I to list (name)'s contributions to our profession and community, the credits would be longer than those that roll across your latest movie screen. You've read them everywhere, so I won't repeat them tonight. Let me just say we're honored that you're here.

◻

The letters after (name)'s name sound like alphabet soup. Ph.D. CPS. CPAE. CPE. But I'll try to translate all those distinguished titles into plain English: This is one successful tycoon. Give him a hearty welcome.

◻

Don't you like suspenseful movies, those that keep you on the edge of your seat? Don't you like the part where the detective or the private eye cleverly gathers all the suspects and interested parties in one room and then suddenly reveals the true killer? Or the movies where, right to the very end, you don't know which of the nice guys will win the girl?

Well, I feel much the same way tonight. I could turn to several of you gathered here—(names of distinguished guests or honorees for award)—and say "You did it." Or, "You won." Or, "You have been successful." "You have done what it takes to make a successful career and a successful company." The rest of us have the utmost respect for your talent and your achievement.

□

I take great pleasure in introducing our distinguished guest tonight, (name). Her responsibilities are many and heavy. Among them, she is totally responsible for [insert], [insert], and [insert]. With great respect and admiration, I present to you (name).

SELF-EFFACING COMMENTS

I was certainly relieved to see this auditorium fill up at the last minute. The president and I both arrived early, talking about what to expect tonight. When he said that you usually had about 200 people and there were only four people here, I got a little worried. In fact, I just asked him outright, "Did you announce that I was going to address the meeting tonight?"

"No," your president assured me, surveying the empty audience. "But it sure looks like word leaked out, didn't it?"

Well, never mind. What I have to say is good for ten or 10,000.

□

Great. After listening to all of those wonderful things just said, I know exactly how a waffle feels when somebody smothers it with syrup.

Well, never mind. I've always had a sweet tooth. Just let me enjoy it. As you can imagine—where I'm concerned—such introductions are rare.

□

That meager applause didn't bother me. I've had the wind knocked out of my sails before. In fact, when the program chairman introduced me at an engagement last week, she said, "We have only one speaker today. So, when he is finished speaking we can sit back and relax and enjoy ourselves because the rest of the program is going to be entertainment.

◻

Thank you, (name) for those gracious remarks. About the only thing you didn't say about me was that I was born in a log cabin. And you were right. I wasn't born in a log cabin. But my family did move into one as soon as they could afford it.

◻

Thanks, (name) for that introduction. If I'd known I was going to be that good, I'd have gotten here earlier to get a better seat.

◻

Thanks for such an introduction. I think the three most difficult things in the world to do are these:

1. Hang on to a bucking bronco
2. Eat melted ice cream with a fork, and
3. Live up to that flattering introduction you just gave me.

◻

I think I should warn you at the outset—I'm just a mediocre speaker. But there's a bright side to that. You never know when you have a bad day.

◻

I know some of you had doubts about my being here tonight. The state of my health and all. In fact, after I sent in the photo they used in the publicity brochure, someone from your office called, quite concerned. She said, "Mr. (name), if you look like your photo, are you sure you're well enough to accept this invitation?"

◻

Before I get into my talk, I just want to remind you that I come free—no fee attached. And you usually get what you pay for. That reminder out of the way, let's talk about. . . .

◻

Speaking on the designated topic, I feel a lot like the bureaucrat who addressed a group of farmers about the government's policy on drought. After the program was over, the speaker asked a farmer in the audience how he thought the talk was received by the rest of the group. The farmer answered, "You did okay, but a good hard rain would've done a heck of a lot more for us."

Likewise, I don't know what I'm going to say that will lessen the impact of [insert]. But I'll do my darnedest.

◻

I noticed that some of you were already yawning before I got up here. But I'm not offended. On the contrary, . . . I take it as a compliment. In expectation of my talk, you were yawning to take in more oxygen to the brain so that you'd be more alert. So, if you yawn, as I get further into the talk, don't worry about it—I'll just talk with more fervor.

◻

Thank you for this opportunity to address you as a group. I've always loved motivational speakers, and now I am one. In fact, I still remember the first really superb motivational speaker I ever heard—(name). He encouraged us as new employees just embarking on our career to improve the world—to go out and establish a sound financial policy for business and for government, and to eliminate poverty and crime in the world. As you can see, the results speak for themselves. So, I feel fully capable of motivating you to do likewise today.

◻

That was such a glowing introduction I hardly recognized myself. But didn't it sound good? I can't wait to hear what I'm going to say.

◻

You know, you're lucky this is an after-dinner speech. They say that hearing is considerably dulled by eating—I suppose that nature's way of protecting us from boredom.

◻

I'd like to introduce myself—you'll see me listed on the program before you. I'm "speaker pending." If my talk's interesting enough, they'll fill in the real name later.

◻

You've heard of "Who's Who" listings. Who's Who in Science. Who's Who in the Arts. Well, I'm more in the category of "Who's He?"

◻

Some of you have probably spent a lot of time tracing your family history, your roots. But I never did like research. So I just decided to offer to speak somewhere and let the meeting planner and newsletter editor do that research for me. In that introduction, you've just heard and read more about me than I knew myself. You did a fine job, (name). Thank you. May I have a copy to send to my folks?

◻

Thank you, (name), for that wonderful introduction. Praise has many effects on man. It makes a wise man modest, but a fool more arrogant. Now, listen up, you dunderheads, and I'll tell you how to set the world straight.

◻

Hello. That was a wonderful meal, and I see some of you are still sipping your coffee. You may want to put those cups aside, however, now that I'm speaking—the caffeine may keep you awake.

◻

They say a prophet is not respected in his own country. Well, I'll have to admit that's so in my case. My own company sometimes has a less-than-high regard for my abilities to forecast the future in our industry. And as I was rubbing my Pet Rock, drinking my New Coke, and listening to my quadraphonic sound system, I tried to figure out the problem about credibility. Nevertheless, I have a few ideas to share about the future. . . .

◻

I want to begin by welcoming each of you and especially those of you I know personally. I only wish that my family could have been here. My father would have really enjoyed that introduction. My mother would have believed it.

◻

Thank you, (name), for allowing me time on the program. I promise to be brief—no matter how long it takes me to get my ideas out.

◻

Hello. I want you to know that I take speeches and pre-meeting promotional literature very seriously. In case you don't recall, your invitation promised, "The lunch will be delicious, the networking opportunities excellent, and the program brief." I can handle brief.

◘

As you may know, you don't pay speakers to address your group. And, of course, that's fine with me as long as I know your money is going elsewhere for a good cause. (Name of meeting planner) did offer me a small honorarium, which I refused. And she seemed rather happy because she said that you all contribute individually before each program. You'll be happy to know that she put the honorarium intended for me back into the group's fund. She said that contribution would bring you pretty close to your total goal—for a coffeepot.

◘

For those of you whose sense of guilt got you out of bed this morning after such a long week, I offer my admiration.

◘

I'm going to speak today about [insert program topic], and you're going to listen. I hope you don't finish before I do.

◘

As I stand before you, I can't help thinking about the man who was killed in a recent flash flood. He made his way to heaven, and at the Pearly Gates he was asked to give his case history—to tell the story of how he died and came to heaven. This he obligingly did. St. Peter thought the story so interesting that he asked the new arrival if he would agree to give a talk to the other angels in heaven, telling them all about the flood and his demise. The newly arrived resident of heaven was very much flattered, and he immediately accepted the invitation. As he flew away, a kind young angel tugged at the sleeve of his robe and said, "Sir, I think I ought to tell you that Noah will be in the audience."

That's exactly how I feel about addressing you this morning—a roomful of Noahs—on the subject of . . .

◘

Yesterday as I thought of this talk, I grew a little panicked because I know how valuable your time away from the job is. Taking out my notes, I tried to eliminate everything that you might already know about [insert topic] and concentrate on just the few important insights I might be able to add to your considerable knowledge.

So, in conclusion, . . .

¤

Thank you for allowing me this slot on your program. A keynote, after-dinner speaker. I'm flattered. Up until this meeting, I was just an after-snack speaker.

¤

Good evening. I appreciate the opportunity to address a group such as this, my peers in the industry. If I don't seem larger than life, it's because I'm not. But try to keep in mind that it's not I who speaks, but life within me. And believe me I've had an eventful life. I chose to make my own mistakes . . . to learn by doing rather than simply observing others' experiences.

¤

When I was first contacted about this speaking engagement, I got the impression that your conference organizers were searching for more than a chief executive officer. They were also obviously looking for someone who could adequately—and perhaps even eloquently—address the very complex topic of total quality in the American workplace. Naturally, I was quite impressed with my selection as keynote speaker . . . until someone told me the story of two little old ladies walking through a cemetery. They spotted a tombstone that read: "Here lies John Smith—a chief executive and a quality expert." One lady looked at the other and said: "Isn't it a shame they have to put two people in one grave."

Well, I *am* a chief executive. . . . But I'm really not sure about being an expert on quality.

—Marshall McDonald
President, FPL

¤

My parents didn't have much formal education, but having seen my report cards, they would catch the irony of my offering counsel to a roomful of Ph.Ds—and in chemistry, no less!

—Richard K. Long
Director of Corporate Communications
Dow Chemical

¤

I'm reminded of the fellow who was once introduced at a similar luncheon meeting as the most gifted businessman in the country—evidenced by the fact that he had made a million dollars in California oil.

When he rose to speak, he appeared a bit embarrassed. The facts as reported were essentially correct, he said, but he felt compelled to state that it wasn't oil, . . . it was coal, . . . and it wasn't California, . . . it was Pennsylvania, . . . and just to keep the record straight, it wasn't a million, . . . it was a hundred thousand, . . . and it wasn't me, . . . it was my brother, . . . and he didn't make it, . . . he lost it.

Matters of fact aside, though, I'm grateful for those kind words and for this opportunity to talk with you today.

◻

Before I start, I'd like to assert that I'm better than sunshine. Pardon me, but I just feel the necessity of saying that. After the last time I spoke, I heard a nice little lady walking out with her husband say what an inspirational speaker she thought I was. And her husband turned to her and snapped, "Thirty minutes of bright sunshine would have done me more good."

Well, that hurt my feelings, and I just want to remind you that the sun isn't out today. So there's no use making a comparison.

◻

Let me say at the outset that I'm considered a very good speaker. In fact, at my last engagement as the crowd was leaving, several came by, shook my head, and told me how much they had enjoyed the talk. Except for one old geezer. He shook his head and told me it was the sorriest speech he'd ever heard. Talk about embarrassed. I was. But then the president made me feel a lot better. He overheard the comment and rushed over to assure me, "Don't give that comment a second thought. That guy's a half-wit. He's never had an original thought in his mind. Just repeats what he hears everybody else saying."

◻

I'm really pleased that you invited me to speak in such nice surroundings. The accommodations and acoustics are wonderful. Not like the last place where I spoke. There was so much hall noise and interruptions that I couldn't even hear myself. Of course, a couple of attendees assured me that I hadn't missed much.

◻

I think it's important that you get to know me—my personality and all—before I start into my real speech. And, of course, in this kind of a situation, it's a little difficult to get to know each of you intimately. So maybe I'll just tell you a little about myself. I'm kind of a "life-of-the-party" type. But then I guess that gives you a pretty good idea of how dull the parties I attend are.

◻

I feel that I should warn you—you're guinea pigs tonight. Yes, I'm trying out some new ideas and I'd like your honest feedback when I finish. To tell you the truth, I'm thinking of writing a book on this subject, and I'd like to have your opinion after I'm finished. I've already talked to a publisher, who once commented to the press that every public speaker has a good book in him. When I phoned him to talk about my particular subject and expertise, I reminded him of his earlier remark. And he reaffirmed that belief: "I'm still sure that's true that every speaker has a book in him—and I think that, in your case, that's where it should stay."

◻

I've been selected as your speaker. You're my audience. It's my job to talk to you and it's your job to listen. If you finish before I do, let me know.

AUSPICIOUS OCCASIONS

Good morning. This is a very important day for all of us. In a few minutes, after this ceremony, you will no longer be "just a group of employees." [Or, "you will no longer be in the XYZ Building." Or, "you will no longer be employees of (company), but of (new company name)."] Instead, you will be part of a much larger purpose [or mission or organization].

◻

As you listen to these next comments, I hope you'll take them to heart because they come from my heart. For all of us, this day is of monumental importance. It marks the beginning of . . .

◻

We gather today at a turning point of our careers and our organization. We need wisdom, foresight, commitment, and patience to tackle the formidable task before us. That task is to . . .

◻

Welcome. This is a day of progress and growth. . . . Of giving and receiving . . . Of celebration and fear . . . Of zeal and commitment . . . Today is the occasion of . . .

◻

Today marks an anniversary. (Number) years ago we numbered our membership in two digits. We administered a budget of $X. We boasted completion of our first community project. Today, (number) years later, our membership has swelled to (number). Our budget stands at $X. Our organization has just completed its (number) service project to the city. Like all anniversaries, such victories demand celebration. Let's pause and give ourselves a hearty slap on the back.

◻

Today demands the attention of the entire city. Struggle. . . . Pain. . . . Patience. . . . Victory. These are the phases we've passed through to get to our present occasion. This morning I'm proud to announce to you . . .

◻

What occasion could get the attention of an entire industry? What progress could arouse the curiosity of old-timers who've "seen it all"? What novelty could trigger the curiosity of neophytes to the field? Answer: Today we are unveiling our . . .

◻

Today is an emotional one for many of us. And emotion is never something I've been ashamed to show. Emotion melts ignorance into knowledge, . . . gives passion to persuasion, . . . turns mediocrity into growth. I'm talking, of course, about the . . .

Closings

GENERAL CLOSES

Thank you for your attention today. The nodding heads, the smiles—it's very evident some of you are into assertive listening, and I've appreciated that. Good night and good work.

□

I wish you all good health, great happiness, and glowing success in whatever situation you find yourself.

□

Thank you for attending tonight. The concern you have shown by your presence has been a very meaningful gesture to all those involved. On their behalf, I again say thank you.

□

Well, there you have it—my news, my philosophy, my experience. It's up to you to improve on it—and I hope you will.

□

Now comes the hard part—it's time for you to think. I ask that you think briefly about [insert]. That you think hard about [insert]. And finally that you think creatively about the future. With all my best wishes. The rest is up to you.

□

Have a good night and a good life.

◻

I hope we've grown together tonight in our sharing and in our understanding of this situation. Voicing the issues has certainly brought us closer to resolution.

◻

As so many before me have added to my life in similar ways, I hope I've added to yours in some small way. God bless.

◻

I don't think I'll ask for a show of hands of those who can now explain all the intricacies of (subject). But if you're still confused, at least I hope it's because of a broader knowledge base. Thank you for your patience on this complex issue.

◻

I want to close by expressing my appreciation for your participation tonight. Your encouraging nods. . . . Your questions. . . . Your examples. . . . You have made my job very pleasant and I thank you.

◻

If there's one thing we in this room can all agree on, it's that you've done an excellent job of sharing your feelings with each other. I hope I've been equally enlightening with new information you'll find useful. Let's thank each other.

◻

I want to say thank you for your time and your emotional energy in listening to what I've had to say. Please continue to give it some thought. That's all I can ask.

◻

Thank you for your generosity in allowing me this forum today to share my ideas with you. I trust that we'll both reap some benefits from the exchange.

◻

Thank you very much for the recognition you've offered me by inviting me to address you tonight. With sincerity I say that it has been an honor for me.

□

As we celebrate together, let's remember that tonight is more than an event. We are part of a much larger process—a process of learning, growing, creating. I look forward to what the future holds for all of us.

□

The food has been good, the networking better, and the program best. I thank each of you who've had a part in making this a memorable evening. Have a safe trip home.

□

Thank you for your enthusiastic attention—at least, it has seemed that way from my vantage point. I hope I've helped to make the path a little clearer and the future a little brighter.

□

This event has been our way of saying thank you for your commitment to the organization and your caring—so freely offered to the community. We hope you and your families have enjoyed the evening. Thank you for sharing with us on this occasion.

□

After this last half hour, I simply can't identify with a former Congressman of mine. After one of his political rallies, a constituent came up to him and said, "Mr. Congressman, I've heard you talk for almost an hour now, and I still don't know where you stand on the issue."

"Fine," the Congressman said. "It took me two days to write it that way."

It took me almost as long to prepare for tonight, and, unlike the Congressman, I've intended to be *very* clear. This issue is important to me and to you.

□

Let me remind you of the father who always wrote a note to the teacher on his son's first report card each semester. "The opinions expressed by this child are not necessarily those of her father's side of the family." The opinions I've expressed tonight are not necessarily those of my entire organization; they are my own. But I hope you'll agree that each of us must make up his or her own mind about these issues and then express those opinions to influence whomever we can. Change is inevitable.

◻

Let's never look back unless we're planning to head that way.

◻

In closing, all I ask is that you consider thoughtfully the ideas I've shared. Mull them over while you're waiting in line at the supermarket check-out or sitting in traffic. Ideas have a way of growing on you. I hope this one will take deep root and have a significant impact on your future.

◻

In thinking of our heritage and what I've tried to say here tonight, remember your spelling. *American* ends with four profound and prophetic letters, "I can."

CALLS TO ACTION

Your attentive support has made my job rather easy tonight. I've tried to share four ways to [insert]. In return, I hope you'll spread the message to your colleagues and friends.

◻

I know that we've all been told that there's nothing much we can do about the situation. Many of us may feel like the little girl who kept standing up in the front car seat. Finally, her mother pulled the car off onto the shoulder of the road and yanked the child down in the seat, fastening her into the seat belt. The little girl pouted and then after a minute snapped at her mother, "I may be sitting down, but in my heart I'm still standing up."

Well, I identify with that feeling. This situation has us sitting down, but in my heart, I'm still standing up. And I'm asking that each of you stand up with me. I challenge you to find a way to change things at every opportunity.

◻

As I see it, we're all in this together. We're at a decision point as a group and as individuals. We can sit and think. Or we can band together and act. I prefer to act. How about you?

◻

I've not really said all I want to say on this subject, but I'm going to stop because my plane takes off in exactly two hours. However, I hope you'll take off on these ideas immediately—within the hour. Tell a friend.

◻

Thank you for your invitation, your attention, your support. All that remains is your action.

◻

I'm tired of hearing the same answer to every question: "It depends." If you, too, are ready for some straight answers, demand them. I encourage you to get vocal every chance you get.

◻

I think many of us feel like the executive who had employees waking him up before dawn one morning. One called about a problem in Detroit and asked him to get on a plane and come help him out. Before he could get dressed, another one phoned from the plant across town to tell him about another problem and to ask what to do. Within the next hour, he'd had three more such calls. Without breakfast, he hurried out to the garage to find that his car wouldn't start. So he called a taxi. And when the taxi driver pulled over and asked him where to, he muttered, "It doesn't matter—they've got problems anywhere you take me."

If we're honest, we'll have to say that our organization has problems—lots of them. And any of them can use our attention.

But my suggestion is that we get focused. I've tried to outline here today four key steps we need to take immediately. I challenge you to get their address and head in that direction.

◻

Together we can accomplish great things—things more important and more meaningful than I've even outlined here tonight. You will be the final source of those good ideas. You will be the driving force that launches us in the right direction. More power to you.

◻

Write. . . . Phone. . . . Fax. . . . Throw a tantrum in the middle of the street. . . . But do *something*. Your job depends on it.

SELF-EFFACING COMMENTS

From the looks on a few faces, I think you're about through with my talk. All you have to do to get me to sit down is to start clapping. . . . Did I hear someone applaud? Thank you. (Be seated.)

□

(Glance at your watch.) My, my, how time flies when you're having fun talking . . . and philosophizing . . . and telling people how to set the world straight. Here it is, already eight fifty-eight and three quarters. Let's call it a night.

□

Well, I'm finished with what I had planned to say. Before I sit down, does anybody have a present for me? I don't mean to be presumptuous or anything, but at the last place I spoke they gave me a new stereo system. Well, not exactly. They gave me an extension cord and said that the next time they invited me back, they'd give me the stereo to go with it. (Glance around.) No gift? Well, thanks anyway.

□

In wrapping up my talk, let me say that I'm a little disappointed about tonight. There are two people in the audience—former colleagues of mine whom I'd asked specifically to attend to give me their opinion on the talk. Both have gone to sleep. But then I guess sleep *is* an opinion. Maybe I'll just keep polishing on this talk before I wake them.

□

Well, it's ten o'clock and you're still here. (Glance at meeting planner.) (Name), I don't know what to do now. You see, here was our plan. If you were still here after dinner, (name) was going to talk about [insert]. Then if you were still here at eight, (name) was going to talk about [insert]. Then if you were still here at nine, I was supposed to give you my views about (subject covered). And then if you were still here at ten—we didn't discuss what to do then. But, not to worry, I have a wallet full of grandbaby pictures. And in the trunk of my car I still have slides from our Colorado vacation. Oh, . . . I see there's a little shuffling around now. Maybe we'd just better wrap this up without the extras.

□

Let me say in closing that I hope you couldn't tell I ate before I spoke. A former pastor of mine always used to refuse a meal when a parishioner offered it, saying "no thanks," because he had to preach later. And more than once I heard members of our congregation say that as far as they were concerned he might as well have eaten. Well, I didn't eat. How was it?

◘

I want to close by sharing one little theory I have. To me, the mark of a gentle, considerate person is that he or she listens attentively to someone with very limited knowledge tell him what he already knows a lot about. Thank you for being so considerate tonight.

PART II: GENERAL TIPS FOR SPEECHMAKING

General Tips
for Speechmaking

GAINING VISIBILITY FOR YOUR CAREER AND CORPORATION

A friend of mine, Larry Rogers, makes few waves in our social circle. Quiet and unassuming, he has been a member of our group for almost five years. But I'd bet fewer than a third of our acquaintances would recognize his name on a membership list. Smart? Sure. Successful? Sure, you should take a look at his paycheck. But nobody in our social circle has an inkling. Why? He never *says* anything.

But at work it's another story. I was conducting an effective writing seminar for a large financial services firm, when the participants' lunchtime conversation turned to communication skills in general.

"You should hear one of our VPs. Talk about the golden-tongue orator! He has everyone eating out of his hand. He gives speeches for just about every occasion, and audiences just hang on his every word."

"So, who is this guy?" I interrupted the amens of the others.

"Larry Rogers, our corporate lawyer. You know him?"

My mouth gaped. My friend, Larry, who said fewer than 50 words on any given social encounter?

Since that time, I've learned that on behalf of his company, he frequently addresses Wall Street, gives interviews to the national media, and speaks at corporate board meetings—not to mention the rah-rah speeches of day-to-day internal business.

Evidently, the two "split" personalities and reputations could be attributable to his taking communication skills seriously only on the job.

But what a major difference that becomes. Good ideas alone aren't enough; good ideas are floating around everywhere. If you don't believe it, listen to the cabbie who knows a solution to the city's transportation problems or to the techies who develop new software programs.

But if you never get great ideas to the right people, what good do they do? Ideas are only good if they can be communicated. Speechmaking catapults a professional to the forefront of his or her career, and speechmaking confirms success.

For the business person who aspires to motivate people, lead organizations, sell ideas, inspire creativity, and deliver quality, communication becomes everything. Nothing can light a fire to your career path or your corporation's profit like the visibility gained through speechmaking.

Think message. Think audience. Think results.

MAKING A SPEECH "YOURS"

If you've been in the workforce for a while, you've probably heard hundreds of farewells to employees, presentations of awards, holiday greetings, dedications of new buildings, and motivational speeches. And you've also noticed some general guidelines in this book at the beginning of each of the categories on such speech occasions. Obviously, there are similarities in these speeches and all those you've heard through the years.

So how can one of these speeches, or any other, ever really be uniquely yours? In the same way, old songs take on a new identity when they're performed by different artists. Do Elvis, Sinatra, and Sammy Davis, Jr. sound the same singing *My Way*? Of course not. The artist makes the crucial difference in three ways: audience, delivery, and attitude.

First, let's look at customizing for your specific audience. The key is immediacy. As Ronald Reagan so aptly put it about the tough economic times: "Recession is when your neighbor loses his job. Depression is when you lose yours."

Immediacy of your ideas to the needs of an audience generates attention and interest.

As a child listening to your parents tell you about all the starving children in China who would love to have your plate of spinach, you weren't too concerned with poverty. But after ten months without a job and only $188 in your checking account, poverty gets your attention.

Immediacy makes the difference.

When you read an article in Sunday's newspaper about the cost of funerals in today's society, you glance over the statistics, shake your head in amazement, and turn to the next article. But if your mother is dying of lung cancer and your siblings have already begun to argue about the funeral arrangements, you pay more attention to the options and costs detailed in the article.

Immediacy makes the difference.

Therefore, the key to gaining an audience's attention is not to speak to them as business people *in general*. What is their immediate interest in/need for/use for your information? To focus specifically, you need to consider the following:

- What is their educational level?
- What is their income level?
- What are their prejudices and biases about your subject?
- What are their problems?
- What do they fear?
- What are their challenges?
- What are their goals and wants?
- What's taboo with them?
- Will they appreciate humor or is this a solemn issue with them?
- What is their attitude about hearing you? Passive? Manipulated for having to attend or participate in any way? Competitive with you and each other? Unified with you and the others in the group? Resistant to your ideas and philosophy? Afraid they can't do what you're asking? Challenged to adopt your ideas? Eager to try out your information?

With the answers to these questions in mind, you can go a long way in customizing your remarks to minimize or encourage their feelings and reactions.

A second way you make a speech uniquely yours is your delivery style.

Psychologist and social scientist Albert Mehrabian has done an often-cited study that shows content accounts for only 7 percent of the impact of speeches. That's right, only 7 percent. So why did I write *Part I* of this book? To save you time. After all, you have to have *some* ideas to express in the first place, and these ideas here help you collect your thoughts in an organized, succinct format.

And your words in presenting those ideas can work for or against you. Simple words and short sentences help your audience grasp those grandiose ideas quickly. Remember that listeners don't have a written script, so they can't go back and pick up the idea they missed because of a long, tangled sentence. They can't check a dictionary for the word that totally blocked their thought processes.

A good speech involves much more than talking through the ideas in a recently published journal article or ad libbing a monthly report.

Had President Bush told the American people that he wanted a "more benign, more docile cosmos" rather than a "kinder, gentler nation," would he have carried half the country? Ideas and word choice count.

But back to Mehrabian's study: The other 93 percent of your impact while speaking results from your voice quality (38 percent) and your physical appearance (55 percent)—in other words, your delivery style. *How* you say what you say, not just what you say. You always have to decide what tone to take with your audience—that of expert, teacher, motivator, critic, or peer.

Translated, that means your delivery is a combination of who you are and how you present yourself. Do you want to preach to them or do you want a "we're all in this together" tone? There are occasions for both. Bush needed to overcome his "wimp" label. "Read my lips. No new taxes," did that for him. Granted, the idea came through clearly, but his effect resulted largely from his tone and expression—his delivery.

Consider your own voice and its impact on your audience. Can't you remember your mother's impact with these two very different statements and tone: "Billy Ray, Jr., come in this house right this very minute." Versus: "Oh, Billy—did you draw these pictures yourself?" Examine the content of these two statements: taken alone, the ideas are neither positive or negative. But you'd recognize the tone of each anywhere, right?

Delivery makes a difference.

Volume, pitch, quality, and pace give your voice its impact. In today's business environment, wimpy voices go unheard. Volume gets attention. Also, you want to aim for a lower pitch. Tension or relaxation in the vocal cords largely determines pitch. Stress makes you sound higher pitched, revealing insecurity and nervousness. Relaxation and confidence come across in a lower pitch. Authoritative voice tones are low and calm, not high and tense.

Voice quality involves such things as a breathy sound, a tense harshness, hoarseness, nasal tones, or a deep resonating solemn sound, slurring of words, accents, diction, and so forth.

Pace is the rate of speaking. You should know the pros and cons of both fast and slow deliveries to determine the effect you want. A fast rate reveals excitement and energy and commands attention so that listeners do not miss what you say. A slow speaking rate, on the other hand, adds drama and emphasizes key points.

And don't forget the use of silences. They effectively involve your audience in introspection.

The disadvantages to both slow and fast deliveries? A fast delivery may create difficulty in your audience's understanding your words and reflecting on your ideas. A slow delivery may give your listeners' minds time to wander. Worse, slow delivery may convey the impression that you don't know what's coming next or don't really have much information to offer.

With variety, you can achieve just the effect you want.

To add emphasis, vary your voice volume, pitch, quality, or pace: A deep resonant, precise articulation of the fourth-quarter profits followed by a slangy conclusion, "There ain't nothin' doin'." A quickly delivered rah-rah for the sales team, followed by a slow sincere thank you for their efforts. Variety.

Variety in voice volume, rate, and pitch also leads to an enthusiastic delivery. Don't equate enthusiasm, however, with hysteria. We're not talking about an unnatural acting career, a style that pits you against a football coach on the sidelines at the Super Bowl. We're talking about your natural speaking style—your natural speaking style when you're talking one on one to a close friend about your chance for a promotion and a huge raise.

Be your naturally enthusiastic self—only in front of a group. That's not to say that you comment on everything with the same fervor in your everyday conversations. "These files need to be updated to reflect last quarter's quotas" will not be delivered with the same feeling as "We just landed the $300 million contract with Universal!"

Those who argue "It's just not me" when encouraged to adopt a lively speaking style need only to hear themselves with friends around the lunch table. In such settings, most people have a lively voice and an animated face with glowing eyes and nice smile. Their hands and arms gesture appropriately without their giving any thought to the conversation at all.

So to determine what your *natural* style is, catch yourself while talking on the phone to a colleague about the latest Wall Street gossip, or the neighbor about the airport traffic. You'll hear your natural self. Feel what it feels like and hear what your voice sounds like when you're enthusiastic about your subject.

Think of your speech as a conversation with an audience larger than one. The idea is to duplicate that feeling, tone, and animation when you're in front of a group. That's the natural you, and that's your most effective delivery style.

Your delivery either supports or discredits your ideas. You may be completely serious about and confident with what you have to say. But the audience may perceive you to be insincere because of poor eye contact, a slouched posture, a bored expression, or limp gestures.

Eye contact is the most noticeable mannerism. If you want to make the audience yours, look at them. When you've caught the eye of someone in your audience, you've established a bond. You've signaled your interest in that person and your sincerity in what you're saying. In fact, we often hear it said, "I bet she couldn't look me in the eye and say that." It's extremely difficult to turn away from someone who is looking at you.

Use your eyes to build a bond with your audience, even though they may have heard your sentiments time and time again. Don't flit your eyes around the room as if they're afraid to land on anyone's face. Don't stare at your notes. Don't look around, through, or over your listeners' heads.

Simply glance around the audience and sweep in the view of everyone. Hold your eyes on different individuals to establish personal contact with them. Let your eyes fall on one individual, hold that contact, make your point, then move to the next pair of eyes. What the audience notices that you're said to Joe, they'll take as intended for them also. One or two sentences delivered to each person establishes intimacy for even the tritest words.

Your delivery—particularly your body language—conveys to your audience how you *feel* about them. That's attitude, the third way to make a speech uniquely yours.

If you sense a friendly atmosphere, you tend to walk and stand closer to the audience. If you're afraid, you cloister yourself behind a podium or table and lean away. If you want to shield yourself from challenges and establish authority, you can choose to stand on a platform, elevated above your audience.

Why do you think negotiators and heads of state spend weeks and months choosing just the right setting for their talks? Podiums, tables, or raised platforms put artificial barriers between you and your audience. Your audience wonders if these props are in place to protect you from them or to keep them away from you.

Here again, in your use of physical space as part of your presentation, your attitude shows.

Your attitude about your audience and subject also comes across when you choose either to memorize, read, or speak from notes. When you read, the audience often wonders if you believe what you're saying, if the ideas are yours at all. Unless you're a terrific actor, memorization can make you sound like a robot.

Speaking from a well-written practice script that has been learned and committed to brief delivery notes is the best of all worlds. (More about this technique later.) You have memorized openings, closings, and transitions verbatim, but can still present your key points and illustrations, using fresh wording and only a phrase to jog your memory.

Your attitude about the subject and audience also comes across with your openness to questions and your attention to the accuracy of what you say.

Consider integrity and genuineness. Audiences want to listen to someone they feel has the same integrity they have, someone who holds the same moral values, has the same problems, and the same upbeat attitude about life. They want to know that what they see is what they get. They want to believe you when you give facts, offer goals, and relate experiences. They want you not to hide behind your content—formal, emotionless, and indifferent.

They want to see your personal involvement with them and with your subject. If you're emotional because you really feel conviction about what you're saying, then you're on solid ground with an audience. When you feel that you are faking enthusiasm and sincerity, back off and cool down. Both you and your audience will be the judge about your enthusiasm, because genuine enthusiasm is contagious.

Whatever your ideas or your delivery, your attitude must reveal a determination to give value. How much salary are the members of your audience worth per minute while they listen to you? If you don't have the time to prepare, don't want to make the effort to customize, and don't have the proper attitude toward your audience or subject, then let someone else have the stage for this occasion.

To sum up: To make a speech yours, take stage when the spotlight falls on you. Approach the front of the audience with deliberate, purposeful steps rather than as if you were being dragged forward against your will. Stand with your weight evenly on both feet, get your bearings, gaze out and take in your audience. Greet them and then respond to your introduction, acknowledge the occasion, or simply begin your planned remarks.

Just remember that these first few seconds are crucial as your audience takes stock of you and your attitude about the occasion and the subject. Impromptu comments about something that's happened earlier in the meeting always impress your audience with your wit, your freshness, and your openness in departing from "scripted" comments.

And when you've finished, end with impact rather than whimpering to a close. When your ideas run their course, simply stop. Add nothing. Don't mumble. Just smile and physically "close up shop." Pause and sweep your audience one last time with confidence that they'll agree with what you've just said. Take your ending time as seriously as you expect airlines to do. Land on time and with precision.

To make the audience and speech yours, take charge completely. Use your posture, body language, attentive gaze to the audience, voice tone and fresh comments delivered in a natural style to convey to the audience that your purpose is to speak to them specifically.

It's your speech, you deliver it.

SELECTING THE APPROPRIATE SLANT, TONE, AND LENGTH FOR YOUR SPEECH

Generic subjects make poor speeches. Never attempt to give a speech with the "Big Black Hole Theory" as your message. You always need a context—a slant, tone, and length appropriate to the specific audience. The way you handle your message makes the crucial difference in the audience's acceptance or rejection.

Take the subject of sales quotas. Let's say the actual sales volume of your company has been falling behind projections by about 25 percent each month for the last four months. That's the information you want to convey. But you'll need to fine-tune that message even in the planning stage.

To the board of directors—

Message slant: The sales slump should have been expected because of new competition in the arena, a reorganization of the marketing territory, and the general economic slump in the state. We should have foreseen this slump and brought our projections in line with reality.

Tone: Just informational. Don't panic.

Timing: three minutes

To the marketing managers—

Message slant: We need to strategize about what we can do to generate an increased demand for our services and products—despite the economic slump and general market conditions.

Tone: Cautious warning. Let's work together on some real plans.

Timing: 30 minutes

To the salespeople themselves—

Message slant: If any sales force in this industry can turn the situation around, you can. We believe in you, and we're going to give you all the help we can to fight the new competition and to increase market awareness of our products and services. Here are four key benefits we want you to emphasize to your prospects. . . .

Just let us as managers know what else we can do to help you. You can do it. Go get 'em.

Tone: Motivational and didactic. Serious, but upbeat.

Timing: one hour

If you don't know what your goal is in delivering information, neither will your audience.

If you've kept in mind the "one page equals two minutes" rule as you've prepared, you probably have the total length about right. But one more consideration: Timing should underscore emphasis. Have you spent only one minute on a major reason to spend $10,000, and seven minutes on an anecdote in the speech introduction? If so, now is the time to reshuffle your information so that timing corresponds to the importance of the idea.

To emphasize a key idea, elaborate. Add facts, statistics, quotes, anecdotes, or other details. To lengthen the entire speech, come up with additional key points. Don't simply try to add more words to the points already well made.

On the other hand, you may discover that you need to cut some information. Always keep in mind the audience's interest. Think of your speech as a road map. If your audience wants to take only the interstate highways to get to their decision destination, don't draw in all the farm-to-market roads along the way. You'll merely clutter the map.

When your speech runs too long, you'll be tempted to cut the flesh and leave the skeleton. That is, you'll want to retain all your key points and omit the stories, quotes, visuals. Don't. Remember that these tidbits make your main points memorable. It's far better to make one point memorable and useful than to present seven key ideas the audience forgets before they walk out the door.

Sometimes you can condense your presentation without leaving out substantive ideas by simply improving sloppy wording. If you've written a draft, keep the language tight. Note how succinct the quotes included in these model speeches are. For a stronger impact, convey ideas in nouns and verbs; avoid the adjective and adverb clutter. For a stronger impact, count on nouns and verbs.

If you're writing a script either for practice or delivery, remember that one page (about 250 words) is about two minutes of spoken delivery. To be accurate, read and time your presentation several times. Keep in mind that you tend to present your talk more quickly in rehearsal than in real life. So always leave yourself a safety net. Count on the fact that a written presentation will take longer to deliver with ad libs, visuals, audience reaction, and extemporaneous comments that the audience evokes.

As you prepare and practice, record on your outline or script the timing of each portion—especially long anecdotes. Distractions, late starts, questions, and other interruptions may force you to do some on-the-spot adjustments to end on time. These notations help you make those spur-of-the-moment decisions about what to eliminate or add if you run long or short during the actual speech.

Nothing endears you to an audience like brevity. Every moment past your allotted time builds frustration.

As you can see, your slant, tone, and timing are built-ins—not add-ons. Always have these in mind as you determine key points, select illustrations, and work on phrasing. Slant, tone, and timing become your drawing board.

DEVELOPING THE BEST ANECDOTES AND ILLUSTRATIONS

When running short on time, beginning speakers will generally cut the anecdotes and the illustrations from the speeches. Just give the audience facts, they tell themselves, the rest is fluff.

Not true.

Anecdotes and illustrations make ideas understandable and memorable. They give vague concepts specific interpretations. We don't understand the "bad economic climate" until we know that means our relatives can't sell their house in Dallas, . . . that the computer company won't deliver the equipment unless we prepay the invoice, . . . or the tax base for our child's school has declined by $40 million dollars.

Always prefer to cover two points with several illustrations rather than to cover ten points with no illustrations. Anecdotes and illustrations breathe life into your sentiments.

The important question then is not whether to add or to omit illustrations, but which ones have the greatest impact. For the most part, the best are those that are brief, personal, and closely related to your specific audience and subject. Those that also appeal to the emotions are a bonus.

BRIEF: In general, the longer the story, the better the punch line or the emotional wallop must be.

Don't confuse speechmaking with lovemaking. In lovemaking, the longer the romance and anticipation, the greater the satisfaction. Just the opposite is true in giving a speech. Anticipation of a point or punch line can build hostility in the reader. When an audience tunes into a story, they are making an investment of time in its outcome; the details along the way are rarely significant within themselves. When your listeners get to the end of the story, they must feel that it has been worth their investment of attention.

On the other hand, to convey the major idea of your speech, a long story may be far more memorable because of its length and perceived importance that bears its telling. I once told an eight-minute, blow-by-blow narration on a speaking tour across the country to illustrate one major point—poor customer service. I wanted the audience to feel the growing frustration of such a lengthy ordeal. But such a lengthy anecdote for one point is rare.

Length conveys importance of the idea. Don't mislead your audience with a long story for a short point.

PERSONAL: Search for the story or illustration that you can make your own. Of course, source books of biographical sketches, quotes, and maxims serve as excellent references for one-liners. And you can start your own anecdote file with clipped articles, stories, cartoons, and statistics as you read newspapers, magazines, and journals. One tip: File them by subjects you're interested in *as you go*; illustrations not quickly retrievable are of little value to you.

If you choose a "canned" story or illustration, then personalize it. If you're talking to accountants, the hero in the story becomes a number cruncher. The buffoon of your punch line becomes your Uncle Joe rather than "the farmer." The department store may become a computer shop.

But there is no substitute for the personal experience story—your experience or that of a colleague or acquaintance or your real Uncle Joe.

Don't say that computers have increased rather than decreased the paper blizzard that floods our office. Instead, tell me how many documents *your* office generated in the process of correcting an incorrect billing on the Hooker account.

Don't say that quality service should be the aim of everyone in your organization. Instead, tell me how a rank-and-file employee, such as Joan Croy in your office, discovered a defective gadget in Customer Jones's typewriter and repaired it on the spot during her lunch break when she was technically off the clock.

Illustrations—whether anecdotes or statistics—carry far more weight with audiences because they are woven of common people, common circumstances, and common feelings.

For example, a headline from the Scripps Howard News Service reads: "Taxes cost 163 minutes for every eight working hours." That puts the "high cost of taxes" in perspective; we work almost three hours out of eight to pay them. Then the writer goes on to illustrate other facts: Food and tobacco cost 59 minutes; transportation, 40 minutes; medical care, 39 minutes; clothing, 24 minutes; recreation, 20 minutes; and all other expenses, 50 minutes.

Bombarding your listeners with numbers confuses them so that they recall none. To make those you select meaningful, bring them within the understanding of your audience. Make them personal.

RELATED TO SUBJECT: In addition to being brief and personal, a statistic, anecdote, or other illustration must be closely related to your point. Most speakers violate the "illustrations must be related" rule when they are searching for humor. Yes, humor adds a light touch to an occasion and gives audiences a warm fuzzy feeling of a shared laugh. But humor for humor's sake rarely works. Use humorous stories only if they relate to your point. And if you tell a long story, you're getting more impact for the minutes if more than one detail of the illustration or anecdote makes a point.

In selecting related statistics as illustrations, use them with care. That means they should be up to date and relate to your audience's current needs and circumstances. Nothing destroys credibility like having numbers that are ten years old.

Also, make sure your statistics aren't misleading. If your competitor's profit increased by 400 percent last year, that may mean that he sold four quilts rather than one. "Averages" are often deceptive. You can describe a hiker crossing a desert at 125 degrees and then plunging into a mountain stream at 41 degrees, and conclude that the temperature on his vacation averaged a pleasant 83 degrees.

Be wary of using too many statistics and round off the ones you select. Just remember that it's easier to gather statistics and facts than to make them relevant and memorable. Don't get sidetracked on the first and omit the second.

EMOTIONAL: Make them laugh or make them cry. Nothing makes you or your message more memorable than an emotional appeal. If fund raisers want contributions, stories about orphans and disease move people toward their pocketbooks. If sales managers want to get through a difficult customer's door, they make their sales reps laugh until the task seems like challenging fun.

Humor helps in almost any speech situation. Why? Because humor gives us a personal identification with the feelings of the audience. Humor makes you a human and approachable speaker—not robot-like. He laughs; therefore, he is.

You can add a humorous touch with a joke or one-liner. But, again, the funniest stories are usually your own personal experiences told with pizzazz you've practiced. The TV show Candid Camera and a similar show based on home-video shots have made millions off the fact that people love to laugh at ordinary people caught in funny, everyday circumstances.

Be concise, be personal, be relevant with your stories and statistics. For a bonus, add emotion.

ADDING FLAIR TO YOUR WORDS

Have you ever seen a novelist's first draft or a speech writer's first script? If so, then you know that an excellent speech represents several drafts of hard work. I once heard prize-winning short-story writer Grace Paley laugh about the problem when she was supposed to be the expert. "I try to let my students see my own struggles with rewrites. Sometime I even take one of my own drafts to class—it's usually somewhere around the seventh or eighth draft, but, of course, I tell them it's the first."

Force Yourself to Edit

If you're an excellent speaker, you'll never be satisfied with a first draft. Editing paves the road to perfection.

First, in editing be aware of the subtle differences between the written and spoken word. As a writer, you can use longer sentences and a multitude of sentence patterns. You can also decide to be formal or informal in word choice and tone.

By contrast, as a speaker, you need to use shorter sentences, simpler words, and easy-to-hear words. The best speakers also use a less formal tone—contractions and the "you" approach.

A president may *write*: "Finally, corporations must examine one remaining classic manufacturing enterprise, namely, the production of major household appliances found in most cultures around the world."

But she'll be wiser to *say*: "Let's take a look at a classic manufacturing enterprise—appliances such as refrigerators, washers, garbage disposals. You'll find them everywhere."

The difference makes it apparent why we have so many deadly speeches: Many speakers try to "present" an article published in some journal or monthly sales report to the board of directors.

If you want a good feel for the differences in your own spoken and written words, select a written report and read it aloud so your ear can help you with the tone. (If you need a prop, hold the telephone receiver and pretend you have another person on the line.) Ask yourself: Would you really *say* those words? If not, change them for a speech.

Another consideration in determining speakable words is the use of foreign phrases and other difficult-to-pronounce words. Former president Lyndon Johnson was notorious for making his speechwriters change words that he found difficult to say.

We all have them. In recording an audio series for Nightingale-Conant, I discovered that I couldn't say the word *error*. After two days of trying to correct the problem, we had to replace every occurrence with *mistake*. So consider having a friend make you aware of words you may have been stumbling over or mispronouncing for years. A friend's cor-

rection is much less embarrassing than an audience member's mention of
your goof.

As a final consideration in your editing, add emotional appeal. Some
words sound like their meaning. For example: "She *harangued* him and
hammered at his confidence." Or: "She *clobbered* the intruder." The hard
sounds help convey the meaning.

Choose words that are specific and visual, words that make the listener
feel: For example, here's a ho-hum sentence: "Accountants prefer to eliminate
these retirement benefits for our elderly." An emotionally charged example:
"Beancounters want to cut off the money to your retired grandparents."

Ho-hum: "Withdrawal of capital can be quickly achieved with these
alternatives to lobby service." Improved: "You can dash right up to the
automatic teller, get your money, and be on your way."

As you edit, also cut out the fat. Think lean.

Judge for yourself what editing does for the following speech excerpt.

~~Your own~~ Enthusiasm *is your* ~~serves as an~~ investment in ~~Whitall~~ *your*

customers. If you ~~do not~~ *don't* feel comfortable in investing ~~your~~

~~enthusiasm and energy~~ in them, ~~and their needs at their corpo-~~

~~rations,~~ how can ~~these same people~~ *they* feel comfortable in investing

in ~~the things you sell to them?~~ *your product?* An Enthusiastic ~~attitude~~ is con-

tagious ~~to those around us in the marketplace.~~ And unfortu-

nately, *so is it,* the lack of ~~enthusiasm is also contagious. No matter~~

~~what creates your feelings of~~ *Whatever the source of your* passion ~~or excitement~~—whether

you love to win or hate to lose— ~~people discover that there is~~ *you have*

power in ~~exemplifying a deep feeling of pride and~~ enthusiasm.

~~about what they do for a living.~~

And don't be afraid to show your customers that your power

and enthusiasm have made you *a* successful ~~person.~~ Everyone

~~you come into contact with~~ wants to be part of a success story.
So the more successful *we look and act,* ~~people dress, the more successful people live, and the more successful people behave,~~ the more *we* ~~products and services they~~ sell ~~to their prospects. People in the market to buy~~ *Customers* don't want to throw *good money* ~~their hard-earned money~~ after ~~unsuccessful sales reps~~ *bad people.* They *chase* ~~are drawn to buy from~~ enthusiastic,

successful people.

Remember Rhythm

According to some people, you'll never be a great dancer if you don't have natural rhythm. But that's not true with drafting a good speech. You can plod and clop along in a first draft and then go back and add the rhythm with a few simple techniques: triads, variety in sentence length and pattern, and alliteration.

Let's take them one at a time. First, triads. That's the use of three's—three words, three phrases, or three sentences. For some reason, people like to hear speakers talk to the beat of three:

> Thank you for your invitation, your attention, your support. All that remains is your action.

> Today is a day of progress and growth. Of celebration and fear. Of zeal and commitment. Today is the occasion of . . .

> He gave us hope. He gave us courage. He gave us love.

Triads work wonders for your style.

A second consideration is sentence construction. Sentence pattern and length are to writing what inflection is to speech. When sentence patterns are inverted, cumbersome, and long, even the most skilled speakers have difficulty in breathing in the appropriate places and inflecting the appropriate ideas. That doesn't mean that you'll never have a long sentence in your speech text. You may. But it should be preceded or followed by a short one that packs punch and gives your listener time to catch up.

Sentences that are parallel also add beauty and help the audience anticipate and follow equal ideas:

We gave for varied reasons: That the lonely could find companionship. That the bereaved could find comfort. That the frightened could find peace. That the sick could find health.

We are one nation—black, white, brown. We are Protestants, Jews, and Catholics. We have Irishblood, Indian blood, German blood. We are intellectuals and of common thinking. We are lighthearted and somber. We are engineers and beauticians, artists and plumbers. We make our home in the East and in the West. We are liberal and conservative, rich and poor.

Finally, don't forget how easily you learned nursery rhymes and how easily you still recall song lyrics. Why? For the most part, they rhyme. The technical term for that is alliteration—repeated sounds in words.

Here's an excellent line from a speech delivered by James Baker, CEO of General Electric:

U.S. business faces a threefold choice in the eighties: automate, emigrate or evaporate.

And another from C. J. Silas, CEO of Phillips Petroleum:

A generation ago, we feared tornadoes more than terrorists, . . . Cholera more than crack, . . . and anthrax more than Amtrack.

Others:

Americans eat peppermint and pistachio. They listen to Mozart and Michael Jackson. They drive Cadillacs and Camaros. To Americans of our century, freedom means an array of choices—from lifestyle to livelihood.

We wish you health, happiness, and hope.

To add punch to your own speeches, make ample use of triads, alliteration, and sentence patterns that are both varied and, on occasion, parallel—depending on the effect you intend.

Like dancers with fancy footwork, those people who "have a way with words" have learned these simple techniques to add rhythm to their speeches. The result is music to an audience's ears.

PRACTICING YOUR DELIVERY

To Write or Not to Write a Complete Script?

That's the question. For assurance that the words will come when you need them, many speakers like to have a complete draft in hand. A draft helps you time a speech and polish your prose.

If you choose to draft a version, try dictating it so that your sentences and choice of words will be closer to being usable than those from a draft that has been composed by writing. Then edit your draft, using the techniques mentioned in the previous section.

Once you've polished the prose, you're ready to throw away the script—almost. You want your polished draft for your *practice* but not necessarily for your *delivery*. And your practice will depend on your delivery method. Let me elaborate:

To Read or Not to Read Your Script?

Reading from a full script, speaking from an outline or notes, and memorizing—these are your delivery choices until technology makes it possible and affordable for all of us to have a portable teleprompter the size of our pocket calculator.

Here are the pros and cons of each delivery method.

Reading from a Full Script

You'll be tempted to use this method because preparation time is less—if time is the sole issue. If effectiveness also matters to you, consider the pros and cons:

Pros—

- A script quiets your fears that you will go blank. Every single word in black and white in front of you provides a security blanket.
- Your timing will be perfect. You will know exactly how long each point takes, and with practice in reading, you will know that you can end on time.
- Your language will be more exact, precise, colorful, and grammatically correct than if you speak extemporaneously. You'll have opportunity to rework and polish each sentence.
- You'll have something "official" to give to the media if you're a spokesperson for your organization. Scripts are often necessary if you have to gain official approval of your exact wording from your company's public affairs officer or if you're otherwise concerned that you'll be misquoted. You can, however, always provide a written text to the media for their quotes and still deliver the thoughts extemporaneously.

Cons—

- You'll have little eye contact with your audience. No matter how much you've practiced your upward glances, you'll be tempted to read more and more. Particularly in the all-important beginning when you either win or lose your audience's attention. The reciprocity of the situation is lost. When you speak to an audience eye to eye, you have their attention because they have yours. When you stare at the script, their temptation is to reciprocate by looking at their own notes or glancing around the room at others' reactions.

- Your words lose their genuineness and intimacy. When you can't look your audience in the face, you lose one of your best techniques for credibility. The effect is the same as when a lover who speaks a language different from his sweetheart pulls a scrap of paper from his back pocket and reads, "I love you for your beautiful personality, your thoughtfulness, and your sensitivity." She gazes at his eyes while he gazes at the paper.

- You won't sound natural. Despite the skill of an experienced speaker, you'll have difficulty not sounding stilted—much like the "average Joe" testimonials on TV commercials.

- Your gestures will be nonexistent or contrived. To be effective, gestures should come from the gut. Reading stifles that unconscious signal to gesture where necessary.

- You'll be tied to a podium without the freedom to move toward your audience.

- You may lose your place. The danger is that you'll frantically find yourself paused in an inappropriate spot groping for the next phrase or idea.

- If it's an audience you know well, they'll contrast the way you usually talk and gesture with this different image and focus on the disparity between the two.

Speaking from Notes or Outline

By far, this is the most effective delivery method for the majority of speakers. Here are the pros and cons for your own evaluation:

Pros—

- You can maintain the all-important eye contact throughout.

- Your ideas will seem genuine and intimate because they will be spoken in your own spontaneous way with fresh inflection and emotion.

- Your gestures will be natural.
- Notes will provide you with an outline for security but freedom to move around and interact with the audience.
- You will have no fear to add or delete ideas, facts, or illustrations as necessary to suit audience needs or reactions. You'll eliminate the fear of losing your place and your poise or of trying to find a spot in the script to jump back in.

Cons—

- Your exact phrasing will not be as precise as when read from a polished script.
- Your timing will vary.

Memorizing Your Speech

The final presentation method is memorization.

Pros—

- If you work very hard to memorize a script verbatim with all the appropriate inflection and gestures, you will sound like a genius—although maybe a robot genius.

Cons—

- If you have a memory lapse, you will feel like an idiot and your audience will think you foolish for being so "unprepared."

How to Learn Your Material—Whichever Delivery Method You Choose

To Read from a Full Script

Whether or not you intend to use your script in actual delivery, prepare it for practice with inflection and timing. First, consider the layout of the page. Always double or triple space. For ease of reading, consider laying it out in two columns (as shown on the next page). Your eye can grasp shorter lines much easier than longer ones. That's why newspapers and magazines use short-line, column layouts.

Rather than our own death,
it is the death of our
friends that hurt us.

But it's not of death that
I want to talk today.

While good men die, their
contributions do not.

I have chosen to talk about
living and giving.

In a word, John was a man
who gave.

He gave us encouragement.

I've never known a decision
so heavy,

a deadline so pressing,

a crisis so confusing,

that John could not put a spring in
my step when I walked out of his
office.

He had a way of putting things
in perspective that made the
situation bearable, if not
actually beneficial.

He gave us time.

He attended meetings just to offer
emotional support when we needed it
with clients and bosses.

He handled paperwork that piled up
when we had to be out of the office
on other business.

He gave us laughter.

You may also skip extra lines between paragraphs to signal yourself that you're finished with an idea.

If you decide not to use the two-column arrangement, then you probably will want to add further markings to your script to help you grasp ideas in a glance and deliver them with the proper pace and emphasis: Mark a single \ to indicate a pause; mark a double \\ to indicate a longer pause. With a highlight pen, mark key words and phrases that need special emphasis. Choose certain colors to help you quickly grasp the layout of your ideas. For example, use green for basic key points, red for examples and statistics, blue for the introduction to a long anecdote.

As for ease of handling your script, don't break a sentence, paragraph, or list between two pages. And never type the script in all uppercase type; upper- and lower-case lets your eye quickly grasp where sentences begin and end.

Leave pages unstapled so that you can lay them aside more easily as you read each one. You may also want to insert margin notes for use of visuals, demonstrations, or other movements away from the podium.

If you plan to use a full script in delivery, always, always deliver your speech from the same copy you used to practice. Your mind will "photograph" chunks and the first words of a section will help your brain recall the remainder.

When you deliver your speech, don't try to hide your script. The audience will know you're reading, and trying to discreetly hide the script looks deceptive and silly. Simply slide each page to the side as you finish it.

Finally, concentrate on the meaning of what you're saying rather than the phrasing. With concentration on concepts, your inflection, pauses, and gestures will improve.

To Speak from an Outline Only

If you agree that the outline-only delivery method lends the advantages you need, prepare two kinds of delivery aids: a full practice outline or script (laid out and marked as previously described) and a brief delivery outline.

A practice outline is a detailed outline on multiple pages or note cards. Again, the benefit of such detail is that it serves as a memory crutch for practice. But the negatives are that you will fumble with the pages during delivery and refer to the outline too frequently, losing eye contact and destroying credibility. For your actual delivery, construct only an outline of key words on a single page or on a few note cards that will trigger your memory with just a glance.

Try what I call a half-and-half outline script: Write the opening statement and the transitions for each point in polished form. Then express the meat of the idea only in key words. Those ideas will remain spontaneously fresh in the final speech.

Here are a few other guidelines to help you handle your notes or outline during delivery: Always number any note cards, but feel free to reshuffle them as needs change. Note how much time each point or illustration takes so that you can make an on-the-spot decision about what to eliminate or add if time runs short or long. Memorize your opening, your closing, and your transitions between points.

No audience will mind that you use notes or an outline. After all, they want to know you're prepared. The issue is *how* you use them. To avoid depending on them too much, practice with your detailed outline. Then use only key words or phrases on your final outline to force yourself to look at your audience and deliver your points with conviction and freshness.

To Memorize a Script Verbatim

Prepare a written text (laid out and marked as previously described) and read it and reread it and reread it. Practice from the same script because your eyes will "photograph" copies of the page to aid memorization.

Break it into chunks and memorize one chunk at a time, devising some acronym or other mnemonic device to remind you of the correct order of the chunks.

My suggestion is not to memorize your script verbatim. You'll fear going blank, particularly if there are any distractions. Memorization also makes the audience uneasy. At first they marvel, and then they worry that you'll make it to the end.

But learning your material is a must.

Read your outline, notes, or script over and over. Read it aloud. Time yourself on each section and record the timing in the margins. Connect the ideas in some acronym and learn to predict the next thought before your eyes catch the next prompt.

Then stand in front of a mirror to practice so that you can see how often you are able to glance up from your notes.

After you've grown less and less dependent on your script or notes, memorize the opening, the transitions between key points, and the closing. That will allow you to maintain the all-important eye contact at the most important times—when you're making a first impression and your audience is deciding whether you're worth listening to, and at the conclusion when they fix in their minds how good you were.

As you practice, don't be tempted just to read through your notes without actually expressing the key ideas in complete sentences. As someone has said, "There's no substitute for scrimmaging." The time required to express your ideas aloud in complete sentences and in the correct order will add polish and confidence to your "real" speech. Particularly pay attention to your delivery of any funny stories. They, more than any other part of your speech, succeed or fail based on delivery.

Do it live, aloud, alone. Do it in front of a mirror, an audiotape, or a videotape. Video is by far the best because you will be able to see distracting mannerisms, poor posture, and weak gestures. If a video is unavailable, an audio is the next best thing. You'll catch irritating voice fillers (*aahh, uh, okay, right?*) and repetitive phrases (*Let me emphasize that* . . .).

Additionally, you'll become more aware of your rate of speech, the tendency to let words trail off at the end of sentences, mumbling, or poor diction. You will also note where to add emphasis and variety. Another benefit of audiotaping is that once you record your speech, you can listen and fix the material in your mind as you complete other tasks such as driving to work or eating. Tape. Listen. Rehearse again. Tape. Listen. Retape. You'll hear dramatic improvements, and, again, these improvements will build your confidence.

Finally, you can practice in front of friends, family, or colleagues and get their feedback. If they're interested, your enthusiasm and confidence will grow. If their attention wanders, you need either more practice or better material!

MAKING NERVOUSNESS WORK FOR YOU

If you hear someone say he or she isn't nervous before a speech, you're talking either to a liar or a very boring speaker. If speakers don't have a certain amount of anxiety, their adrenalin will not be flowing to push them to a peak performance.

The secret is to perform *despite* the nervousness, actually making it work for you rather than against you.

"Stage fright" often begins long before we're on stage. If you're like most, the condition overtakes you the moment someone phones to ask if you could "put together a few words for Charlie's retirement banquet" or "kick-off the district meeting with a little encouragement to the sales staff."

Fears come in all flavors. We fear that our information or comments are not exactly what the audience expects, needs, wants, or agrees with. We fear they'll challenge our authority or attack our performance. We fear making an embarrassing misstatement or omitting a key point or illustration that would render the entire message murky. We fear embarrassing ourselves in any number of ways, some rational and some not.

What shakes our normal confidence in our ability to perform on the job is the absence of feedback. In a one-on-one conversation, we get verbal nods, smiles, questions, and other encouragements that help us to communicate clearly. Before a group, that feedback comes to us differently. We simply have to be our own inner motivator to keep the energy and enthusiasm flowing.

So how do you tweak that nervousness and make it work for you in the absence of encouragement from a one-on-one contact? First, the physical things: Take a few deep breaths and exhale slowly. Let all the muscles in your body go limp, then tense them, then let them go limp again. Yawn, dropping your jaw and keeping your tongue flat against the bottom of your mouth. Suck in a few short breaths and you'll yawn yourself into relaxation. Take a brisk walk or jog before showing up at the event.

Second, the psychological things: How do you talk to yourself to rid yourself of irrational fears? Try these tracks: "What's the worst thing that can happen to me if I bomb this speech?" "Will the *Wall Street Journal* run a story about my fiasco on the front page?" "Will these people physically assault me?" "Who will even remember what I said three days from now?" "Will my career take a nosedive if I blow this opportunity?" "Will I never have another opportunity to redeem myself with another speech?"

In case of a poor speech, time is on your side. People quickly forget exactly *how* you said something and tend to remember only that you spoke. If you can live with the answers to any of these questions, your performance will be uphill.

When you feel those butterflies, get them in formation and visualize the swarm as a powerful push propelling you to a peak performance.

HANDLING DISTRACTIONS/ INTERRUPTIONS/HECKLERS

If it can go wrong, it will. If you speak routinely, it's simply a matter of time until you must deal with some disaster. The lights go out and plunge the entire room in total darkness for half an hour. The screen for showing the sales figures stands lopsided so that all your visuals look as though somebody wrote them lying down. Plumbers are next door pumping the water from the burst pipes. The carpenters are tearing out the wall at the back of the room. The lighting flickers, causing migraines for the people seated in the center of the room. The meeting next door scheduled simultaneously with yours boasts six sopranos singing the Amway "fight" song.

The only answer to these disasters is to check out every possible glitch beforehand. If you have disasters over which you have absolutely no control or no warning—such as a power failure or improperly working equipment—simply stop your speech and locate someone who can help.

If the distraction is outside noise, call an unscheduled break and see if you can deal with it yourself. If not, make a joke of it and continue. Continually referring to the noise and showing irritation increases the distraction. If you ignore it, your audience will generally follow your lead.

Being human, you'll find hecklers much more difficult to ignore. Keep in mind, however, that hecklers generally create audience sympathy for you and create hostility for themselves. If you can ignore them without showing irritation yourself, continue your speech and your audience will listen all the more carefully to what you say and sometimes "handle" the hecklers for you.

If hecklers do gain attention so that the audience can't listen to you, you can always ask them to give their name and their company before they state their objections. Hecklers are much braver when they can hide behind anonymity. But put on the spot to give a name and associate their organization or company with the disturbance, they seem to give their behavior second thoughts.

If the hecklers begin their harassment before your speech, try to make them see you as a person rather than a "company representative." Physically move toward them and make eye contact. Courteously ask why they are protesting. Your sincere approach sometimes defuses their hostility, regardless of whether it changes their views, and gives you peace during the speech. Remember that only you control the microphone.

When you find yourself in front of an out-of-control audience for any reason—freak accident, power failure, malfunctioning fire alarm—you simply have to let the air clear before you regain control. After the situation is again under control, tell a personal experience or joke related to what just happened. Or simply acknowledge the interruption, and then begin again. The audience will empathize with you and give you their attention all over again.

HANDLING QUESTION–ANSWER PERIODS

Next to the invitation itself, the offhanded comment, "Oh, by the way, you should allow a little time at the end for questions," is the greatest cause for concern for many speakers. Why? Several reasons: They fear not knowing the answer to a specific question. They fear that someone will question their authority or the credibility of their information. They fear stammering and faltering with unplanned answers. They fear a hostile audience or participant. They fear losing control of the audience and the situation. They may even feel "put upon" for being placed on the spot with an unpopular answer or an unpopular subject.

And any or all of these may cause embarrassment.

Why, then, should speakers put themselves through the anxiety of anticipating these predicaments and devastating results? First of all, the audience expects time for questions—as their God-given right to force the speaker to "meet the press" so to speak, particularly on controversial points.

But in addition to audience expectations and needs, questions also benefit you, the speaker. First, questions allow you to apply the key points specifically to your audience's situation. Audience analysis, of course, is part of your preparation, but questions give you one last opportunity to make specific application. Questions also provide feedback on how clear you were and offer a chance to correct wrong impressions. When you get an off-the-wall question, you immediately recognize that one of your key points has been perhaps misleading for or misunderstood by your listener.

Another advantage of question-answer periods is to establish further rapport with your audience. Your answers show that you care about individual needs and understanding. They show genuine goodwill in giving value to your audience. Here's your opportunity to be spontaneous and witty. And nothing shows your depth of knowledge, credibility, and communication skills as vividly as unrehearsed fielding of unplanned questions.

Finally, questioning periods give you "leeway" in judging the appropriate timing. Five or ten minutes either added or subtracted from your speech can be corrected in the time alloted for questions—a reassuring cushion for you, particularly on a first-time speech run.

Let's get into the mechanics, then, of handling question-answer periods effectively.

Anticipate and Prepare for Questions

Audience analysis, the first step in preparing a speech, should always include consideration of questions the group will have about your information and opposing viewpoints. Plan for these questions specifically in your question-answer period and prepare succinct responses.

Here's an acronym we use to coach students in formulating a strong, memorable, spur-of-the-moment answer:

    S = Summary (One-sentence summary statement of your answer)

    E = Elaborate (Key points to support your answer)

    E = Example (Specific illustration that will make the key points memorable)

    R = Restatement (Restatement of summary)

Question: "Do you think leasing space in this building will solve our overcrowding problem permanently?"

Answer:

(S) "No, I can't see leasing more space here as a permanent solution."

(E) "The extra space available is not suitable for the kinds of shelving we want to install. For another thing, the extra space does not open to the outside corridor, and therefore, the traffic to the registration desk will still create the main peak-hour waiting lines. And neither will the extra leasing space accommodate the additional 200 or so visitors we plan to have during the spring."

(E) "If you'll remember, two years ago we tried—with no success—to alter the traffic pattern by leasing more space on the bottom floor. People just would not walk to the end of the hall to take the alternate route. You remember Frank Tanner's comments about his people not even having time to *reach* the coffee machine in 15 minutes, much less get a cup of coffee."

(R) "So, no, I don't consider leasing more space in this building as a permanent solution to the overcrowding problem."

With this format, you should find it much easier to be a SEER and to think on your feet. The idea is to have a thinking format to gather and present your ideas in a concise way for maximum impact and recall.

One last tip: You may want to avoid a particular issue in your prepared remarks on the lucky chance that the matter won't surface in the question-answer period. But don't count on it. Be prepared with an answer or at least an acknowledgment of any opposing viewpoint.

Encourage Questions When They Are Slow to Come

Don't assume that if the group voices no questions there are none. Audience members hold their tongues for any number of reasons: They haven't shifted gears yet to active participation. They think that a question is stupid and that they should have understood your information the first time around. They may also think their question and your answer would be of limited interest and, therefore, hate to monopolize others' time for their own clarification. They may feel particularly inept at wording their question. They may not want to risk others' hostility with a controversial viewpoint or question. They may have understood your speech so thoroughly that they have no questions.

And your greatest three worries: They may not have understood your talk well enough to ask a question! They may have no interest at all in your subject! Or they may have written you off for credibility reasons.

To encourage questions, make sure your body language shows openness to the audience—upturned palms, wide-open arms, alert posture, raised eyebrows, a smile, movement toward the audience. All these gestures and movements show that you welcome their interaction.

Extend an invitation to questions with comments such as: "What questions do you have?" rather than "Do you have questions?" The least effective invitation is to mumble, "Are there questions?" as you glance up briefly, leaf through your notes again, or leave the stage.

Affirmations from you after questions ("Excellent question," "Thank you for asking that," "I'm glad someone brought that up because . . .") also encourage other listeners to take a risk with their own questions.

If you anticipate difficulty in generating questions, you can distribute index cards at the beginning or end of the speech, asking participants to jot their questions on the cards and pass them to the front. That way, you can weed through the cards, selecting the best ones. This procedure gives you maximum control and flexibility while still being responsive to the audience.

You can also generate questions with an opinion poll: "How many of you think that it would be feasible to raise this amount of money in six months' time? In a year?" They raise their hands after each. "Lisa, you responded on six months. What gives you that confidence?" Such probing relaxes the group, encourages openness, and starts momentum for expressing opinions.

Pose your own question: "A question many groups frequently ask and one that may also be of interest to you is . . ." Or: "A question Bill Maxwell raised at our last meeting may still warrant discussion. He wanted to know if . . ." Or: "An issue I didn't get into in my earlier remarks is . . . Do any of you have a particular concern about how . . . ?"

Or you may want to repeat questions or comments overheard at the beginning: "I overheard someone earlier express the idea that . . . How many of you agree?" This help on your part gives audiences time to consider their own questions and shows that you're taking their questions seriously.

Maybe most important of all: When you do receive a question, be brief in your answer. If you take ten minutes to answer the first one or two, some participants will fear antagonizing less-interested audience members by asking another question that may lengthen your speech another half hour.

Determine Whether to Repeat the Question

If the sound is so poor in the room that questions from the audience can't be heard, certainly you should repeat them for all to hear. You may want to repeat some questions, if not all, simply to give yourself time to think.

But to repeat a question in a small-group setting where everyone obviously heard is redundant and makes you sound like a parrot.

And you never want to repeat hostile questions because it's difficult to do so without sounding hostile or defensive yourself. The other danger is that you reinforce the negative thought or the opposing viewpoint in your audience's mind.

Maintain Control of the Audience

Set boundaries at the beginning of the session as to what kinds of questions you will take, the number of questions you have time for, and who will respond to each.

"I'll ask you not to bring up the issues of X and Y for security reasons." "We won't let ourselves get into the Z matter because of the current litigation." "I prefer to deal with questions only in the area of A and B rather than C, which headquarters can more appropriately handle." All these comments at the beginning set the stage for your control of what is to follow.

Then when someone asks an irrelevant question, you can defer the answer to a private dialogue afterward and not waste the group's time or seem unresponsive to their needs. You will also limit the occasion for questions unrelated to your topic or expertise.

And no one says that you must answer all the questions. If you consider a question out-of-line, confidential, personal, irrelevant, or of little interest to the rest of the group, you can always deflect it, reroute it, challenge it, or simply defer answering it. "I'm afraid that's out of my area of expertise; would someone else like to respond?" "Jack, I'm curious about why you're asking that question; didn't you and Mark work those issues out earlier?" "Do we really need to answer that question, or would it be more advantageous to focus on . . . ?"

Finally, take questions in turn and don't let a few monopolize: "I regret that we'll not have time to finish with all the questions from those of you who are so perceptive with additional thoughts. But we do need to wrap this up. I'll be around here for a few minutes if any of you would like to follow up one on one."

Listen to the Question

Listening to the questions may not be as easy as it sounds. If you're nervous, if you're lambasting yourself about a previous error, if you're worrying about the time, or if you're threatened by the hostile body language of someone in the room, it's easy to miss the point of what the questioner is asking. Poor listening may cause you to fumble a question you could have easily fielded.

Compounding the matter is the fact that the asker may give too much background or irrelevant information before getting to the real point. And the asker may not have a clear understanding of what his or her real question is!

To avoid giving an off-base answer, clarify with a probing question of your own: "Let me see if I understand your question correctly. You want to know if . . . ?" Or: "Is your question thus-and-so? Or are you really asking if it is possible to . . . ?"

Give your best effort to understanding the true question rather than concentrating on preparing your reply to contradict or refute the asker's viewpoint. Finally, show that you are listening with attentive body language, such as leaning forward, head tilted in reflection, with steady eye contact.

Think Before You Answer

Even when an answer pops quickly to mind, pause before rushing ahead. With frequently asked questions, it's tempting to give the canned answer when, with a little forethought, you can customize your answer, making it even more responsive to the asker.

To allow even more thinking time, you can use props such as removing or replacing eye glasses, taking a sip of water, striding to another spot in the room before turning to face the group, or tilting your head and rubbing your chin as if reflecting on the brilliance of the question.

You can also buy thinking time by commenting on the question itself: "That's a tough question." "That's a perceptive question." "I anticipated someone asking that and I don't know if I'm going to have an answer that you'll agree with or find completely satisfying, but . . ."

You may say honestly: "Let me think about that a moment" and then repeat the question to yourself aloud, "Ummm, what would I recommend if . . ." Such a repetition renews the audience's attention as they anticipate why the question required serious reflection.

You may refuse to answer at all: "I'm not at liberty to answer that now." "That piece of the puzzle is still in the works now. May I get back to you on that later?"

Overview Your Answer Briefly, Then Elaborate

The question-answer period is not the place to redo your speech. When asked a question, respond with a headline message, then elaborate very briefly. Your audience will understand the elaboration much better within the context of your overview answer.

Here are a couple of examples of this technique: "In a word, my answer is yes. Management is aware of the problem and we're trying to correct it. Last week, for example . . ." Another example of overviewing and then elaborating: "I don't think it's too expensive, no. It costs less than X and Y. Here's how I think we can finance the first phase . . ."

Direct the Answers to the Entire Audience

Begin your answer while maintaining eye contact with the asker, and then after a few seconds glance away and sweep the entire group. Direct the remainder of your answer to everyone and make your comments generic enough for their interests also.

Remember that you do not have to satisfy every questioner completely because some will never stop their follow-up questions. Others may persist in presenting their own viewpoints even after you've given your answer. Just make your point briefly, break eye contact with the asker, then turn to the entire group and ask for the next question.

Use Your Answers to Reinforce Your Points

"I'm glad you brought that issue up because it will give me opportunity to elaborate on . . ." realigns the question with one you really want or need to answer. You can also refocus the question to make it bigger or smaller: "The larger issue that most of the industry will be concerned with is . . . ; therefore, let me put my answer in a larger context." Or: "Yes, that is the big-picture problem, but let me bring it a little closer to home with the more direct issue of . . ."

Go in either direction with the question to reinforce what you think is the essential viewpoint or message of interest.

Polish Your Techniques
for Handling "Problem" Questions

Show-Off Questions

These are the questions asked merely to show the asker's own knowledge of the subject or accomplishments. Recognize the reason behind the question, then comment only briefly and go to the next question. If this kind of questioner persists, you may have to add a comment such as the following to keep him or her from monopolizing the situation: "I'm not sure I'm understanding your question in all this. Would you please ask the specific question again."

The asker will generally fumble into focusing on a question that you can answer briefly and use to regain control.

Off-the-Subject Questions

If the question is completely off the wall, you may simply gaze at the asker momentarily and then move on without a response at all—as if you didn't quite understand the point.

You may ask if someone else has a similar concern. If so, answer briefly. If not, ask for permission to hold the question until the end, "if there's time."

Or you may comment: "Interesting idea, but how does that relate to Y?" The asker will usually mumble that it doesn't and acquiesce or ask a more relevant question.

"That's interesting and something worth further thought, but right now I'd like to spend our time focusing on . . ." will usually put the matter to rest. Or: "I hadn't expected a question of that nature. May we discuss that later—just you and I?" The asker will usually be reinforced by the personal attention offered and you won't lose the rest of the audience.

Limited-Interest Questions

When possible, bridge from the limited perspective to the larger issue at hand: "With reference to your specific situation, my opinion is that . . ., but the larger issue here seems to be . . ." Continue by making application to the entire audience.

Ask: "Does anyone else here have that concern?" Pause and look around, then continue: "Well, let me give you a brief answer and let's talk about that later one on one—will that be more helpful?"

Then break eye contact and move on.

"Dumb" Questions

Don't chance cutting someone off with what sounds like a "dumb" question but may be a very intelligent one after all. Rather, the "dumb" question may be a result of advanced, complex thinking that may not have occurred to you. The question may be quite relevant and you simply don't understand the relevance because of limited expertise. Probe further to make sure you understand completely: "I'm afraid I'm not following the question. Would you explain further exactly how X relates to Y?"

Rambling or Long-Winded Questions

You may interrupt with, "Excuse me, but do I understand your central question to be . . . ?" Or: "Excuse me, but I think I now have the drift of your question. My response is simply that . . ."

Unintelligible Questions

If you cannot understand the question because the asker has a heavy dialect or is fuzzy with the wording, pick one phrase or part of the question to deal with and frame a question that you think he or she may be asking.

Multiple Questions

In response to long, complex questions· with irrelevant information thrown into the pot, you may have difficulty remembering everything that was asked along the way. When that's the case, either answer the questions you remember, answer the last one, answer the most important one, or ask the questioner to repeat them slowly while you write them down. Then respond one by one.

You can defer some of them with: "If I understand completely, you've asked me four good questions. Let me answer the first two and come back to the others later if there's time."

Hypothetical Questions

Be careful that you don't get trapped here. Express your disagreement with assumptions and say so when you think such a situation is highly unlikely. End with: "I prefer to concern myself with the real here-and-now in formulating policy on this issue. For the present situation, I still consider . . ."

Or refocus with: "James, we have so many real-life situations at hand that I'd rather stick with those concrete facts, if you don't mind." Or: "There are so many unknowns and variables in hypothetical questions that it would be difficult to give a meaningful answer to that concern. In the case of Z, is your interest more about . . . ?"

Forced "Yes or No," "A or B" Questions

If you can answer with a simple yes or no, do so. But if you prefer not to see the matter in black or white, say so: "I think we have to be careful here not to back ourselves into a corner with either answer. Either simple answer can keep us from seeing the extenuating circumstances that might alter . . ." Or: "I don't think a simple yes or no would do justice to the issue." Or: "I think we'd make a mistake to put it in either-or terms. There are so many issues that can affect . . ."

Finally, you can expand your options: "I think we have more than those two alternatives. Rather than A or B, a third possibility is to . . ."

Questions You Don't Know the Answers To

You may defer the question to someone in the room with more expertise in that area: "I'm not sure I can adequately elaborate on that. Jeff, will you offer your expertise here?" You will win respect for your honesty and the support of the more experienced person you deferred the question to.

Never be afraid to say simply, "I don't know. I'll have to check on that information and get back to you." And then do so.

Hostile Questions

If you expect hostile questions, you may request that all questioners state their names, companies, and titles before they ask questions. Some will think twice before they blurt out a hostile comment and risk associating it with their company. Anonymity is great protection.

Try to determine the reason for any hostility. By acknowledging and sympathizing with the legitimate feelings of the asker, you may defuse the hostility and help him or her receive your answer in a much less hostile manner.

The questioner's hostility may be a reflection of his business agenda or his personality and may have little to do with you. Simply let the asker vent his emotions, and then go to the next question after a brief statement of your opinion.

Some questioners use a pseudo-courteous tone to wrap a hostile question. If so, reply just as courteously, but without the sarcasm.

You may even try a little humor or drama before answering, such as throwing your hand across your heart as if you'd been shot. "You may have hit me on that one." Then proceed to answer as calmly as you can.

For frivolously hostile questions, you can relay the question back to the asker or to another person: "Mr. Jones, I feel uncomfortable in responding to that question. Maybe you'd just like to tell us how you would answer that question were you in my place?"

If you think the hostility is limited to one person's viewpoint, you can let the group respond on your behalf: "Do any of the rest of you agree with that viewpoint? Does anyone else want to respond?" The silence will be a great answer. Or you may add your own in a courteous way.

Don't feel that you have to refute the opposing view in great detail, particularly if the hostile view was not well supported itself. Simply comment: "No, I don't think that's the case." No elaboration. Your answer will sound authoritative and final and will put the asker in the position of being rude and argumentative if he/she rephrases and continues.

If you can easily do so, rephrase a legitimate question minus the hostile tone: The question is: "Why are you *demanding* six years' funding up front?" Repeat the question aloud: "Why do we think six years' funding at the outset is necessary? Well, first of all . . ."

Above all, do not match hostility with hostility; instead, try to remain congenial in your answer. The audience will almost always side with (or at least empathize with and respect) the person who remains the calmest and most courteous.

Remember that the way you answer questions will always be remembered more clearly and for much longer than the content of your answer.

Conclude the Question-Answer Period with a Summary

Don't let your speech limp to a close after the last question with, "Well, if there are no more questions, that's about all, folks." Instead, firmly conclude with your prepared closing remarks. Here is where you actually use your prepared closing—that pithy quote or challenging question that will leave your audience charged and ready to act. In fact, some speakers prepare two closings: the one that ends their prepared speech and leads into the question-answer period and then one that wraps up the entire session with high impact.

If you're lucky, you may happen to get a question that's a great lead-in to your prepared closing. If so, use it as impetus to your conclusion and you'll look even more eloquent and in control.

Maybe the very idea of questioning got off to a bad start when we as children were told never to question our parents' decisions or commands. And schools sometimes reinforce the idea that questions negatively challenge the instructor's authority. Certainly, we all remember the loud-mouthed smart aleck whose every question was a challenge. Or maybe we've seen too many *LA Law* dramas where the judge instructs the witness in a booming tone: "Just answer the question."

Don't let those experiences keep you from making your speech all it can be. Allow questions and watch your audience's mood, interest, and body language switch from low gear to high. Questions clarify, tailor, and reinforce your key message. To your audience, they are your statement of openness, genuineness, courtesy, and goodwill.

APPEARING ON VIDEO OR TV

The higher you advance in your career, the more likely your chances for appearing on camera—as panelist on an early morning talk show, as an interviewee on a newscast, as the "endorser" of a company training program, as the spokesperson for corporate policy and procedures regarding your latest merger or acquisition.

If your overall appearance doesn't command respect, your message will float into never-never land. Good looks and expensive clothing don't necessarily have to be part of the picture on the screen. But you must look confident, authoritative, and professional. Can you communicate all that simply through appearance? Certainly. Even before someone opens his mouth, appearance has created much of the total speech impact.

For on-camera speeches, you have to pay special attention to clothing, make-up, and gestures to make sure the real you gets translated on the screen. First, your posture and mannerisms: Most people notice that they have a rather stern look on camera. To lighten up your facial expressions, try to adopt an "amused" expression. That is, lift your eyebrows slightly and keep your gaze and chin turned slightly upward. Sit or stand straight and keep your gestures close to your body, moving your hands between waist and head only.

Be careful about sudden movements toward the camera—extending your hands or shifting your weight and recrossing your legs. Such gestures look aggressive and even make your hands or arms look much larger as they plunge forward. The camera greatly exaggerates wide, sweeping gestures and pointing figures, and may make you look hysterical rather than authoritative. Remember to keep your palms upward and open to welcome intimacy with the audience rather than crossing your arms defensively across your chest.

Eye contact is what generally throws speakers off-stride. When you are used to the warm feedback and encouraging nods of a live audience and instead face a cold camera, you tend to become mechanical yourself. Instead, force yourself to gaze into the camera as if into a lover's eyes. Caress the camera with your eyes to show sincerity and warmth.

Or try to visualize the camera as a colleague sitting directly in front of you, nodding or raising an eyebrow at everything you say. For practice, sit in front of a mirror and talk to yourself with gestures and all. See how you look; "feel" your facial expression and the warmth from the mirror. Your subconscious can remember that feeling so that it doesn't seem so foreign and cold to you in a studio.

Clothing is easier to handle because you can prepare ahead of time without having to account for nervousness and the resulting forgetfulness. Camera lenses have difficulty in balancing certain extreme colors such as black, white, and red. Also, you want to avoid fabric patterns that "move"—stripes, dots, plaids, shimmering prints. Plain colors at the center of the spectrum package you best for the screen.

If you wear glasses, avoid ornate ones that shine and call attention to themselves. Touch the frames with powder to tone down the shine. In fact, avoid any accessory that "stands out"; you want the audience to remember you and your message, not the necktie or necklace you were wearing.

Where make-up is concerned, the idea is to look natural. The days of the necessity for heavy make-up on screen are over. That means that you should avoid bright, shimmering colors in lipsticks, eyeshadows, and blush, which the camera will accentuate and "play with" to your disadvantage. Powder any shines on the forehead, nose, chin. Cover dark circles or shadows under the eyes, which will be even darker on camera.

In general, if you are understated in your own mirror, your coloring will be fine under the bright lights of the camera.

This attention to your movements and gestures, clothing, and make-up will add the polish that enhances your professional appearance and important message.

APPENDIX: REAL SPEECHES

"Where Have All the Risk Takers Gone?"

Recapturing America's Conquering Spirit
C. J. Silas, Chairman & Chief Executive Officer
Phillips Petroleum Company
The Forum Club of Houston
March 29, 1989

Thank you for inviting me to share my views.

Let me begin by saying how much I appreciate an organization like the Forum Club. You welcome a diversity of views. Yet you share a common goal: to enrich and improve this community.

You may not agree with what I have to say this afternoon. But I know that all of us would agree, as Sam Houston once said, "It is in the diversity of opinion that democracy may rest secure."

By now, you know that the subject of my remarks is risk. And in case there's any doubt, . . . let me assure you that I wouldn't be in the petroleum business for very long if I wasn't just a little bit in favor of risk. In fact, I feel so strongly about the necessity of taking risks . . . that I spoke on the subject last month here in Houston . . . at a meeting of the British American Business Association. My remarks that day focused on the U.S. energy situation.

But today, I'd like to address the business community at large . . . because it seems to me there's a nagging question that overshadows all of us. It's a question about risk. And it's a question I invite you to examine with me this afternoon. The question is this: "Where have all the risk-takers gone?"

Houston's a good place to begin looking for an answer. Many of you are leaders in this community . . . or pacesetters in the business world . . . because you took the risks necessary to reap the rewards.

At the same time, Houston and other oil towns like Bartlesville, Oklahoma—where Phillips is headquartered—are still reeling from the effects of careless risk: risk fostered by the belief that oil prices had nowhere to go but up.

Today, both Houston and Bartlesville are slowly coming back to life. But we seem to be more cautious than we were ten years ago—more content to lick our wounds—and less eager to jump back into the fray. What has happened in our industry is indicative of what's happened in American society.

Having been burned by Love Canal, Three Mile Island, the recent scare over Chilean grapes, and a host of other troubling events, we've exchanged free enterprise . . . for frightened enterprise. Henry Fairlie wrote an article called "Fear of Living" . . . which appeared in a recent issue of *The New Republic*. Fairlie calls our modern-day fear of risk "Strikingly an American phenomenon." He says, "In America, the threshold of tolerable risk has now been set so low . . . that the nation is refusing to pay the inevitable costs of human endeavor." And he goes on to say, "This morbid aversion to risk calls into question how Americans envision the destiny of their country."

We all know that our great nation began as an experiment— sparked in the fires of oppression . . . and forged on the anvil of risk. Our founding fathers declared their independence from the richest and most powerful empire on earth. And in so doing, they wrote that they would back their cause with their "lives . . . fortunes . . . and sacred honor."

Since then, our nation has grown and prospered because—in our hard-won freedom—men and women have been rewarded for dreaming great dreams . . . and for risking it all to see their dreams come true. Today, however, it seems that far too many Americans are demanding the impossible:

- We want all the advantages of our modern world . . . without any of the risks.

- We want a strong national defense . . . without actually having to serve in the armed forces ourselves.

- We want enough energy to run our microwave ovens and satellite dishes . . . without any power plants, strip mines or oil wells in our back yards.

- And we want our absolute safety guaranteed at every turn . . . without the government raising our taxes, and without business raising the prices we pay for goods and services.

Why are we drifting toward a riskless society? There are many reasons. I'd like to share four reasons with you—all based on fear.

Reason Number One: The fear of being poor. Generally speaking, you and I are more financially secure than our parents were. Not only do we earn more money, drive nicer cars and live in bigger homes, . . . but we have a number of safety nets that many of our folks went without—from health-care and retirement plans . . . to unemployment compensation. Yet, instead of easing our cares about financial ruin, . . . these safety nets seem only to magnify the possibility of ruin.

So we pad our safety nets even more:

- We demand more pay, . . . greater benefits . . . and bigger dividends.
- At the same time, we insist upon fewer taxes, . . . lower prices . . . and reduced insurance premiums.

The hypocrisy of this mind-set was captured well by the Apostle John . . . nearly 2,000 years ago in the Book of Revelation. John describes a church in Asia Minor . . . whose members bragged that they were "rich, increased with goods, and in need of nothing." John records the reply from Heaven, where the people are judged, not as rich, but as "wretched, miserable, poor, blind, and naked." In 20th-century terms, this church in Asia Minor was materially bankrolled . . . but morally bankrupt.

Our fear of being poor is one reason we're drifting toward a riskless society.

Reason Number Two: The fear of being sued. This fear has intensified over the last two decades. It affects business most directly—since business is the prime target of tort, or liability, law. But more importantly, it saps the strength of the American economy . . . and siphons the wealth from American consumers—the very people tort law was designed to protect.

Peter Huber has written a work called, "The Legal Revolution and its Consequences." In that work, he says tort law was "set in place in the 1960s by a new generation of lawyers and judges. . . . Some grew famous and more grew rich in selling their services to enforce the rights they themselves invented." Huber goes on to say that our desire to make others pay for our misfortunes . . . produces a hidden "tort tax" on goods and serv ices. This "tort tax" accounts for 30 percent of the price of a step-ladder . . . and 95 percent of the price of some childhood vaccines.

Last year, the Conference Board surveyed a number of the nation's chief executive officers. The survey showed that the threat of liability had led about half of the CEOs' businesses to discontinue product lines . . . and nearly 40 percent of their businesses to withhold new products. Let me share one example with you.

A few years ago, a leading manufacturer of a whooping cough vaccine announced that it was getting out of the market . . . because it could no longer afford liability insurance. Whooping cough used to kill 7,000 American kids each year . . . and infect 200,000 more. New vaccines have all but eliminated the ravaging effects of this illness.

Yet, the medicine is not totally risk free. About ten children die each year as a result of severe—though extremely rare—side effects. The parents of some of these children have won multi-million-dollar suits against the various makers of the vaccine. These suits have prompted insurance companies to drastically increase the liability premiums that the makers of these vaccines must pay. And these premiums, in turn, are the reason at least one maker of the vaccine has decided to get out of the business.

Now, . . . no one wants to lose a child. And to lose a son or daughter in the process of giving them a vaccine that's supposed to prolong their lives . . . seems especially ironic and sad. Yet when the lives of ten children can be leveraged against the lives of 7,000 more, . . . something is desperately wrong in our courts— but more to the point, something is wrong in our hearts.

Our fear of being sued is the second reason we're drifting toward a riskless society.

The third reason is the fear of being victimized by modern society. A generation ago, we feared tornadoes more than terrorists, . . . cholera more than crack, . . . and anthrax more than Amtrak. We realize that while modern technology has lengthened our lifespan, . . . it also has created some new and frightening risks:

- Chemicals can vaccinate us against a wide variety of diseases . . . or spread death—in the form of chemical weapons—across remote villages on the Iraqi border.

- Lasers can remove cataracts from the human eye . . . or guide nuclear warheads with deadly precision.

- And plastics can be formed into milk bottles . . . or fashioned into explosives that look like radios and pass undetected through airport security.

Television has brought the feats—and failures—of modern society into our homes. Who can forget that hot summer night when Neil Armstrong took "one giant leap for mankind. . . ." Or that cold winter morning when the *Challenger* burst into flames in the Florida sky?

The same medium that brought us the Beatles from Ed Sullivan's studio . . . brings us a daily fare of war and famine from the meaner stages of the world. We sink deeper into our La-Z-Boys, . . . swallow the lumps in our throats, . . . and switch to something less objectionable, like professional wrestling. At night, we retreat under the covers and wish for the good old days . . . when only old people died—and they did it quietly in their sleep.

The fear of being victimized by modern society is the third reason we're drifting toward a riskless society.

The fourth reason is the fear of being beaten at our own game. The rise of the global village frightens many Americans. We see ourselves no longer as the undisputed kings of the mountain . . . but as squatters in the valley of economic sameness. We worry that the Japanese and West Germans have reduced us to also-rans . . . while our borders have become the dumping ground for the failed economic enterprises of Asia and Central America.

Robert Reich calls this mind-set . . . the myth of the mob at the gates. He argues that Americans see ourselves as a nation under siege from Arab sheiks and Asian hordes. And we insist that these invaders are best fought off not by attacking in the marketplace . . . but by retreating behind our castle walls.

Reich makes a strong point. We crank out inferior products . . . and demand a premium price—declaring that we have every right because, after all, we're Americans, and our products are American made. We dig protective moats around our markets . . . instead of building bridges that could lead us to new conquests. And we screech about the mob outside . . . when in fact the real threat is from the enemy within.

Perhaps we're very much like the people one playwright described as . . . "Dying of hot heads . . . and cold feet."

This afternoon, I've shared with you four reasons I believe we're drifting toward a riskless society:

- Our fear of being poor
- Our fear of being sued
- Our fear of being victimized by modern society
- And our fear of being beaten at our own game

At this point in my remarks, I feel a little like Thomas Carlyle, the Scottish philosopher who lived in the 1880s. One Sunday morning, he was getting dressed to deliver a speech to a large audience. His mother was sitting near the front door. She asked, "And where might you be going, Thomas?" He replied, "Mother, I'm going to tell the people what's wrong with the world." His mother tugged gently on his sleeve and said, "Yes, Thomas. But are you going to tell them what to do about it?"

Carlyle's mother gave some pretty sound advice, . . . which I plan to heed this afternoon. I hope you agree that there is no such thing as a risk-free society, . . . that our clamoring for one will never produce it, . . . and that a proper *perspective* on risk . . . is far more beneficial than a nationwide *prohibition* of risk.

If you do agree, then let me challenge you to see the issue of risk in our society as a battle that must be won on three fronts:

- The personal front
- The corporate front
- And the community front

First, the personal front. I believe, . . . unless American business leaders are more fully convinced that risk is a necessary—and beneficial—element of doing business, . . . we'll continue to wander outside the gates of the global village.

Have you really stopped to consider the risks involved in everything we do? Some of you own compact cars rather than luxury sedans. Do you realize . . . that in making the decision to buy a compact car, you risked safety for the sake of economy? Let me ask you: In a head-on collision between a four-door sedan and tiny hatch-back, . . . which car would you rather be in?

Or . . . maybe some of you have decided to wait another five years to have children. Do you realize that if you're a 30- year-old woman . . . waiting until you're 35 to have children doubles the chances of having a child with some kind of genetic defect?

Or . . . maybe you're an unmarried man who plans to stay that way. Do you realize that you can expect to die ten years earlier than men who are married?

I understand that for some of you . . . that's a price you're willing to pay. But my point is this: You and I take risks every day. And to think that we can create a business environment in a riskless vacuum is more than naive—it's bad business.

So the first front in our battle against the riskless society . . . is the personal front.

The second front is the corporate front. I'm convinced that many companies flounder . . . because their people fail to see the company as a *community* of risk-takers. In their minds . . . and in their methods, . . . they've created a department of risk—in which the only risk-takers are the ones who eat in the executive dining room. The typical employee feels alienated from the risk-taking process . . . but vulnerable to its consequences.

Doesn't it make more sense to promote the concept . . . that *every* employee is a risk-taker . . . and *everyone* shares in the consequences?

Four years ago, Phillips repelled two hostile takeover attempts . . . and launched a company-wide restructuring program. We tried to impress upon our shareholders, customers and employees that remaining an independent, integrated company was a better alternative for all of us . . . than being busted up and sold for scrap. We also made it clear that such an alternative was risky:

- We'd have to sell two billion dollars of assets.
- We'd have to lay off several thousand employees.
- And we'd have to tighten our purse strings by trimming capital spending, expenses—even our common stock dividend.

We asked our shareholders to be patient. We asked our customers to be loyal. And we asked our employees to roll up their sleeves—to find ways to cut costs without cutting corners, . . . to assume greater responsibility, . . . even to work longer hours for wages that would be frozen for an indefinite period of time.

Not everyone thought we'd make it—especially when oil prices hit the skids in 1986. I remember one writer who described Phillips as a company hanging on by its bloody fingertips. Well, our 1988 annual report has just come out. And in it, we've got plenty of good news to share:

- An 18-fold increase in earnings over 1987
- A 44-percent appreciation in shareholder value
- A 142-percent replacement of hydrocarbon reserves
- A strong capital spending program . . . which includes the building of a major ethylene plant southeast of Houston
- And a new employee stock-ownership plan . . . that enables our employees to buy Phillips stock at a fixed, below-market price

I believe we succeeded in 1988 because *all* of us— shareholders, customers and employees alike—shared in the risks and rewards. We were willing to see ourselves as a community of risk-takers.

The third front in our battle against the riskless society is the community front. And by community . . . I don't mean only the cities and towns where we have plants and offices. I mean every place we meet the public:

- Every place they see our drilling rigs
- Every place they fill up with our gasoline
- Every place they see or hear one of our ads

Having properly identified our community, . . . we find there are several services we need to perform within that community. First, we need to *inform* our community about risk.

At times, that means being willing to tell people what they don't want to hear.

Second, we need to *educate* our community about risk—so that all the consequences of what we do are seen in their proper context. All of us tend to fear what we don't understand. And what we fear, we oppose. Information and education help reduce fear in the community.

Finally, we need to *involve* our community in the decision-making process. We understand that we must not only comply with the *letter of the law* as it's established by legislative and regulatory agencies, . . . but we must comply with the *spirit of the law* as it's seen and felt by the people whose lives we touch every day. We understand, as Thoreau once said, that it takes two to speak the truth—one to speak, and another to listen.

I'll close with this: This summer, we'll celebrate the 20th anniversary of the landing on the moon. Some of you, no doubt, were involved in this historic project that helped open the frontier of manned space travel. As we celebrate, . . . we're sure to be reminded that three men lost their lives in the first *Apollo* spacecraft. And while their loss was tragic, . . . we must also remember that their deaths left us undeterred. The *Eagle* landed a year and a half ahead of schedule.

Henry Fairlie described that conquering spirit as: "The American gusto that blew like a fresh wind around the globe . . . showing what could be accomplished in so short a time by a nation that did not shrink from risk." Twenty years from now, will Americans be asking, "Where have all the risk-takers gone?"

The answer depends on whether we shrink from risk . . . or soar again on the wings of our conquering spirit.

Thank you very much for your kind attention.

"White Hats and Honesty"

Marshall P. Bissell, President
New York Life Insurance Company
Managers Meeting, Orlando, Florida
March 17, 1979

Do you remember the old-fashioned western movie? Its square-jawed hero was firm, forthright, clean-shaven, and he always wore a white hat, except in the presence of a lady. The villain, on the other hand, was cruel, craven, and thoroughly corrupt. He inevitably had a menacing mustache, smoked small black cigars, and he always wore a dark hat which, as I recall, he never removed in anyone's presence.

In a way, the ethical ideals we learned as children from our parents were shaped and dramatized in Hollywood's "B" movie morality plays: Virtue did indeed triumph; the good guys always beat the bad guys; and the hero (or heroine) was a veritable paragon of honesty, integrity, and trustworthiness.

More recently, the astounding success of a movie like "Star Wars" proved that, even in our seemingly less-innocent modern society, an uncomplicated story of heroes overcoming villains will still attract record crowds.

But real-life Lone Rangers or Luke Skywalkers have been in short supply recently. We are, in fact, coming to the close of a decidedly unheroic decade. Political figures, for example, have lost the credibility they once had, as a cynical electorate has simply stopped listening to glib rhetoric and empty promises. Far too many corporate executives have embraced a balance-sheet morality which has encouraged bribery, price fixing, and even an offer to finance the overthrow of an elected government. Policemen and firemen have abandoned their posts in a number of cities to walk strike-picket lines, heedless of their oaths, the law, or simple public safety. Even that quintessential American hero, the professional athlete, has become a muscled mercenary who defies contracts, jumps teams, and decries as inadequate an annual salary which many people could not earn in two lifetimes.

As inflation has raged; as unemployment has soared; as government has almost institutionalized its inability to respond to the needs of its citizens; as industry has carelessly manufactured but carefully promoted questionable and even dangerous products—I seem to sense a kind of despair in the American people. Too many people appear to see themselves as victims of forces they cannot control.

What is, perhaps, most important about the public reaction to these large, faceless institutional forces is that they once were heroic models. Having fallen from grace like Milton's renegade angels in "Paradise Lost," they have become, to a disenchanted and angry public, the new villains.

The business community, for one, has been attacked for both real and imagined sins. Such recent legislative remedies as the Foreign Corrupt Practices Act of 1977 are Congress's attempt to mandate morality in the marketplace. The Act's harsh penalties may, in fact, force most businesses to observe the letter of the law. But it is the spirit of the law which should concern all of us. And, in this instance, I agree with Stanley Sporkin, Director of the Securities and Exchange Commission's Enforcement Division, when he acknowledges that "No law, by itself, no matter how strictly administered, can effectively root out bribery and corruption unless business is committed to a policy of compliance."

I mention the Act because I am troubled that some companies have not made that commitment. Indeed, they have resisted it. As you know, the Foreign Corrupt Practices Act was a response to the many instances of bribery of foreign government officials and other intermediaries by American corporations and individuals. These incidents were reported in exact and discouraging detail for months.

Yet, a recent article in a leading news magazine reveals that some of the most blatant violators, including a number of America's most prominent corporations, continue to complain that the Act keeps them from successfully competing in the international marketplace.

They are, in effect, insisting on the freedom to violate the law in order to protect or increase profits. The fact that this attitude is limited to a small number of companies is little comfort. I suspect the shell of public cynicism will harden further in response to this request for the government's benediction of bribery.

Our task is to crack that shell. I don't think we'll accomplish anything by silence. And our efforts will be doomed to failure if we try to divert attention from the sins of the business community by casting government as some sort of supervillain. Certainly, no one will even listen to us if we con centrate on simply quoting Hobbes and Adam Smith, while pining away for the seemingly lost glories of the free enterprise system.

No, I think the task for honest businesses, and honest businessmen and women, is far more difficult.

Frankly, we must change people's minds. We must show them that their perceptions are understandable, but grossly inaccurate; that their suspicions are unfounded; and that their despair is unnecessary.

But how?

First of all, we won't do it by simply *saying* we want to regain public confidence and respect. We will do it, however, by making the qualities of honesty, integrity, and trust living values in all of our personal and professional undertakings.

In fact, it comes down to this: We must do what is right precisely because it is right, even if we are alone. What is wrong remains wrong, even if, theoretically, everyone does wrong.

That standard of ethical behavior has characterized our industry, and particularly our Company, for a long time. That is why I believe we have a leadership responsibility in this effort.

Think about it for a moment. Our industry operates in a very fragile marketplace. With the exception of the policy contract itself, we don't offer a plug-in, energy-saving product that the consumer can see or touch. We, in fact, offer nothing except our word. As the "Promises to Keep" slide presentation demonstrated so well, in exchange for premiums, we vow to keep our word.

The relationship, therefore, between agent and policyowner, demands complete understanding and trust. It is, in many ways, like a marriage which can be destroyed by even small instances of deception, dishonesty, or disrespect.

But in a very real sense, the marriage is a union of policyowner and company. The agent may do the proposing, but it is New York Life, and everyone involved in the marketing process, that the policyowner weds. Therefore, the responsibility for a sale rests on all of us: agents, general managers, regional officers, and Home Office executives.

But the agent is visible. By representing the Company, he or she becomes, in the eyes of our policyowners, New York Life. That is why I place such heavy emphasis on honesty and trust and why I place such heavy responsibility for the ethical behavior of our agents on the individuals in this room today.

Let me be very clear when it comes to ethical behavior: There is, quite simply, no compromise. Earlier this year, at the General Agents and Managers Conference in Boston, I stated New York Life's unequivocal opposition to the twisting and stripping practices which have besmirched our industry. I do so again now, and I will continue to speak out against those who commit or condone such practices because I am convinced that they destroy credibility and invite the kind of regulation which will cripple our ability to serve our policyowners with distinction.

Let me again be very explicit: Any kind of dishonesty on the part of an agent, whether it is in a sales presentation or in providing candid counsel to a policyowner who has placed his or her trust in New York Life, demands prompt remedial action. If, as general managers, you discover such activity, your response must be swift, sure, and, if necessary, severe.

Every New York Life agent deserves the opportunity to wear the hero's white hat. In point of fact, nearly all of them do. Your job—and you know it far more acutely than anyone—is to help the few who don't, or exercise final judgment if they persist.

Our industry has enjoyed a tradition of trust over the years. You provide the essential bridge between Field and Home Office, and so each of you has responsibility to maintain and enhance that tradition. You must, in fact, be an exemplar, a person who reflects the qualities we want and need in our agents; a person who proves to the experienced agent as well as the apprentice that success and advancement are the result of a commitment to integrity.

That's why each of you is important to the Company. You know that one of your most critical assignments is to motivate agents to achieve certain sales objectives. When they do, they and their policyowners benefit. But I want you to be particularly sensitive to another possibility, and that is the unintended but nonetheless real creation of an atmosphere within which the sale becomes an objective to be reached at almost any cost. Under this kind of stress, an agent may feel justified in "bending the rules" to secure that sale.

But the rules need not be bent. Indeed, by dedicating ourselves to the highest principles of ethical conduct, I believe we can all make our lives more deeply and personally rewarding. And, like the narrator in Thornton Wilder's "The Bridge at San Luis Rey," we will be comforted in the years ahead by our ability to look back and say, "We come from a world where we have known incredible standards of excellence."

As a Company, our commitment to those standards imposes on us an obligation we freely accept. It is a pledge to keep the interests of our policyowners foremost in every business decision we make.

Our investment policy, for example, proceeds from that pledge. Certainly, we seek to discover, and act upon, prudent growth opportunities. But implicit in that search is yet another responsibility: to invest our policyowners' resources in activities which preserve the environment, which help reverse urban decay, and which help solve vexing problems which might otherwise burden succeeding generations.

The FACTS system, too, is another way we honor our commitment. The system gives policyowners swift access to vital information about their insurance protection. It protects that infor mation and safeguards each individual's privacy, while controlling the cost of administration. It seems clear that by making every Field Office a kind of Home Office away from home, we will provide that often hard-to-achieve combination of better service at low cost.

My point is this: The fabric which is New York Life derives its strength from each individual thread of ethical and honorable conduct. Let any of those threads weaken or break, and the entire cloth will unravel like an old, worn-out sweater. All of us in this room are charged with the task of keeping that fabric whole, and we do so not only by expecting—even demanding—high standards, but by setting a good example.

Therefore, when, as general managers, you require from your agents uncompromising ethical conduct, your criteria become the norm. Exceptional behavior becomes unexceptional. Excellence becomes the rule.

Your job is one of the most demanding, challenging, and dif ficult assignments in the Company. We recognize that. The General Managers Compensation Plan is but one way to acknowledge your responsibilities.

It is easy, I know, to *talk* about honor and honesty. We live in a world which often pays lip-service to these qualities, and then ignores them. What is practical is sometimes placed in opposition to what is right.

In my view, there is no such opposition. What is right is truly practical; what is idealistic is truly realistic. In effect, therefore, compromise with our highest ethical standards and aspirations is nothing less than an aberration. The opposite of "honesty" is not "realism"; it is "dishonesty." The opposite of "integrity" is not "pragmatism"; it is "corruption." The opposite of "trust" is not "compromise"; it is "cynicism."

As individuals and as business professionals, our goal is to make the real and the ideal synonymous.

One step toward that goal is a clear and specific statement of Company policy and objectives on the subject of business ethics. The American Institute of Certified Public Accountants is considering recommending that such a statement become part of a company's internal audit controls.

Chairman of the Board Brown has decided to voluntarily distribute such a statement to all employees and agents, and he will be doing so within the next few days.

"The standards we raise," Mr. Brown points out in his statement, "depend on the personal integrity of each employee and agent. Toward that purpose," he says, "each of us has a solemn obligation."

"Always do right," Samuel Clemens once wrote. "This will gratify some people—and astonish the rest." He was right, of course. That is our task now and for the years ahead: to gratify our policyowners, to astonish our critics—and to speed toward the day when no one will be astonished.

"Always do right." It has been on New York Life's agenda since 1845. It always will be.

Reprinted with permission from Marshall P. Bissell, President (Ret.), New York Life Insurance Company.

Remarks at a Dinner

Honoring Tip O'Neill
President Ronald Reagan
Washington, D.C.
March 17, 1986

Reverend clergy, Mr. Prime Minister (Garret FitzGerald of Ireland), Mr. Speaker, ladies and gentlemen, I want to begin tonight by saying how touched I am to know that Tip wanted me here this evening. [Laughter] Why, he even called me himself last week and said, "Mr. President, make sure you don't miss the dinner Tuesday night." [Laughter]

But to be honest, I've always known that Tip was behind me [Laughter]—even if it was only at the State of the Union Address. As I made each proposal, I could hear Tip whispering to George Bush, "Forget it. No way. Fat chance." [Laughter]

I think it was inevitable, though, that there'd be a standoff between us. Imagine one Irishman trying to corner another Irishman in the Oval Office. But despite all this, Tip wanted me here. He said that since it was March 17th, it was only fitting that someone drop by who actually had known St. Patrick. [Laughter] And that's true, Tip, I did know St. Patrick. In fact, we both changed to the same political party at about the same time. [Laughter]

Now, it's true that Tip and I have our political disagreements. Sure, I said some things about Tip, and Tip said some things about me. But that's all history. And anyway, you know how it is, I forget. [Laughter] I just follow that old motto "Forgive and forget." Or is it "Forget and forgive." [Laughter]

Ladies and gentlemen, I think you know Tip and I've been kidding each other for some time now. And I hope you also know how much I hope this continues for many years to come. A little kidding is, after all, a sign of affection, the sort of things that friends do to each other. And Mr. Speaker, I'm grateful you have permitted me in the past, and I hope in the future, that singular honor, the honor of calling you my friend. I think the fact of our friendship is testimony to the political system that we're part of and the country we live in, a country which permits two not-so-shy and not-so-retiring Irishmen to have it out on the issues, rather than on each other or their countrymen.

But in addition to celebrating a country and a personal friendship, I wanted to come here tonight to join you in saluting Tip O'Neill, to salute him for the years of dedication and devotion to country. Tip's recollections of politics go back, of course, far beyond my own. [Laughter] He's seen some who play the game well and others who do not. He's seen some who love politics and some who came to it only out of a sense of duty. But through it all, Tip has been a vital and forceful part of America's political tradition, a tradition that he has truly enriched.

Yet Tip O'Neill represents far more than just this political tradition. Deep within, too, is the memory of places like Back Bay and south Boston, the docks, the piers, those who came off the ships in Boston Harbor seeking a better land, a better way for their children. And they found that something better. They rose above the prejudice and the hardship.

Tip would see one of his contemporaries become president—John F. Kennedy would be 68 today, had he lived. And Tip can remember those golden hours better than most in this room. And then, not too many years later, there was another of immigrant stock who would become Speaker of the House. In so short a time, so much leadership from one city, one place, one people. How fitting that Boston College, a place that became to so many of those new arrivals a symbol of moving upward and onward; how fitting that Boston College, whose towers on the heights have reached to heaven's own blue for so many, should sponsor this salute to Tip O'Neill. Tip, you are a true son of Boston College and our friend. And we salute you.

You are also a leader of the nation, and for that we honor you. But you also embody so much of what this nation is all about, the hope that is America. So, you make us proud as well, my friend, you make us proud.

Thank you. God bless you all.

"Creating a New Order of Things"

Alfred S. Warren, Vice President
General Motors Corporation
NASA/AIAA Symposium Quality and Productivity
Washington, D.C.
December 3, 1986

"It must be remembered that there is nothing more difficult to plan, more uncertain of success, nor more dangerous to manage than the creation of a new order of things. For the initiator has the enmity of all who would profit by the preservation of the old institutions, and merely lukewarm defenders in those who would gain by the new ones."

—Machiavelli, *The Prince* (1513)

Good morning. I'm Al Warren. That was a quote from The Prince, the famous book by the 16th-century political scientist, Niccolo Machiavelli. Machiavelli's ideas aren't to everyone's taste, but he knew a thing or two about today's topic: cultural change. It may seem strange to have a representative of an automobile manufacturer speaking at a conference on aeronautics and astronautics. But I think there are some real similarities between GM's business and yours. Of course, GM is not just an automobile company. We've long been involved in aeronautics and the space program. We were the first to use integrated circuits in an airborne computer. We were there when the first man walked on the moon. And now that Hughes Aircraft is part of the GM family, we're more involved than ever in flight, space, and satellite technology.

But more important, I think all industry in the U.S. faces some similar challenges. The outward causes may differ, but we're all looking for ways to become more efficient—ways to improve our quality and productivity. If you operate in the private sector—like we do at General Motors—the reason for pursuing greater productivity and higher quality is quite simply competition. On the public side, there's the pressure of budget cuts. We're all looking for ways to do the job better at lower cost.

The world is changing. That's certainly true in the automobile business. Today, the worldwide automobile business is becoming more homogeneous. It wasn't always that way. For a great many years, the American automobile industry was different from the rest of the world. American cars were bigger and required more fuel than foreign models. American drivers enjoyed lower operating costs than their foreign counterparts and could afford more luxurious models.

But times have changed! Thanks to OPEC and the economic and technical strength of overseas manufacturers—particularly in Japan—America is more than ever part of a world market. Perhaps I should modify that slightly. When I talk about a global automobile industry, I'm essentially speaking of North America, Japan, and Western Europe. Two of those three markets—Japan and Europe—are characterized by overcapacity and low profits. The North American automotive business remains the richest and most profitable in the world.

For that reason, auto producers from around the world are coming here in increasing numbers, seeking part of those profits. Nissan, Honda, and Volkswagen already have assembly operations in this country. Soon, they'll be joined by Mazda, Mitsubishi, Toyota, and others.

In the face of this competition, it is absolutely essential that GM become the highest-quality, lowest-cost producer. That's the key to surviving and thriving in the future. And the management of GM has been planning to achieve that goal for several years. It's easy to say that you plan to remain the world's leading automobile company. But it takes plenty of hard thought, hard work, and hard cash to make it come true.

We started to implement our strategy several years ago. We reorganized our operations here in the U.S. and in several other parts of the world. We diversified into areas like home mortgage financing and industrial robotics. And we made several acquisitions including Electronic Data Systems (EDS) and—as I mentioned, Hughes.

EDS is spearheading the development of new computer systems and data-processing capability for GM. Soon we will have an information-sharing network, unique in the industry, for employees, suppliers, plants, dealerships, and staffs to draw upon.

Complementing this ability is Hughes. Hughes has few, if any, equals in the field of systems engineering. And systems engineering is what GM needs to create the factories of the future and the 21st-century car. Hughes is also one of the premier electronics companies in the world, and the car is well on its way to the day when all its functions will be electronically controlled. In the works right now are electronically controlled anti-skid brakes . . . active suspensions . . . satellite navigation . . . collision avoidance systems . . . and electric power steering. We expect Hughes to play a big part in the development of the electronic car.

As another part of our competitive plan, we've built or are building six new assembly plants and refurbishing 12 others. The automated assembly equipment in these new plants will actually give us capacity equivalent to an extra plant. At the same time, we're improving our quality and lowering our cost.

In 1984, we announced a $2.5 billion press plant modernization—to upgrade the operations at the plants where we stamp body panels. Most of that spending is behind us now, and the results have been fantastic. For example, in Mansfield, Ohio, 21 of the world's largest and most modern transfer presses will produce parts at a rate of 100 million per year. Mansfield is the equivalent of one-and-a-half traditional plants. In all of our stamping plants, we have—or soon will have—100 of these presses. That will give us the equivalent of another stamping plant. When we set out on this program of modernization, we knew there would be a period of overlap—time when some of our older plants continued to operate as newer plants came on stream. Just about a month ago, we reached a point where we could announce that the time to begin phasing out 11 of our older plants had come.

It's a significant step. It will result in annual fixed-cost savings of $500 million. As a result, our competitiveness will increase, we'll be able to maintain our leadership, and enhance the job security of the great bulk of our work force.

We realize that these closings will have a human impact. They will affect the people who work in those plants, their communities and states. We're committed to working with our salaried and hourly people, with union officials, and with government leaders to reduce the impact of these necessary changes.

Transition teams will be established at each affected plant with appropriate counseling. And we're looking into government programs to assist displaced workers.And we have a variety of programs in place at General Motors to cushion the impact. In fact, the American auto worker has probably the best transitional package in the industrial world.

One such program is called JOBS—that's short for the Job Opportunity Bank-Security Program. This program was developed by the union and the company during our 1984 negotiations and gives us a way to work together—jointly—to promote growth and secure jobs. Under this program, no employee with a year or more of seniority can be laid off as a result of new technology, outsourcing, negotiated productivity improvements, or the transfer or consolidation of work resulting in less work content.

Employees who qualify for the JOBS program will be placed in what we call a job bank. People in the job bank are placed in special training programs, or work as replacements for other workers, or can even work in nontraditional assignments. And, of course, they're eligible for jobs that may become available in other GM facilities. JOBS is a joint program run by GM and the UAW. Each GM facility has a committee including the plant manager and other management representatives and the local shop committee.

To my mind, JOBS has an importance far beyond just its possible application to these upcoming plant closings. It is a way to persuade people to let go of the rock of tradition and swim across the river of change. The really important feature of this job security program is that it encourages productivity initiatives from everyone in the organization. GM and the UAW agreed to foster such gains. In fact, local bargainers may even consider changes in the National Agreement to achieve higher productivity.

With a program like JOBS, employees no longer need fear such improvements. They should welcome them as a long-term tool for achieving greater job security. Before, when a team of engineers came in to study their jobs and find ways of making them more efficient, workers would understandably be afraid of losing their jobs and the ability to support their families.

Now, a GM employee knows if his job is eliminated by a robot—or other new technology—he will be protected. Through retraining, he may even end up maintaining a string of robots. The new jobs will be more interesting and satisfying.

JOBS is one example of the way GM and the UAW are responding to the competitive challenge. It's one way that we have realized that the company, the employees, and the union have more in common than in conflict—that we can work together to make a better future.

Another joint program—one that's been around much longer than JOBS—is the Quality of Work Life—or QWL—program. QWL, too, makes it possible for workers to contribute to the success of the organization. It also helps us convince people to swim that river of change with us. I'd be the first person to admit that we at GM are still learning to tap all the abilities our employees bring to their jobs. The great thing about QWL is that it allows us to search jointly for new ways of encouraging employee involvement. It's another avenue that allows people to contribute to the success of the business. QWL emphasizes self-direction and self-control. It gets people at all levels involved in problem solving, data analysis, and making decisions.

Many plants with QWL programs have experienced improved quality, productivity, decreased absenteeism, and improved management-union relationships. Those are *not* the goals of a QWL program. But when they occur, we're very happy to see them.

One of the most outstanding QWL programs in GM operates at Delco Remy battery plant in Fitzgerald, Georgia. Each employee is assigned to a team and given extensive training in decision-making skills. Supervision is strictly advisory. The teams make decisions on production, maintenance, repairs—everything that relates to their jobs. On the quality side, Fitzgerald has received just about every recognition possible, including top ratings in GM's internal quality evaluations. The plant has also done an outstanding job on reducing costs.

Fitzgerald is just one outstanding example. In several other plants, workers meet regularly, develop new ideas, and get together with engineers to plan, train, and research new approaches to their jobs. That not only makes for a better, more satisfying work experience, it also tends to help make a plant more competitive in the long run. There are many fancy definitions of QWL, but they all boil down to treating people as adults when they are at work. Quality of Work Life means giving people dignity and respect.

That's something we in American industry have to do more of. One of the employees at our plant in Tarrytown, N.Y., said before QWL was introduced, GM was only interested in people from the neck down—concerned with their muscles not their brains.

Well, today America needs all the brains it can get. We have to tap into the decision-making ability of every man and woman.

When men and women are respected in their communities—deacons in their churches, city councilmen, directors of local charities—when they own homes, raise families, and make hundreds of personal decisions each week, they want respect at work, and they deserve it.

And only by giving them that respect are we going to benefit from their ideas. We need the contribution they can make. I learned that very early on in my GM career. I was troubleshooting at a GM plant and there was a machine that wasn't working. Engineers and managers were scurrying about trying to find the problem. Finally, one of the hourly workers pulled me aside and said, "Do you want to know how to fix that machine?"

He was the operator, and—not surprisingly—he knew what was wrong. Nobody had bothered to ask him. If we can tap into that knowledge—the experience and ideas that employees at all levels have—we'll be well on our way to achieving our goals.

I'm not suggesting that QWL is a panacea. It won't solve all our problems.

Higher quality and greater productivity are multifaceted goals. But they are the only guarantee of a successful future. All the job-security agreements, benefit packages, and QWL programs aren't going to mean much unless we're doing the best possible job in every area of our business. At the same time that we are trying to make the best possible use of our immense human resources, we have to tackle many other challenges— challenges in design, engineering, manufacturing, and marketing.

At GM, we're tackling those challenges. As I said, we're modernizing our plants and building completely new operations. These plants are not only using new systems, new processes, and new equipment; they're also making completely new products. That transformation hasn't been without problems. Some of those problems have been reported extensively. Maybe they've even been exaggerated.

We're learning how to operate this new equipment in these new plants and how to design, engineer, manufacture, and service new high-tech products.

One thing we've learned in the process is that we need to do much more up-front education and training of our work force before high technology is introduced. In a couple of our new plants in Michigan, employees went through a million man-hours of training before the first cars were produced. But in the future, we're going to have to do even more—and perhaps different—training. Recognizing that, we've created a joint training process with the UAW at a new Human Resources Center just north of Detroit. That's another challenge we've recognized, and we're gearing up to handle it.

On top of all these challenges, is the overriding concern of integrating human and technological resources. That's been a challenge as long as I've been with GM, and I think we're doing better than ever.

Does that mean all the problems will soon go away? Of course not! But the longer we face these challenges, the more experience we accumulate in overcoming them, the better job we're going to do in the future.

In the long run, the benefit of our "strategy for the 80s" will be obvious. By achieving higher quality and greater productivity, we'll be insuring jobs for the future. And at the same time, we'll be giving people work that is more interesting and satisfying.

There are big changes to be made. And as shrewd old Machiavelli knew, there are plenty of people who don't want to see change. The joint approach I've been describing this morning is new to many Americans. To make it work, we're going to have to change the way both workers and managers see the world.

But I'm convinced we've already started to swim that river of change. And I know we'll make it to the other side. We're crossing the river at GM and organizations all across the United States are doing the same thing.

This country has a history of facing change and making it happen. We were the first to fly an airplane, the first to land on the moon, and the first to send a space probe to Neptune and beyond.

We can do what must be done. We have the people. We have the technology. And in combination, they're going to make us winners!

Harvard Business School Club of Washington

50th Anniversary Dinner Speech
Philip Caldwell, Chairman of the Board
Ford Motor Company
Washington, DC
March 31, 1983

Among the many luxuries we can seldom afford is the luxury of reminiscence. There are, however, some occasions when the best of maxims should be thrown to the winds, and sentiment should claim its rightful place.

Tonight, I confess, I cannot resist a glance over my shoulder—for we are celebrating a birthday, an anniversary . . . a half century of this club which was founded exactly 50 years ago today.

March 31, 1933, was hardly a happy time in the history of American business. The Ides of March again turned out to be a fateful period of the year.

Just 25 days before, President Roosevelt had closed the banks, and depression changed the economic climate in this country and across the world.

It was a time of shattered hopes. Many lost faith in the ability of American business to manage. Indeed, the very system of market enterprise was thought to have failed.

That was the depression we called The Depression—until this one came along.

It was also the year that Adolf Hitler became Chancellor of Germany, and the biggest theatrical success on Broadway was appropriately titled "Ah Wilderness."

Nevertheless, we survived the Depression and World War II and went on to prosper. By 1950, when I served the club as president, I think it is fair to say that we were pretty well convinced of our ability to manage ourselves, our businesses, and our country.

Moreover, what we had learned at Harvard became an essential ingredient in developing our prosperity, and at the same time, a matter of envy for the rest of the world.

The most influential business book of the 1960s was first published in France. It was called "The American Challenge," and it was written by a Frenchman—Jean-Jacques Servan-Schreiber. His thesis was that the challenge to the industrial countries of Western Europe was no longer military. It was the power of American management. He argued very persuasively that Europe, in particular, must learn the things that all of us here had been privileged to learn at the B-School.

Our circumstances in those days certainly could not contradict his thesis. The United States emerged from World War II as the principal economic, social, political, and military nation in the world. And with good reason.

The jet engine and penicillin were invented in Britain, but they were put into production here. The rocket motor was developed in Germany, but we were the first to the moon. An enormous American research and development effort also produced some notable national achievements, of which perhaps the most significant was the transistor.

My own company, which many years earlier had invented the moving assembly line, added yet a further dimension to efficient mass production. It was called "automation"—a word coined by one of my manufacturing predecessors. The first assembly operation in the world to use robots was our car assembly plant in Kansas City.

The "just in time" technique, that the Japanese call kanban, was invented by Henry Ford. Eiji Toyoda told me himself in Tokyo, last year, there was no mystery to the development of Toyota in Japan. He merely came to see the Ford Rouge Plant in 1950—and then went back to Japan and built the same thing.

The revolution in retailing mechanization was led by National Cash Register, and the office revolution by IBM.

Escapism was invented in Hollywood. Housework was saved from drudgery by Mr. Hoover, and the New York garment business transformed our outward appearances, as the sustained faith in the basic virtues of America transformed our inner souls.

People came here to learn. I sometimes think that the only reason the Japanese were so quick in developing a camera industry was so they could come and photograph what we were doing.

The essential question that follows this important catalogue of American achievement, of course, is not how have the mighty fallen, but why?

In the early '60s, the United States was still producing more cars and trucks than the rest of the world put together. Now we are number three—behind Japan and Europe. This reordering of the standings in the international production league also applies to many other industries—from steel to textiles, television to copiers . . . from ships and shoes to sealing wax and machine tools.

There have, of course, been some enormous international forces at work—tempests big enough to force any industrial ship off course. Many of these contrary winds arose from the government quarter, either because of a lack of policy, or from conflicting priorities.

The United States blithely ignored the first energy crisis in the fall of 1973, and remained wedded to a policy of cheap energy and gasoline at 30 cents a gallon. Washington decided the way to save energy was to require auto makers to build fleets twice as efficient as they were in 1974, but they forgot consumers had to be persuaded to buy them.

In 1978—as recently as that—a glut of Japanese cars—all small—sat unsold on the docks, and the U.S. auto industry was offering rebates of up to $500 to sell its small cars, and could not get enough production out of its plants to satisfy the demand for the big ones.

Moreover, the law discriminated against U.S. manufacturers because our cars had to have 75 percent American content to be counted with U.S.-built cars toward meeting the fuel-economy requirements that came into effect that year. After all, the U.S. auto industry, in good times, consumes 22 percent of the nation's steel, 62 percent of its rubber, 20 to 25 percent of its machine tools, a third of the flat glass, and provides one out of nine jobs in manufacturing and creates $150 billion of GNP.

Unfortunately, Congress did not impose the same requirements for American content on cars made abroad, and more and more cars and trucks were imported with no U.S. content at all.

We turned ourselves into the most litigious society in the world. Once upon a time, if you had a row with your neighbor you gave him a piece of your mind. Now you take him to court. Critics sometimes point out there are more lawyers in the state of Delaware than in all of Japan.

In 1979 we had a second energy crisis. Americans began to learn a new word—"ayatollah"—and experience a new and unforeseen deprivation. There were lines at the gas pumps because of faulty allocations of gasoline by the federal authorities, and our industry and our economy were sent into a tailspin overnight.

What did we do about it?

If you were to send for Mr. Gallup, and ask him to do a survey to answer that question, it is a certainty that 20 percent would say "I don't know," 30 percent would say "not much" and 50 percent would say "nothing at all."

And yet, as its response, there is one industry in this country that is well on its way to the biggest industrial revolution in history. It happens to be the auto industry, and I would like to spend a few minutes creating the groundwork for a very positive Gallup Poll—at least in this room tonight.

The auto revolution is—if you will—the greatest story never told.

When the industry embarked upon this enterprise, it didn't seem to matter very much what caused the circumstances that made it imperative. That was when we at Ford Motor Company decided we would stop looking back. It didn't much matter who put the dirt in the carburetor, whose crystal ball wasn't working, or who was to blame.

The responsibility we decided to distribute was the responsibility for future success, rather than past misdeeds.

Detroit decided to re-equip, to modernize, to retool, to invest and to commit, not merely to survival, but rather to a new and expansive future.

Since then, the U.S. auto industry has moved forward to rebuild, re-equip or retool no fewer than 47 new engine and transmission facilities and 89 assembly plants. To illustrate the magnitude of that effort, just one of Ford's new engine plants has a continuing line of computer-controlled machine tools that stretches one-third of a mile in one direction . . . then back again for another third of a mile, and forward again for still another third of a mile.

The same kind of transformation was also being undertaken in the plants of more than 5,000 auto-industry suppliers. At Ford, we committed ourselves to replacing every single vehicle in our product range over as short a period of time as we could manage . . . as we could manage efficiently and with excellent quality.

The total cost of this revolution to the U.S. auto industry was $80 billion. It is sometimes pointed out that this is a great deal more than it took to put a man on the moon. I prefer to remember that it is about the same, in today's dollars, as the cost of the Marshall Plan. But unlike the Marshall Plan, virtually every dollar came from private resources.

At the outset, the television commentators and the newspapers told the world the U.S. auto industry was failing. In 1980 the industry's combined losses totaled $4.2 billion. Yet, in that same year, its combined investments totaled $11.4 billion. Nobody talked about that. In fact, our government leaders and many academics were being critical that U.S. industry was not making capital investments, and that top management was interested only in short-term results.

In a little over two months' time, my own company will have cause to celebrate a birthday, much as we are doing here tonight. We shall be 80 years old. In this endeavor to renew our products and our facilities, we have spent almost as much money in the last four years as we have earned in our entire history.

It has taken time for our tree to bear fruit. One plants a seed in the auto industry, and it takes a minimum of three years to come up. More often, it takes five.

But the fruit from those seeds is beginning to ripen now. This model year Ford is bringing to the U.S. market alone no fewer than eight new cars and trucks—a $3 billion effort. The dramatic, aerodynamically styled Thunderbird and Cougar made their bows in February. The new, small, rugged, but very attractive, four-wheel-drive utility vehicle called Bronco II is now in production. The beautiful new front-wheel-drive Ford Tempo and Mercury

Topaz will be in production in a few weeks for sale in May. The all-new Mustang convertible is ready for the spring selling season, and so is the Turbo Thunderbird which will challenge the best from home and abroad.

All these new Ford products are making an authoritative statement about the U.S. automobile in terms of both form and function, and even more importantly, in terms of quality, fuel efficiency and value.

Ford quality has improved an average of 59 percent compared to 1980 models, and by independent survey last year our customers told us that Ford cars had the highest quality of any cars made in America. We have improved the average fuel economy of Ford cars by 74 percent since 1975—and we now have the LTD and the Marquis with more miles-per-gallon than even our smallest cars of a decade ago.

I know there are soothsayers who would dismiss these efforts as unimportant—who would let our basic wealth-producing industries atrophy—who would prefer instead to leapfrog into some kind of service economy or hi-tech super-world.

I don't agree with that view. There is no record of any country becoming, or remaining, a great power by relying upon service industries. I do not believe that video games or fast food restaurants can give us the fundamental basis for a healthy economy or a healthy society.

Nor do I believe that our national defense depends exclusively or, perhaps even primarily, upon the military. It is the vigor of our basic industries—and not the missile count—that best provides the real security of our country.

Most of the economy has been shrinking but one can find growth, if one wants to look for it in the statistics of the Department of Labor. Those statistics will tell you of the professions or crafts that have increased substantially in recent years.

Between 1972 and 1980 there were only three professions which more than doubled in size: economists, psychiatrists (presumably because of all those economists), and writers (because, I suppose, we had to have soap operas to take our minds off the activities of both the economists and the psychiatrists).

But I must not digress. One of the reasons that I have talked about the auto industry is that I want to emphasize the management challenge that this revolution represents.

In pursuing this new path, we had to ensure that we were down to fighting weight. Since 1979, Ford Motor Company has taken more than $3 billion dollars out of our annual operating costs. Slimming does get rid of the fat, but it does not necessarily tone up the muscles. We were determined to make better use of our intellectual muscles—and that means people.

We, therefore, with the UAW, embarked on an employee-involvement program. We stopped asking people to deliver just their bodies to the workplace. We asked them to bring their minds, their ideas, and their enthusiasm.

At Ford, we have encouraged the voluntary establishment of problem-solving groups in all our plants and offices. This program started a little tentatively at first, for not everybody was a believer. Quite soon we had people knocking on a lot of doors, and asking when was their group going to get started.

We brought prototypes of new vehicles to the men and women on the production line—before we were locked into tooling—and asked them for their suggestions. "How," we said, "do you think you could put it together better?" We got a flood of ideas and a great many have been incorporated into our vehicles beginning with Job One.

Ford now has nearly 1,100 groups in all our major plants and facilities in the United States. And the movement is spreading—almost like a crusade—into our plants overseas, and into those of our suppliers.

These new approaches to management have also had a profound effect upon our executives.

Over time, it seems that most companies tend to build up bureaucratic layers of organizational and administrative barnacles. They create structures and superstructures that become comfortable traditions.

But the comfortable way to manage also creates a price tag—most often a stiff one.

What we are after—and I would be the first to insist that we are not there yet—is a "purpose-centered" organization rather than one that is "procedure-centered."

Some bureaucracy and form is essential. There is a place for the "seat of the pants" manager, but I have known many like that who only end up with shiny suits. A measure of control is necessary in all human activity, but it does not have to be all-embracing.

Our new look at people resources didn't stop with the hourly employees. We removed layers of management as well—streamlined control, pushed decision making down the line, and enhanced communications up the line.

We have reduced our salaried-staff headcount by nearly 30 percent in the North American automotive business alone, and when I say staff, I mean all staff. We used to have 51 vice presidents. Now we have 41.

These changes within Ford Motor Company, which are still imperfectly apparent to the outside world, are important lessons at a time when the whole country is experiencing change.

At Ford, we are taking the initiative to lead rather than to be led by change—to call upon the vigor and inventiveness which once brought our country out of the Depression that dominated the country at the time this club was formed.

I said earlier that this is a time to take stock in the strength of American business and industry. That is no less a goal or ambition for a nation than it is for an individual company.

What more do we need to make it possible for somebody like me, standing here 50 years from now (at our 100th anniversary) to point to genuine achievements, and the return of growth and prosperity to our country? It seems to me that some choices are very clear.

- We can devote ourselves to time-wasting arguments over missiles, or we can rediscover the true basis of our national strength and economic security—the one for which we do not need any kind of control agreement.

- We can accept the prospect of unbalanced fiscal and balance-of-trade budgets, or we can balance both.

- We can lose ourselves forever floundering in the maze of currency exchange rates—based on the myth of U.S. dominance in the world—or we can manage the dollar and restore some reasonable order into the world's monetary system.

- We can stay wedded to a system of taxation that is out of joint with all the other trading nations of the world, and contributes to our serious and growing negative trade balance, or we can have the courage to demand that our tax system should be as modern as the plants that contribute to it.

- We can accept regulation and government by agency mandate, or we can put our trust in the enterprises that created this market-driven economy. Isn't regulated enterprise a contradiction in terms?

- We can stop looking at the other end of the rainbow in the hope of some miraculous revelation, and start appreciating the miracles we are performing at home.

In making choices such as these, I would hope that we will be administering preventive medicine and restoring our country to good health, rather than always reacting only to curing the fevers of the time.

Above all, if we have the will, we can remember the nature of Servan-Schreiber's "The American Challenge"—and make it happen again.

As I pointed out at the beginning, that American challenge that so concerned Europe in the '60s was the challenge of American management. It was, in a way, an unspoken compliment to the school which produced all the members of this club and many others.

But there are times when it seems to me that even Harvard Business School—and the others who follow behind its pathfinding initiatives—could do with a re-resolution of the principles upon which it was founded.

I am disturbed when people tell me that the Business School has become a kind of employment agency, a door through which its best and brightest present-day graduates—like so many Alices—slide down a plush chute to end up in consultancy work so they can pay off their school debts faster.

The United States needs to invent. It needs to manufacture. It needs to sell. It needs to trade. It needs to adapt. It needs to manage. It needs to know what it stands for. There has never been a greater need for our best business schools and our brightest managers to provide the nerve, the vision, and the leadership to do these things.

Would it not be more satisfactory to us all if we could remind the country once again of those ideas of wisdom that one of the School's most distinguished professors used to insist upon when I was his student many years ago?

"There are many different elements of management," he would point out. "Some will tell you that this is first or that is first. You may take your pick. But I believe that the first requirement of good management is to love your product. If you want to be a success in business, you must love your product."

Nothing that has happened to me, in all the years that have followed, has convinced me there is any more fundamental precept to guide our actions. Loving our products, whether in business or in representing our country, and knowing what we stand for and being proud of it, will lead more quickly than we might think to a new "American Challenge."

Printed with permission, courtesy of Ford Motor Company.

"Are You a Good Coach or a Great One?"

Marvin E. Showalter, Chairman
Credit Union Executives Society
Annual Convention & Exposition
Orlando, Florida
June 26, 1988

I don't know how I could ever live up to an introduction like that if I wasn't already a credit union executive. (Pause.) And I'm not saying that to pat myself on the back or to try and be funny.

I just happen to think that when it comes to being participants on the world's financial playing fields, credit unions, by and large, are the winners of the day. And as executives and directors, we coach the teams of financial professionals that more people are coming to respect and appreciate as time goes on.

You know it, I know it, our members know it and even the competition is starting to sit up on the bench and watch. That means that when our credit union teams are ready to move into play, we must have our strategies set, our goal in sight and be ready to run at the sound of the gun to make our best professional efforts count. That's called "Going for the Gold." And that's what this year's convention is all about.

Good teams have good coaches and great teams often have great ones. That's as true in business and finance as it is in sports. I think what we have here is a gathering of many of the top professional credit union "coaches"—both paid and voluntary—from among our membership and around the world.

And, like any good coach, you're here to learn how to help your credit union team players maximize their skills and achieve top performance on the financial playing field that is your field of membership or your community. That's why I'm here.

(With vigor!)

But if that's true, then I guess I'm also your coach for this year's event. In that case, listen up! Because there are a few things I'd like to say before we get under way, and I'm only going to say them once . . . or maybe twice.

You can be sure that my expectations for your performance here will be high, and that the workouts will be grueling. No pain, no gain, and I plan to make sure everyone does their part to contribute to this year's convention team!

I will expect all of you to be down here bright and early every morning for continental breakfast. I will expect you to be seated front and center at Monday's and Wednesday's luncheons. And I expect to see full participation at the refreshment breaks, both mornings and afternoons. (Pause.) The food's not important. You're in training, so eat whatever you want. (Pause.) What *is* important is the opportunity you'll have to network before, during and after the breakfasts, breaks and luncheons, and the wealth of information you can uncover from your fellow team members.

But for gosh sakes, don't always hang out with the people you came with! You already know what they think. This is your opportunity to meet some new team members and gain some fresh perspectives. That's how networking works.

(*Optional, if the audience is with you.*) Anyone caught violating this rule is going to give me ten laps around EPCOT Center . . . without the benefit of the monorail!

I also expect to see each and every one of you attending the events and general sessions. The CUES staff has gone to a lot of trouble to bring in some of the top outside trainers in the business. I want to make sure you get your money's worth when it comes to tips, techniques and new ideas.

And when it comes to topics, what we don't have, you don't need. This year's scorecard includes everything from power communications to setting the pace in your day, from multiple-subject events to a regulatory relay that includes some of the NCUA's top performers.

But you have to be in there participating, talking it up, rolling up your sleeves and getting down to specifics. Remember what the great American philosopher Yogi Berra said about such things: "You can observe a lot by just watchin'." (Pause.)

Imagine how much more you can take in by getting in there and swinging at a few of them.

When it comes right down to it, we're all coaches here this week, looking for ways to inspire our credit unions' teams on to higher performance and greater member service. And remember that good teams have good coaches, and great teams have great ones. That's as true in business as it is in athletics.

As your last training exercise, I want you to turn to a fellow teammate some time today—do it right now if you like—and ask them if they are a good coach or a great coach. And if they say they're a great coach, congratulate them and shake their hand. But if they say they're only a good coach, ask them what it would take for them to become great.

We have most of the necessary tools right here. As members of the same convention team, we're training here in a supportive environment that will nurture our management skills and help them grow. And we've brought in some of the best industry experts to help us in our special workouts over the next few days.

The only thing we're not providing is the will, the drive and the desire to be great. That, we all have to find within ourselves.

Is the fellow teammate you asked a good coach or a great one? Now ask yourself the same question. And between the two of you, decide what it would take to reach that level of greatness.

And before you hit the showers Wednesday, find that person and let them know if you've got what it takes to be a great credit union coach.

Your members will be in the stands cheering for you if you do . . .
. . . and so will we.

Printed with permission. Courtesy of Marvin E. Showalter and Credit Union Executives Society.

Diamond Club Dinner
Welcoming Remarks

Stephen Joel Trachtenberg, President
University of Hartford
Parkview Hilton Hotel, Hartford, Connecticut
February 15, 1987

It's a pleasure and an honor for me to welcome you to this evening's program, and to welcome our distinguished guest A. Bartlett Giamatti, president of the National League.

Bart Giamatti needs little introduction from me, given his standing in the world of major league baseball and of American athletics. He has added a new and illustrious name to a pantheon that includes Abner Doubleday, Lou Gehrig, Babe Ruth, Joe DiMaggio and Mickey Mantle.

Indeed, Bart's identification with baseball and athletics is so complete—his passion for sports so total—that it has given birth to some envy. And envy, as always, has given birth to some rumor.

The rumor being spread by those who cannot stomach his successes is that Bart, like some kind of superspy out of a James Bond novel, is a man with a secret past. Bart, it is whispered, far from having always been the sportsman and athletic raconteur we see before us today, was once—of all things—a *university president*.

And not the president, let me add, of a muscular school like Ohio State or Notre Dame! The president, rather, of an effete Eastern snob school that produces the kinds of graduates who don't like Ronald Reagan, or Cheerios, or Blondie, or engagement parties or bridal showers.

When I heard this rumor the first time, I was shocked. I regarded it as one more example of the kinds of slurs that are always being flung, alas, at those of Italian-American descent. It seems that no matter how many years go by, there are still those who cannot see a last name ending in "I" without suspecting that the person it denotes is a representative of the Mafia with a colorful past and a switchblade in his pocket.

I heard the rumor a second time. I heard the rumor a *third* time. That left me no choice but to go straight to Bart's office and to beg him for an explanation.

I don't have to tell you what palatial quarters he occupies today. Making my way past a battery of secretaries and personal assistants, each of whom asked me for my driver's license and Social Security number, I admired the trophies in their glass display cases, the medals, the inscribed photographs of major athletes and the many other signs of a long and satisfying career in sports.

When I was finally admitted to his mahogany office with its elegant recessed bar, and he had given me a snifter of fine cognac, I posed the question to him.

"Bart," I said, "what about these rumors that you were once the president of—uh—forgive me for saying this—*Yale University*?"

It took Bart a few minutes to recover his composure, and then he offered me the following explanation—which I am happy to present to you today.

Bart admitted that his Italian-American origins had played an important role in his life. But far from seeking to model himself on such figures as Al Capone and Marlon Brando, he had chosen as his personal godfathers the two great Italians known as Dante Alighieri and Niccolo Machiavelli.

Initially he studied them in college and graduate school—to such an extent that he even received a Ph.D. in the field of Romance Languages and Literature.

Then, discontented with the abstract nature of his confrontation with these two cultural greats, he decided to test their outlooks and their philosophies in actual practice—in the world of grim reality.

Machiavelli, as we all know, was the author of what the Germans call *Realpolitik*. What that means is that you have to be prepared to do things that are necessary rather than things that are merely pleasant or moral. "And that," Bart said to me, "is what Yale University all about."

True, he did serve as the school's president for a number of years—but only to experience what Machiavelli was getting at in his most famous work, *The Prince*. Let me quote the words Bart actually used in his mahogany office:

"Steve," he said, "I played that role up to the point at which I could feel Old Nick smiling upon me from his studio apartment in the Inferno. At that point, I knew that I had absorbed the very essence of his outlook, in a manner that might be called Applied Humanities. When I received a note of commendation from Education Secretary Bennett, telling me how well I had embodied the values of the western tradition, I knew it was time to quit."

Specifically, it was time for Bart to live out the values of Dante as laid out in *The Divine Comedy*—especially the books called *Purgatorio* and *Paradiso.*

"Purgatorio," Bart explained, "was when I announced my resignation from the presidency of Yale and had to sit through the resulting farewell dinners. You have no idea what a high-cholesterol dinner will do to you when it is followed by one-hundred-year-old port and fortune cookies."

Paradiso, on the other hand, is his present job as president of the National League and all-around sportsman. Again, let me put it in Bart's own words:

"Steve," he observed with a blissful smile, "I can't see a baseball sailing up into a blue sky without thinking about Dante. After getting a little bit of a boost from Virgil and from his own beloved Beatrice, Dante took off into the wild blue yonder, where goodness reigns supreme. And that, it seems to me, is what baseball is all about. It's why baseball has done so much to shape our wonderful American psyche. It's why baseball is so closely identified with joy, love, loyalty and peace."

By this time, I must confess, I was in tears. Bart led me, blubbering, to the door. And my closing image of him, framed in the mahogany doorway, was of a figure in the tradition, not only of Dante, but of Fiat, Ferrari, Frank Sinatra and Olivetti—all of those products and traditions that have made our lives melodious and stylish.

Bart sits here today as a man who has passed through hell and reached the world of eternal bliss. He has earned his smile, as well as his Ph.D., through almost unlimited tolerance for pain. He has even emerged with a grin on his face, from the presidency of Yale, a school that is *still* trying to compete with the University of Hartford in areas like fund-raising and intercollegiate athletics.

We welcome you tonight, Bart. We welcome your smile and your neatly trimmed beard. We welcome the athletic values that have made you a folk hero in your time and an example to us all. And I personally would like to present you with this token of our affection, awe, esteem and admiration.

Now, in honor of A. Bartlett Giamatti, LET'S EAT!

Printed by permission. Courtesy of Stephen Joel Trachtenberg, President of George Washington University.

Index